English Language Arts and Reading 7-12

Third Edition

A complete content review for Texas Teacher Certification Exam #231

Dr. Jane Thielemann-Downs

Dedication

This text is dedicated to the children and teachers of the great state of Texas. It is only through education that we better ourselves, our community, our state, and our nation.

Disclaimer

Many states offer teacher exams that measure the content knowledge required of an entry-level educator. This book is designed to guide the examinee's preparation by helping the test taker become familiar with the subject matter content, the competencies to be tested, and the test item format. Educator preparation program staff may also find this information useful as they help examinees prepare for a career in English / Language Arts education.

When preparing for this test, emphasis should be placed on the competencies and descriptive statements which delineate the content that is tested. Please note that a portion of the content is included in the sample items found in this text book. These questions represent only a *sample* of items. Thus, test preparation should focus on the complete content delineated for testing. There is no guarantee that the content of this book will completely prepare an examiner for all questions on the test. Readers should consult textbooks, articles, experts, and Web sites for updates, extra resources, for verification of content information.

General Information about this Exam

The purpose of the English Language Arts Content Specialty Exam is to assess whether an examinee has the requisite knowledge and skills that an entry-level educator must possess. The 100 word multiple choice questions and the two constructed response questions are based on the English Language Arts and Reading 7-12 framework

Domain	Domain Title	Approximate Percentage of Test	Standards Assessed
I.	Integrated Language Arts, Diverse Learners and the Study of English	15%	English Language Arts and Reading 7-12 I, VII
II.	Literature, Reading Processes, and Skills for Reading Literary and Nonliterary Texts	40%	English Language Arts and Reading 7-12 I - IV
III.	Written Communication	30%	English Language Arts and Reading 7-12 I, V - VI
IV.	Oral Communication and Media Literacy	15%	English Language Arts and Reading 7-12 I, VIII - IX

Table of Contents

ABOUT THE AUTHOR

JANE THIELEMANN-DOWNS is a Professor of Education in the College of Public Service at the University of Houston-Downtown where she teaches courses in Reading, Language Arts, and Educational Psychology. She has been a member of the faculty at UH-D for 24 years, and currently resides in Houston, Texas.

Additional works by this author:

Thielemann, J. (2013). *English Language Arts 6-12 New York State Teacher Certification: A complete content review for Content Specialty Test (03)*. Booksurge: Charleston, S.C.

Thielemann, J. (2012). *FTCE: English 6-12*, *A Complete Content Review for the 6-12 Florida Teacher Certification Examination*. Booksurge: Charleston, S.C.

Chen, I. & Thielemann-Downs, J. (2011). Preparing for Teacher Certification in Technology Application (Grades K-12): A course of study for the "TExES" Exam #142 and #139. Booksurge: Charleston, SC.

Thielemann-Downs, J. (2011). CSET: English Preparing for the California Subject Examination for English Teachers: A complete content review for: Subtests I, II, III & IV, (2011). Booksurge: Charleston, SC.

Thielemann-Downs, J. (2010). *Preparing for Teacher Certification in English, Language Arts & Reading Grades 8-12, Second Edition for "TExES" Exam #131*. Booksurge: Charleston, SC

Thielemann, J. & Chen, I. (2008). *Technology Application Competencies for K-12 Teachers*. IGI Global: Hershey, PA.

Thielemann, J. (2007). *Preparing for Teacher Certification in English, Language Arts & Reading Grades 8-12. "TExES" Exam #131*. Eakin Press, Austin, Texas

DOMAIN 1:

Relationships among the Language Arts

Diversity of the Student Population

Structure and Development of the English Language

Competency 1: Relationships among the Language Arts

- Understands the continuum of language arts skills and expectations for students in grades 7–12, as specified in the Texas Essential Knowledge and Skills (TEKS).
- Understands the importance of integrating the language arts to improve students' language and literacy.
- Understands the interrelationship between the language arts and other areas of the curriculum and uses this knowledge to facilitate students' learning across the curriculum.
- Understands relationships among reading, writing, speaking, listening and complex thinking and uses instruction to make connections among them in order to improve performance in each area.
- Understands and teaches how the expressive uses of language (speaking, representing, writing) and the receptive uses of language (listening, reading, viewing) influence one another.

Competency 2: Diversity of the Student Population

- Knows how individual differences (e.g., in relation to experience, culture, language, attitude, disability) may affect students' language skills.
- Designs learning experiences and selects materials that respond to and show respect for student diversity.
- Knows strategies for providing reading, writing and oral language instruction for all students, including English-language learners (in accordance with the English Language Proficiency Standards [ELPS]) and students with reading, writing or oral language difficulties and/or disabilities.
- Understands basic processes of first- and second-language acquisition and their impact on learning in the English language arts classroom in accordance with the ELPS.
- Understands how a first language or dialect differences may affect students' use of English and knows strategies for promoting all students' ability to use Standard English.
- Promotes students' understanding of the situational nature of language use and the value of knowing and using Standard English while fostering pride in their own language background and respect for the language backgrounds of other people.

Competency 3: Structure and Development of the English Language

- Demonstrates knowledge of major historical, regional and cultural influences on the ongoing development of the English language (e.g., Anglo-Saxon migrations, emergence of dialects, changing technology).
- Understands and teaches how to research word origins and analyze word formation as an aid to understanding meanings, derivations and spellings.
- Understands and teaches relationships among words (e.g., homonyms, synonyms, antonyms) and issues related to word choice (e.g., connotative and denotative meanings, multiple-meaning words, idioms, figurative language).
- Knows and teaches rules of grammar, usage, sentence structure, punctuation and capitalization in Standard English and is able to identify and edit nonstandard usage in his or her own discourse and the discourse of others.
- Knows how to provide explicit and contextual instruction that enhances students' knowledge of and ability to use Standard English.
- Knows and teaches how purpose, audience and register affect discourse.
- Demonstrates an understanding of informal and formal procedures for monitoring and assessing students' ability to use the English language effectively.
- Uses assessment results to plan and adapt instruction that addresses students' strengths, needs and interests and that builds on students' current skills to increase their proficiency in using the English language effectively.

Domain I: Chapter 1

Competency 1: Relationships Among the Language Arts - *The teacher understands and applies knowledge of relationships among the language arts and between the language arts and other aspects of students' lives and learning.*

The beginning teacher:
- Understands the continuum of language arts skills and expectations for students in grades 7-12, as specified in the Texas Essential Knowledge and Skills (TEKS).
- Understands the importance of integrating the language arts to improve students' language and literacy.
- Understands the interrelationship between the language arts and other areas of the curriculum and uses this knowledge to facilitate students' learning across the curriculum.
- Understands relationships among reading, writing, speaking, listening and complex thinking and uses instruction to make connections among them in order to improve performance in each area.
- Understands and teaches how the expressive uses of language (speaking, representing and writing) and the receptive uses of language (listening, reading and viewing) influence one another. www.sbec.state.tx.us

Key Terms

Content areas
Expressive language
Integrating language arts
Interdisciplinary approach
Literacy skills
Receptive language
Standard English
TEKS
Thematic approach

Relationships among the Language Arts

It is very important that a teacher obtain a working knowledge of the English, language arts and reading skills required of Texas public school students in grades 7-12 as specified in the TEKS, because a high correlation exists between the competencies of the TExES exam and the TEKS. For a complete listing of the TEKS visit www.tea.state.tx.us/.

The TEKS describe the continuum of language arts skills and expectations for students in grades 7-12. These skills include: listening, speaking, reading, writing, viewing and visually representing. The TEKS describe the skills necessary for English and language at each grade level. Each year the TEKS reading and writing skills increase in complexity as students mature and develop in their reading and writing abilities.

The TEKS emphasize the interconnection in literacy development between reading and writing skills as they reinforce each other. Each year, students are expected to spend time reading classic, contemporary, and informational works, and also identify characteristics of various literary elements and structure. Students are also expected to compose and use various forms of writing for specific purposes such as informing, persuading or entertaining. English, language arts and reading skills also require students to compose multi-sentence paragraphs, use varied sentence structure, and apply correct grammar, usage, spelling, and punctuation skills to their work.

Additionally, students are expected to incorporate technology into their work and learn to cite references in their research. Classroom use of technology will undoubtedly continue to expand and will play an increasingly significant role in public education in the years to come as technology becomes more sophisticated and cost effective (Best evidence, 2012).

Integrating the Language Arts

Historically, instruction in American's schools isolated academic subject areas without much emphasis on the interconnectedness of knowledge. Teaching the language arts requires the teacher to encourage students' constant use of language through the integration of the language arts. A typical Language Arts classroom may involve listening and speaking activities such as cooperative learning groups, interviewing, reading aloud, and role-playing. A language arts classroom may require students to participate in reading and writing activities such as reading novels, plays, and poems; studying word families; and writing short stories, plays and essay responses. Teachers should select a wide range of fiction, nonfiction, classic and contemporary literature in order for students to build a greater understanding of themselves and their communities as well as other cultures of the world (Tchudi and Mitchell, 1998).

Today's language arts teacher should integrate technology into learning by requiring students to apply computer and research skills in daily lessons. Using the Internet as a research tool in order to acquire new information, correspond with others via computer for personal fulfillment, critique information found on the web, and site sources in classwork are just a few of the many ways that technology can be integrated into the English / language arts classroom.

Making Connections: Language Arts and Content Area Subjects

A Language Arts teacher should emphasize the **integration of the language arts** with other content areas because the same literacy skills taught in the language arts classroom are required for learning in the **content areas** of science, social studies, mathematics, music and the arts. Postman (1979) stated that the study of biology is not plants and animals, it is the language that describes plants and animals. History is not events, it is language describing and interpreting events. Astronomy is not planets and starts, it is a way of talking about plants and stars.

Emphasizing the interconnection of subjects is known as the **interdisciplinary approach**. In order to increase understanding of content area curriculum and improve academic performance, students should be taught to ask questions, identify and solve problems, and use research and study skills in order to integrate the skills of literacy (Eggen & Kauchak, 2006). Learning opportunities expand when teachers help students read and write about what they are studying Time spent reading and writing connected text is associated with increased levels of work knowledge, fluency, and comprehension. (Moore, et al, 2011).

An effective teaching strategy for integrating the language arts with the other content areas is to teach using a **thematic approach**. This strategy involves arranging the curriculum around specific themes such as: "Man against Nature," "Building Communities," "Criminal Investigation," or "Traveling the Sea." While studying a theme, students may explore the topic using a variety of **literacy skills** and techniques. Teachers should apply the methodology and language from more than one discipline in order to examine the theme, issue or problem. A balance is then created between the content and the process of learning, allowing students to amass facts and develop concepts while practicing important academic learning processes (Eggen & Kauchak, 2006).

When students participate in thematic units of instruction, they apply the following interdisciplinary literacy skills:
- Locating and reading appropriate materials
- Maintaining journals in order to summarize reading
- Listening to well-crafted English read orally
- Reading silently and orally

Expressive and Receptive Uses of Language

All literacy experiences in reading and writing should be considered interconnected as they each influence the other. Reading and writing are dynamic, interactive processes that help students construct meaning. For example, reading a literary work often gives students ideas for writing, and writing can clarify student understanding of what is read. Thus, the **expressive** uses of language (speaking, representing, and writing) and the **receptive** uses of language (listening, reading, and viewing) influence one another. In sum, integrating the language arts during literacy instruction enhances and supports thinking and learning. (Tchudi and Mitchell, 1998)

References

The effectiveness of educational technology application for enhancing reading achievement in K-12 classrooms: A meta-analysis. (April, 2012). *Best Evidence Encyclopedia: Center for Data Driven Reform in Education* (DDRE).

Eggen, P & Kauchak, D. (2006). *Strategies and Models for Teachers* (5th ed.). Allyn and Bacon: Boston.

Moore, D.; Moore, S.; Cunningham, P.; Cunningham, J. (2011). *Developing Readers and Writers in the Content Areas K-12*. Allyn & Bacon: New York.

Postman, N. (1979). *Teaching as a Conserving Activity*. Delacorte: New York: NY.

Tchudi, S. & Mitchell, D. (1998). *Exploring and Teaching the English Language Arts.* Longman: New York.

www.tea.state.tx.us

www.bestevidence.org

Practice Questions

1. Mr. Louis, an 11th grade English / language arts teacher, is planning to have his students read *The Iliad,* the classical work written by Homer in 700 B.C. The story of *The Iliad* is a salute to heroes. It begins after the wars have been raging for ten years. Homer describes the cause of the war (known as the Judgment of Paris). The problems started at a wedding when Eris, the Goddess of Discord, rolled a golden apple on the floor, which was inscribed *for the fairest*. The favored Prince of Troy, Paris, had to decide which of three goddesses would receive the apple. The goddess Aphrodite bribed Paris into picking her; in return, Paris would receive Helen, the wife of Menelaus who was the most beautiful woman in the world. Paris then steals the beautiful Helen and takes her and the Spartan treasure back to the city of Troy. Seeking revenge, the Greek kings band together to sail to Troy to seek the return of Helen and the treasure.

Mr. Louis wants to enhance his students' reading and writing skills as well as their understanding of the characters' motivations and actions by relating classroom assignments to their own personal understanding. Which of the following activities would most effectively integrate writing and reading skills and also enhance student understanding?

   A. After reading the story, students choose a favorite character in the story that has traits and characteristics they feel important for success in life (courage, leadership, truthfulness, etc.), and then write a personal response describing the character and why that character's trait is important to the story's outcome.
   B. Students work in small groups to identify and list the main characters of the story. Then, students note the descriptive words which describe these characters found within the story. Students must then create a rubric of characters and descriptive traits on a chart.
   C. Students work in small groups to draw a plot graph of the story's main events and use it as a guide to discuss the major events and characters.
   D. Students choose an important event in the story, and then write a journal entry describing how it would feel to take part in that historic event.

A is correct. This answer choice matches the question; the activity requires that the student link their reading and writing skills while also enhancing their personal understanding of characters' motivations and actions. TEST TIP: working in cooperative groups supports student-centered learning. However, once students are in groups, pay close attention to the assigned task. Some assignments such as making a list or writing a glossary do not require students to engage in higher order thinking. A cooperative activity that involves students in higher order thinking is most likely the correct answer.

2. Many students in Mr. Louis' 11th grade English class read and comprehend two years below grade level. Which of the following classroom activities would be most effective in helping these students improve their reading comprehension and understanding of Homer's *Iliad* and make connections among the language arts?

    A. Require that students view the film, *O' Brother, Where Art Thou*, a modern movie which mimics the theme of Homer's *Iliad*. Students then work in small groups to create a chart of the movie's main characters which parallel Homer's Iliad.

    B. Require that students read a different version of *The Iliad* written for elementary students, and then base the student's grade on activities completed with the easy-to-read version of the text.

    C. Require that students investigate the origin, significance and meaning of this famous work using additional print and technological resources written on a variety of reading levels, and then write a report to share with the class.

    D. Place students in collaborative groups in order to reread the story using a dictionary to investigate unknown words.

C is correct. This answer choice best matches the question. This activity requires that the students work with additional materials and modes of learning in order to enhance their reading comprehension and understanding of the passage.

3. The students in Mr. Louis' 11th grade English class are reading an historical account of Christopher Columbus' first voyage to America. Mr. Louis wants students to comprehend the reading selection on multiple levels in order to understand the historical significance of the document. Mr. Louis conducts a guided reading lesson during which he leads the class through literal interpretation and comprehension of the text. During the guided reading lesson, Mr. Louis helps students break down long and complex sentences, look for signal words, use context clues for unknown words, and restate difficult parts of the passage.

After the lesson, Mr. Louis wants to extend student understanding of the passage by integrating other language arts skills. Which of the following activities would best extend students understanding and comprehension of the reading selection, and also integrate the language arts skills of speaking, listening, and viewing?

    A. Mr. Louis asks students to write down the difficult words they have encountered in their vocabulary notebooks, and then write a new story in their journals using as many of the new words as possible.

B. Mr. Louis asks students to write a Reader's Theater script based on the reading selection, make simple props and costumes for the characters, and then perform the play in front of their peers.
C. Mr. Louis takes students on a local field trip to the art museum to view a painting of Columbus' landing in America. Students are given the opportunity to make sketches in their notebooks as they view the painting.
D. Mr. Louis asks students to design and color a flag that they think represents Columbus' voyage to the new world; the teacher then posts the flags on the classroom bulletin board.

B is correct. This is the best answer choice because students must review the reading selection as they write their play; they will also use the language arts skills of speaking, listening and viewing as they perform the play in front of their peers.

4. Students in Mr. Sanchez 11th grade English / language arts class have just completed an integrated unit on poetry. The culminating activity of the unit requires that students write their own poems. Before students can submit their final poems for grading, Mr. Sanchez asks students to work in small, cooperative groups to read and discuss their poems. Of the following, which describes the greatest benefit this requirement will have to students?

A. Reading their poems aloud will allow students to compare their work with the work of others in order to determine if their poems should be submitted to the school literary magazine.
B. This activity will allow students the opportunity to identify overuse of emotional sentiment or colloquial expressions and receive feedback from other students.
C. This activity will allow students the opportunity to evaluate their topic selection to determine whether or not it is appropriate for the poetry assignment.
D. Reading their poems aloud will allow students opportunity to consider the clarity of their language and the appropriateness of their word choices using a second learning modality.

D is correct. This answer choice offers the students an opportunity to share their work with others, and has the added benefit of offering students the chance to practice expressive and receptive language skills.

Domain I: Chapter 2

Competency 2: Diversity of the Student Population - *The teacher is aware of the diversity of the student population and provides instruction that is appropriate for all students.*

The beginning teacher:
- Knows how individual differences (in relation to experience, culture, language, attitude and disability) may affect students' language skills. Designs learning experiences and selects materials that respond to and show respect for student diversity.
- Knows strategies for providing reading, writing and oral language instruction for all students, including English-language learners and students with reading, writing or oral language difficulties or disabilities.
- Understands basic processes of first and second-language acquisition and the impact on learning in the English language arts classroom.
- Understands how first language or dialect differences may affect students' uses of English and knows strategies for promoting all students' abilities to use Standard English.
- Promotes students' understanding of the situational nature of language use and the value of knowing and using Standard English while fostering pride in their own language background and respect for the language backgrounds of other people. www.sbec.state.tx.us

Key Terms

Acquired system
Acquisition theory
Acquisition Learning Hypothesis
Advanced ELL
Advanced High ELL
Affective considerations
Affective Filter Hypothesis
Affective variables
Attitude of acceptance
Auditory learner
Authentic assessment
Authentic dialogue
Beginning ELL
Biological factors
CALP (Cognitive Academic Language Proficiency)
Chomsky, Noam
Cognitive processing factors
Cultural accuracy
Culturally pluralistic
Dialect
Dynamic Language
ELL (English Language Learners)
ELPS (English Language Proficiency Standards)
Goals maintenance
Immersion
Influence of first Language
Innatism
Input hypothesis
Intermediate ELL
Kinesthetic learner
Krashen, Stephen
Language acquisition
Language minority students
Learning style
Linguistic factors
Monitor Hypothesis

Monolingualism
Multicultural literature
Natural Order Hypothesis
Perceptual factors
Prior knowledge
Receptive understanding
Semantic mapping
Social class
Social factors
Social interaction
Social language proficiency
Sociocultural factors
Standard English
Subtractive bilinguals
Tactile learner
TESOL (Teachers of English to Speakers of Other Languages)
Tier 1 words
Tier 2 words
Tier 3 words
Transitional program
Usage
Visual learner
Wait time

Diversity of the Student Population

It is important that secondary English teachers become knowledgeable about the students they teach, and project an **attitude of acceptance** toward a student's first language and culture.

This involves knowledge of students' experiences, culture, language, attitude or disabilities that may affect reading skills and language acquisition.

Cummins (1979) describes how first language development can aid the second language learner's academic progress. Students must reach proficiency in at least one language if they are to obtain the same academic progress in a second language. Students who possess a high level of proficiency in their native language obtain an increased awareness of the nature of language, greater flexibility in understanding word associations and an increased sensitivity to the interpersonal cues of language use (Cummins, 1979).

Learning a second language may create positive or negative emotional responses for students. Research suggests that **affective variables** such as student motivation and interest are strongly related to successful second language development (Scarcella, 1990). Teachers must be aware that each student learns a second language in his or her own way. These differences may originate in the student's personality, learning style or developmental stage. The challenge in educating **language minority students** is to create not only an atmosphere of respect and acceptance, but also lessons and programs that respect the students' home culture and language while also enhancing educational achievement in the use of **Standard English** (Scarcella, 1990).

Respecting Diversity

Secondary English teachers need to provide literary experiences that reflect the multitude of backgrounds of the students in today's schools. **Multicultural literature**, defined as literature that represents any distinct cultural group through portrayal and rich detail, can play an important role in developing pride in one's heritage and building positive self-concept. Yakota (1993) explains that students benefit from various experiences from cultures other than their own, and these experiences help students understand differing points of view. Students should be encouraged to investigate and research culturally diverse points of view found within important cultural or historical events (example: differing viewpoints about the discovery of America, the Wounded Knee massacre, the Indian wars in Texas of the 1890s or immigration laws and patterns).

Yokota (1993) provides well-defined criteria for selecting multicultural literature. Yokota

(1993) explains that a literary work should be culturally accurate and that issues should be represented within the literary work in ways that reflect the true values and beliefs of the culture. The criterion of **cultural accuracy** serves as an umbrella criterion. Included with criterion are: richness of cultural details, authentic dialogue and relationships, in-depth treatment of cultural issues and the inclusion of members of "minority" groups for a purpose. (Yakota, 1993).

Yakota (1993) explains that details of the story should be written in such a way as to provide details about the culture described. Details may be a natural part of the story and provide insight into daily life rather than attempting to explain the culture. The literary work should also provide **authentic dialogue** and relationships among characters. Furthermore, the work should provide an in-depth treatment of cultural issues. It is important to give issues a realistic portrayal and explore them in depth so that readers may be able to formulate informed conclusions about the issues. No matter how minor a character in the story, Yakota (1993) explains that each of the characters should be regarded as a distinct individual whose life is rooted in his or her culture.

The intent of sharing multicultural literature in the classroom is to provide vicarious experiences from cultures other than the students' own, and these experiences should, in turn, influence the decisions students will make about living in a **culturally pluralistic** world (Yakota, 1993). Other ideas for promoting an appreciation of multiculturalism include: inviting culturally diverse guest speakers into the classroom, posting information on bulletin boards about famous people of diverse cultures (inventors, mathematicians, etc.) and sharing books written by diverse authors.

Promoting the Use of Standard English

Within American society some students speak with a **dialect**; using words, grammar and speech patterns that differ from Standard English. A **dialect** is defined as a variation of Standard English that is distinct in vocabulary, grammar, or pronunciation. Students who speak a dialect of English or a second language represent all socioeconomic levels and may involve a variety of cultures. Although some of these students may come from mainstream "middle class" America, many will come from groups that experience socioeconomic marginality, and racial or ethnic discrimination (Scarcella, 1990).

Research indicates that students' use of nonstandard English results in lowered teacher expectations for academic performance and lowered assessments of students' work and the students themselves. English / language arts teachers need to be aware of this damaging trend and take every effort to keep expectations high of all students to counteract this trend (Scarcella, 1990).

Teachers need to take care that students are not demeaned or embarrassed because they do not speak Standard English or because they speak a language other than English. The teacher needs to take every opportunity to model Standard English for these students. It is important for all teachers to remember that the primary reason for teaching Standard English is that it allows access to educational and economic opportunities that often are not accessible to such students. (Eggen & Kauchak, 2006). Thus, English Language Learner (ELL) students must learn to use and apply Standard English conventions.

Students with a first language other than English may incorporate grammatical, syntactical or semantic rules of their first language into their expressive language as they speak and write English. For example, a Hispanic child may say "shirt red" instead of "the red shirt," or "her hair is color brown" instead of "she has brown hair." Another example can be found in prepositions. In English the prepositions "in," "on" and "at" are all distinguished by the situation. In Spanish, however, the student may say "put this in the table" instead of "put this on the table," because these prepositions are not differentiated in Spanish as they are in English.

Planning Instruction

The best teaching approach when planning instruction for students who speak nonstandard English or English as a second language is to first focus on understanding the students and accepting their dialect as a valid form of communication and to also model Standard English constantly. Directed lessons that offer explicit instruction in Standard English enhance the student's knowledge and ability to use Standard English independently. It is important to note that learning Standard English is easy for most students whose original language is a dialect of English as long as they have good role models (Woolfolk, 1998).

In order to become competent in the use of Standard English, students should have experience in using English in a variety of situations and purposes. A good pedagogical practice is to set up classroom situations of language sharing. Competence with language is likely to develop during personal interactions in which a more skilled individual guides a student with lesser English skills.

Explicit and Contextual Instruction for ELL Learners

The English Language Proficiency Standards (ELPS), as required by the Texas Administrative Code (19), Chapter 74, Subchapter A, §74.4, outline English language proficiency level descriptors and student expectations for English language learners (ELLs). School districts are required to implement ELPS as an integral part of each subject in the required curriculum. Visit web site www.tea.state.tx.us/ for detailed information.

In order for ELLs to be successful, they must acquire both social and academic language proficiency in English. **Social language proficiency** in English consists of the English needed for daily social interactions. **Academic language proficiency** consists of the English needed to think critically, understand and learn new concepts, process complex academic material, and interact and communicate in English academic settings.

Classroom instruction that effectively integrates second language acquisition with quality content area instruction ensures that ELLs acquire social and academic language proficiency in English, learn the knowledge and skills in the TEKS, and reach full academic potential. Effective instruction in second language acquisition involves giving ELLs opportunities to listen, speak, read, and write at their current levels of English development while gradually increasing the linguistic complexity of the English they read, hear, speak, and write.

The English Language Proficiency Standards (ELPS) describe the English language proficiency levels of beginning, intermediate, advanced, and advanced high. These levels are not grade-specific. ELLs may exhibit different proficiency levels within the language domains of listening, speaking, reading, and writing (www.tea.state.tx.us).

Beginning ELLs have little or no ability to understand spoken English in academic and social settings. These students:

- struggle to understand simple conversations and simple discussions even when the topics are familiar and the speaker uses linguistic supports such as visuals, slower speech and other verbal cues, and gestures;
- struggle to identify and distinguish individual words and phrases during social and instructional interactions that have not been intentionally modified for ELLs; and
- may not seek clarification in English when failing to comprehend the English they hear; frequently remain silent, watching others for cues.

Intermediate ELLs have the ability to understand simple, high-frequency spoken English used in routine academic and social settings. These students:

- usually understand simple or routine directions, as well as short, simple conversations and short, simple discussions on familiar topics; when topics are unfamiliar, require extensive linguistic supports and adaptations such as visuals, slower speech and other verbal cues, simplified language, gestures, and pre-teaching to preview or build topic-related vocabulary;
- often identify and distinguish key words and phrases necessary to understand the general meaning during social and basic instructional interactions that have not been intentionally modified for ELLs; and
- have the ability to seek clarification in English when failing to comprehend the English they hear by requiring/requesting the speaker to repeat, slow down, or rephrase speech.

Advanced ELLs have the ability to understand, with second language acquisition support, grade-appropriate spoken English used in academic and social settings. These students:

- usually understand longer, more elaborated directions, conversations, and discussions on familiar and some unfamiliar topics, but sometimes need processing time and sometimes depend on visuals, verbal cues, and gestures to support understanding;
- understand most main points, most important details, and some implicit information during social and basic instructional interactions that have not been intentionally modified for ELLs; and occasionally require/request the speaker to repeat, slow down, or rephrase to clarify the meaning of the English they hear.

Advanced high ELLs have the ability to understand, with minimal second language acquisition support, grade-appropriate spoken English used in academic and social settings. These students:

- understand longer, elaborated directions, conversations, and discussions on familiar and unfamiliar topics with occasional need for processing time and with little dependence on visuals, verbal cues, and gestures; some exceptions when complex academic or highly specialized language is used;
- understand main points, important details, and implicit information at a level nearly comparable to native English-speaking peers during social and instructional

interactions; and rarely require/request the speaker to repeat, slow down, or rephrase to clarify the meaning of the English they hear. Visit web site www.tea.state.tx.us/ for detailed information.

Adapting Instruction for ELL Learners

Teachers must learn to adapt instruction to increase student proficiency in using the English language effectively. For example, when a lesson requires that students read and comprehend a section of the text, teachers should be aware of the "Three Tiers of Words" needed by ELL students to gain meaning from the text:

Tier 1 words are words that are needed for everyday communications, words that English-speaking students know and that we take for granted. Examples *include find, search, however,* and *finally.*

Tier 2 words are those tiny words that make comprehension very difficult for ELLs. Examples include so, at, into, within, by, if, and then.

Tier 3 words are content-specific words that are generally low-frequency words in English. For example, in science students may be required to understand words such as: isotope, lathe, osmosis, mass, and membrane. http://www.utdanacenter.org

Teachers must remember that explicit vocabulary instruction (direct, purposeful) is critical and must be developed across and within all content areas.

- It is important to pre-select words to teach.
- Not all words are created equal.
- There are no word lists for tier 1, 2, and 3 words.

Moreover, purposeful attention to the reading domain can increase the likelihood that students will attain comprehension of the course content. http://www.utdanacenter.org

Effective Teaching Strategies

The following strategies are suggested for teaching English / language arts / reading to students who speak a dialect of English (Woolfolk, 1998).

- Select materials with care. Allow time for practice and rereading of stories in varying speech styles. Allow students the opportunity to retell stories out loud to varying audiences.
- Integrate the language arts. Allow students opportunities to read, speak, listen and write about literature whenever possible.
- Use technology to assist learning. Software programs for listening, speaking and reading comprehension can promote learning of Standard English.
- Integrate authentic assessment into the grading system. Although great emphasis is placed on standardized testing in today's classroom, students should be given the opportunity to link learning to real-life tasks through authentic assessment tasks. This helps to ensure that "school" knowledge can be applied to problems that students will encounter throughout

their lives as they become responsible members of families, work groups and communities. Offer many opportunities for listening to Standard English. Allow students the opportunity to listen to a passage or story before reading out loud.

- Become familiar with the features of the student's dialect. This will provide a greater understanding to distinguish miscues from comprehension errors. Try not to correct students while reading; rather, correct after the students finish reading the passage aloud.

Additional strategies suggested by Scarcella (1990) for teaching English / language arts / reading to **ELL students** for whom English is their second language include:

- Provide students with continuous and substantial exposure to large quantities of written and spoken English that is comprehensible to ELL students.
- Provide multiple opportunities for students to interact in English with a variety of speakers (both inside and outside school). English teachers need to create speaking and writing tasks that offer genuine opportunities for students to explore, investigate and learn English.
- Do not assume students will volunteer to answer a question in class; instead, develop a lesson plan that will allow all students opportunities to participate actively.
- Do not assume students will ask questions when they do not understand; instead, check students' understanding in a more non-threatening manner by questioning them, using brief quizzes, participating in small group work, etc.
- Provide plenty of **"wait time"** for students to translate and process questions. Allow more time for the student to think about the question and his answer before calling on another student.
- Share classroom assessment methods and techniques with students. Make sure students understand the established grading methods.
- Reduce instruction in mechanical and grammatical exercises and related drills that emphasize the component parts of language.
- Reduce instruction relying solely on comparisons of the first and second language.

Understanding Acquisition and Development of Language and Literacy

Research suggests that affective variables such as student motivation and interest are strongly related to successful second language development (Scarcella, 1990). Teachers must be aware that each student learns a second language in his or her own way. These differences may originate in the student's personality, learning style, or developmental stage.

Although languages and the way different cultures expose their students to language vary, the outcome of first-language acquisition is clear. Almost all children become fluent in their first language. However, this kind of guarantee is not automatic with the acquisition of a second language. It is important for teachers to project an attitude of acceptance toward a student's first language and culture. The challenge is to create an atmosphere of respect and acceptance with lessons and programs that respect the students' home culture and language and enhance educational achievement in the use of Standard English (Scarcella, 1990).

Cognitive, Affective, and Socio-cultural Influences on Language Development

Language acquisition is the process by which humans acquire the capacity to perceive, produce, and use words to understand and communicate. Learning to talk is one of the most visible and important achievements of early childhood. In a matter of months, toddlers move from hesitant single words to fluent sentences (Johnston, 2006).

In very general terms, the two primary factors that influence language development are biological and environmental. However, a major challenge to understanding language acquisition is to understand how language capacities (syntax, phonetics, and vocabulary) are learned by infants from what appears to be very little external input. Opposing theorists try to explain this dilemma; one side purports the concept of **innatism**, explaining that a child is genetically born with innate language capacities, the opposing theorist explain language acquisition as a response to **environmental** stimuli.

Theoretical Debate

The nature of the mental activity that underlies language development as a child grows is widely debated among child language experts. However, in broad strokes, the observable "facts" of language development are not in dispute. Most children begin speaking during their second year and by age two are likely to know at least 50 words and begin combining them in short. Once vocabulary size reaches about 200 words, the rate of word learning increases dramatically and grammatical function words such as articles and prepositions begin to appear with some consistency. During the preschool years, sentence patterns become increasingly complex and vocabulary diversifies to include relational terms that express notions of size, location, quantity, and time. By the age of four to six or so, most students have acquired the basic grammar of the sentence. From that point onward, students use language more efficiently and effectively. Children also learn how to create, and maintain, larger language units such as conversation or narrative. Although there are individual differences in rate of development, the sequence in which various forms appear is highly predictable both within and across stages (Johnston, 2006).

The nature of language knowledge

Noam Chomsky (1959) theorized that verbal communication requires productivity, i.e. the ability to create an infinite number of utterances never heard before. This endless novelty requires an understanding of abstract language knowledge. Ultimately, "rules" for combining words cannot be rules about particular words, but must be rules about classes of words such as nouns, verbs or prepositions. Once these abstract blueprints are available, the speaker can fill the "slots" in a sentence with the words that best convey the message of the moment. Chomsky's (1959) key point was that since language abstractions can never be directly experienced, they must emerge from the child's own mental activity while listening to speech (Johnston, 2006).

Factors affecting language acquisition and development

As the debate between nurture vs. nature continues in many academic circles, several factors in each have been identified as contributing to language development (Johnston, 2006).

Basic Biological / Genetic Makeup

In the nature category, some theorists contend that students are born with an innate biological device for understanding the principles and organization common to all languages. This is to say that language development is programmed into the human design. Language development then simply happens innately and is not necessarily shaped by other outside influences. Many scientists believe that the human brain comes with a "universal grammar" that interacts with the rest of the brain in early development that forms the foundation of language fluency (Johnston, 2006).

Social Interaction

An active and communicative social environment influences language development because this provides ample input for children to process. Some linguists argue that adults play an important role in language development by providing children with repetitious exposure to correct language usage. In addition, social interaction offers opportunities for children to experiment with language – try out new words in new contexts, verbalize complicated and abstract thoughts, and more (Johnston, 2006).

Research indicates that children who are exposed to complex vocabulary and grammatical structures develop language more quickly and more accurately than those from less language-rich environments. Additionally, challenging and stimulating activities that involve language also seem to influence language development (Johnston, 2006).

Opportunities for Usage

Some researchers place more emphasis on the usage of language as an influential factor than biological make up or exposure. Children who are listened to and prompted with stimulating questions to speak often develop their language skills more quickly than those who do not use language as often. A good example is the baby of the family who seldom needs to speak because older siblings speak for them. This influences language development and often delays the natural development (Johnston, 2006).

Sociocultural Factors

There are **sociocultural** factors that influence language variation. **Social class** has a major bearing on the way a child uses language. Emmitt, Pollock & Komescaroff (2003) describe how different classes use different codes of language. A child's sociocultural circumstance dominates a child's use and development of language. In some sociocultural situations, language usage may inadvertently discriminate against **gender** groups and can therefore be considered discriminatory. **Ethnicity** can also be seen as a major factor in language variation. Students who do not speak English as their first language must understand the new language conventions (Johnston, 2006).

Affective Considerations

The **affective** domain includes factors such as: empathy, self-esteem, extroversion, inhibition, imitation, anxiety, and attitudes. Some affective variables may seem at first rather far removed from language learning, but when one considers the pervasive nature of language, any affective factor can conceivably become relevant to language learning (Johnston, 2006).

However, the course of language acquisition is not driven exclusively from within. The structure of the language to be learned, and the frequency with which various forms are heard, will also have an effect. Despite the theoretical debates, it seems clear that language skills reflect knowledge and capabilities in virtually every domain (Johnston, 2006).

Learning a Second Language

Second-language acquisition is as complex as the acquisition of the first language, but with the addition of a wide variety of complicating variables. An interesting metaphor is comparing the addition of a second language to home renovation vs. new construction. Fortunately, people have the ability to learn languages throughout their lifetime because many of the same strategies used for first-language acquisition are also used for subsequent language learning (Clark, 2010).

The individuality with regard to second language acquisition is part of the controversy surrounding the education for ELL (English Language Learners). Numerous options for teaching second language exist in American schools today. True **bilingualism**, in which children are taught in their native language, is offered in some public school programs. Others support a **transitional** program - a program that solely supports the native language until students have learned enough English to be taught in an English-only environment. Still other school districts insist on total **immersion,** a program that requires the child to conform to an English-only environment with a "sink or swim" mentality.

In the United States, a strong belief held by many Americans is that young students are able to acquire languages easily, so if they are in English-only classrooms they will learn English. The lofty goal of having every English-language learner proficient in English in three years represents the thinking of many politicians and educators. They insist that English language learners have spent too much time in native-language and not enough time learning Standard English instruction (Clark, 2010).

Conversation Fluency / Academic Language Proficiency

Early approaches to second language learning viewed language as a set of discrete skills: reading, writing, listening, and speaking. Knowing a language meant mastering these skills including: attaining a basic vocabulary and understanding grammar (Wright, 2010). However, recent research and theoretical developments have broadened our understanding of what it means to "know" a language.

Cummins (2008) explains that there is a difference between **basic interpersonal communication skills (BICS)** and **cognitive academic language proficiency (CALP)**. BICS refers to conversational fluency in a language while CALP refers to students' ability to understand and express (both oral and written modes) concepts and ideas that are relevant to success in school. Cummins (2008) distinguishes three different aspects of language proficiency: **conversational fluency, discrete language skills**, and **academic language proficiency**. Cummins (2008) argues that conversational fluency takes about 1 to 2 years for ELL students to develop. Estimates vary, but research supports that it takes 5 years or longer for ELL students to catch up to native English speakers in academic English (Krashen & Terrell, 1983).

Language for Academic Success

The **TESOL** (Teachers of English to Speakers of Other Languages) standards, known as the English Language Proficiency Standards **(ELPS)** reflect a national effort to delineate what academic language proficiency means for ELL students. According to the Standards, academic language proficiency includes being able to communicate for social, intercultural, and instructional purposes within the school setting and being able to communication information, ideas, and concepts necessary for academic success in language arts, mathematics, science, and social studies.

Krashen's Theory of Second Language Acquisition

Stephen Krashen (University of Southern California), an expert in the field of linguistics, specializes in theories of language acquisition and development. (Krashen, 1982; Krashen, 1996; http://www.sk.com.br/sk-krash.html).

Krashen's theory of second language acquisition consists of five main hypotheses:
1. the Acquisition-Learning hypothesis,
2. the Monitor hypothesis,
3. the Natural Order hypothesis,
4. the Input hypothesis,
5. and the Affective Filter hypothesis.

The **Acquisition-Learning** hypothesis is the most fundamental of all the hypotheses in Krashen's theory and the most widely known among linguists and language practitioners. According to Krashen, there are two independent systems of second language performance: the **acquired system** and the **learned system**. The acquired system or **acquisition** is the product of a subconscious process very similar to the process children undergo when they acquire their first language. It requires meaningful interaction in the target language - natural communication - in which speakers are concentrated not in the form of their utterances, but in the communicative act. The **learned** is the product of formal instruction and it results in conscious knowledge about the language, for example a student's knowledge of grammar rules is increased after explicit lessons given by the teacher.

Krashen's **Monitor** hypothesis explains the relationship between **acquisition** and **learning** and defines the influence of the latter on the former. The monitoring function is the practical result of the learned grammar. According to Krashen, the acquisition system is the "utterance initiator," while the learning system performs the role of the monitor or the "editor." The monitor acts in a planning, editing, and correcting function when three conditions are met:
1. There is sufficient time for the learning to occur
2. The student is focused on form and wants to be correct
3. The student has learned the rule (i.e. grammar rule)

Krashen's **Natural Order Hypothesis** suggests that the acquisition of grammatical structures follows a natural order which is predictable. For a given language, some grammatical structures tend to be acquired early while others late. This order seemed to be independent of the learners' age, first language background, and conditions of exposure.

The **Input** hypothesis is Krashen's attempt to explain how the learner actually acquires a second language. Krashen explains that the learner improves and progresses along the natural order when he/she receives second language input that is one step beyond his/her current stage of linguistic competence.

Finally, the **Affective Filter** hypothesis embodies Krashen's view that a number of affective variables play a facilitative, but non-causal, role in second language acquisition. These variables include: motivation, self-confidence and anxiety. Krashen (1996) claims that learners with high motivation, self-confidence, a good self-image, and a low level of anxiety are better equipped for success in second language acquisition (Krashen, 1996; http://www.sk.com.br/sk-krash.html).

The Effect of First language on Second Language Acquisition

In both first- and second-language acquisition, a stimulating and rich linguistic environment will support language development. How often and how well parents communicate with their children is a strong predictor of how rapidly students expand their language learning. Encouraging students to express their needs, ideas, and feelings whether in one language or two enriches students linguistically and cognitively. Moreover, encouraging students to express themselves while building on their prior knowledge of real-life situations also builds language experience (Clark, 2010).

Young children will become bilingual when there is real need to communicate in two languages and will just as quickly revert back to **monolingualism** when the need no longer exists. If a student's interactions outside the home are in only one language, they may quickly switch over to that language and may begin to have only a **receptive understanding** of their first language. Children are not usually equally proficient in both languages. They may use one language with parents and another with their peers or at school. At the time students are acquiring new vocabulary and understanding of the use of a new language, it may appear that they are falling behind in language acquisition in general; however, it is normal for there to be periods of leveling off (Clark, 2010).

Overall, continued first-language development is related to superior scholastic achievement. When students do not have many opportunities to use language and have not been provided with a rich experiential base, they may not learn to function well in their second language, and at the same time, they may not continue to develop their first language. This phenomenon occurs whether students are monolingual or bilingual with the result that their language level is not appropriate for their age.

It is important to note that language learning is not linear, and formal teaching does not "speed up" the learning process. Instead, language learning is **dynamic**; that is, language must be meaningful and used frequently in order to develop (Krashen, 1996).

Some students who have a first language other than English may incorporate grammatical, syntactical or semantic rules of their first language into their expressive language as they speak and write English. For example, a Hispanic student may say "shirt red" instead of "the red shirt," or "her hair is color brown" instead of "she has brown hair." Another example can be found in prepositions. In English the prepositions "in," "on" and "at" are all distinguished by the situation. In Spanish, however, the student may say "put this in the table" instead of "put this on the table," because these prepositions are not differentiated in Spanish as they are in English.

Tabors (1997) explains that most children understand that learning a second language is a cognitively challenging and a time-consuming activity; however, a child must want to communicate with people who speak that language if acquisition is to occur. Research suggests that students who are in a second-language learning situation have to be sufficiently motivated to start learning a new language (Tabors, 1997).

Cummins (1981) describes how first language development can aid the academic progress of the second language learner. Students must reach proficiency in at least one language if they are to obtain the same academic progress in a second language. Students who possess a high level of proficiency in their native language obtain an increased awareness of the nature of language, greater flexibility in understanding word associations and an increased sensitivity to the interpersonal cues of language use.(Cummins, 1981).

There is consensus that if students do not fully acquire their first language, they may have difficulty later in becoming fully literate and academically proficient in the second language (Collier, 1992; Cummins, 2008). The interactive relationship between language and cognitive growth is important. Preserving and strengthening the home language supports the continuity of cognitive growth. Cognitive development will not be interrupted when students and parents use the language they know best (Clark, 2010).

If experiences and ideas are familiar and meaningful to the child then knowledge acquired in the first language (academic skills, literacy development, concept formation, subject knowledge, and learning strategies) will transfer to the second language. As students are learning the second language, they are drawing on the background and experience they have available to them from their first language. Collier (1995) believes that the skills students develop in their first language form the foundation they must have to be academically successful in their second language.

Literacy not only transfers across languages, it facilitates "learning to read" in another language even when the language and writing system appear to be very different. Reading in all languages is conducted in the same way and is acquired in the same way. The common linguistic universals in all languages mean that students who learn to read well in their first language will probably read well in their second language as well. Researchers agree that reading in the primary language is a powerful way of continuing to develop literacy in that language, and to do so, students must have access to a print-rich environment in the primary language (Collier, 1995; Cummins, 2008; Krashen, 1996; McLaughlin, 1984; Pérez & Torres-Guzmán, 1996).

It is important to note that research has found that when ELL students learn all new information and skills in English, their first language becomes stagnant and does not keep pace with their new knowledge. This may lead to **limited bilingualism**, where students never become truly proficient in either their first or second language. Moreover, supporting **English only** programs gives students the impression that different languages and cultures are not valued equally.

Students who have lost their first language (so-called **subtractive bilinguals**) do not score as well on cognitive and academic measures as students who have maintained or expanded their first language as they acquire the second language (Collier,1995; Ramsey, 1987; Saville-Troike, 1982).

The learner's social skills and style are also important to language learning. Students who are naturally social and communicative seek out opportunities to engage others. If these students are given lots of opportunity to interact positively with others who speak the target language, their language learning is promoted. Personality, social competence, motivation, attitudes, learning style, and social style in both learners and speakers influence the way a child learns the second language. With the variety of programs available to students, these elements become variables that are difficult to factor in and whose effect is difficult to predict (Wong, 1991).

Developing Academic Literacy: teaching methods and techniques

The best teaching approach when planning instruction for students who speak nonstandard English or English as a second language is to first focus on understanding the students, accepting their dialect as a valid form of communication, and constantly model Standard English. Directed lessons that offer explicit instruction in Standard English enhance the student's knowledge and ability to use Standard English independently. Woolfolk (1998) explains that learning Standard English is easy for most students whose original language is a dialect of English as long as they have good role models. In order to become competent in the use of Standard English, students require experience in using English in a variety of situations and for a wide variety of purposes.

Addressing a student's dialect

The following strategies are suggested for enhancing the literacy achievement of students who speak a **dialect** of English (Woolfolk, 1998):

- Become familiar with the features of the student's dialect. This will provide a greater understanding to distinguish miscues from comprehension errors. Try not to correct students while reading; rather, correct after the students finish reading the passage aloud.

- Offer many opportunities for listening to Standard English. Allow students the opportunity to listen to a passage or story before reading out loud.

- Select materials with care. Allow time for practice and rereading of stories in varying speech styles. Allow students the opportunity to retell stories out loud to varying audiences.

- Integrate the language arts. Allow students opportunities to read, speak, listen, and write about literature whenever possible.

- Use technology to assist learning. Software programs for listening, speaking, and reading comprehension can promote learning of Standard English.

- Integrate authentic assessment into the grading system. Although great emphasis is placed on standardized testing in today's classroom, students should be given the opportunity to link learning to real-life tasks through authentic assessment tasks.

Consider Learning Styles

Each of us perceives the world in a unique way; individuals differ in the way that they remember, think, problem solve and make decisions. For example, even though two individuals may be equally knowledgeable about a situation, the first individual may respond quickly to solve a problem while the other is slower and more reflective. (Woolfolk, 1998)

Learning styles or modalities, as described by Dunn and Dunn (1978) include: **visual, auditory, tactile** and **kinesthetic** modalities of learning.

- The **visual learner** learns best by seeing the information (for example, viewing a chart or graph, reading a book, viewing a video).

- The **auditory learner** learns best through hearing the information orally, through lectures or tapes or by talking out loud while reviewing and reciting.

- The **tactile learner** learns best through the sense of touch; these students learn best by using manipulative materials. The kinesthetic learner learns best through direct physical involvement: for example, these students learn best through role play, conducting lab experiments or using hand or body movements which accompany songs.

Teachers must remember the importance of individual learning styles or approaches to learning. It is considered good teaching practice to conduct lessons that use more than one learning modality. A teacher who teaches using a single modality may negatively affect the academic achievement of students who learn better through other modalities (Woolfolk, 1998).

Constructivist Techniques for Developing Academic Literacy

Secondary English teachers need to understand and promote literacy development as an active process for students. In order to do this, it is important that teachers understand and apply the constructivists' theory of learning to the classroom as purported by constructive learning theorist, Jean Piaget. Constructivists believe that students make sense of new information by connecting it to **prior knowledge** and previously acquired understanding.

Prior knowledge refers to the reader's previous or existing knowledge of the subject matter of the text. Research reveals that prior knowledge is probably the single, most influential factor with respect to what the student will learn (Alverman & Phelps, 1994).

Unfortunately, many students in today's classrooms do not have the personal knowledge and experiences necessary to support learning. Therefore, the teacher must make the effort to provide a knowledge base in order to build the necessary background to make learning meaningful.

Setting the Purpose for Reading

Some students may think that recalling, or memorizing text in order to answer questions correctly or prove that they know exactly what someone wanted them to know may be the ultimate proof that learning has occurred. In order to promote literacy development, secondary English teachers must understand that how a student responds to a text and what meaning the student constructs from a text is influenced greatly by the purpose the student has for reading (Cox, 1999).

Students should be made aware that text characteristics and purposes for reading will determine the strategies and skills needed to increase their understanding of a selection (Cox, 1999). The purposes for reading a selection are endless; students can read to solve a problem, search for answers, verify predictions, etc.

Semantic Mapping

Semantic mapping is a visual strategy for vocabulary expansion and extension of knowledge by displaying words in categories related to one another. Creating a **semantic map** is an adaptation of concept definition mapping but builds on students' **prior knowledge** or **schema**. While it draws on prior knowledge it recognizes important components and shows the relationships among the components (Cox, 1999).

Semantic mapping is a very interactive process and should be modeled in the classroom by the teacher at the beginning of the lesson. The steps involved in modeling semantic mapping include:

- write the concept word on the board (for example: write the word "marine" on the board),
- ask students to think of as many words as they can for the concept word, teacher then writes the list on the board or overhead and have students copy it,
- finally, have students work in small groups in order to place the words into categories.

To extend the semantic map-making process and give students additional practice, divide students into pairs or groups and assign a word that originated from a story or important concept to be learned (such as the word "pearls"), or assign words related to the topic in general, such as "sea turtle." As students work, they may find that some brainstormed words defy categorization. This is okay. They can still be offshoots of the semantic map, as not everything will fit into a category (Cox, 1999).

Semantic mapping is an excellent way to teach vocabulary across the disciplines. "marine" is a good word for science teachers who are teaching a lesson about the ocean, as well as for literature teachers who are about to embark on a story involving sea life. A social studies teacher might want to pick a word to explore in depth, such as "war" or "cavalry." Even older students will benefit from looking beyond the standard meaning of a word and into the deeper meaning. This will lend a greater depth of understanding when reading and help students with future writing assignments.

Semantic mapping is a good vehicle for students to share their work with the class, thus "teaching" the concept because teaching a concept to others increases student retention of information (http://www.essortment.com/all/teachersusesem_tvej.htm).

References

Alverman, D. & Phelps, S. E. (1994). *Content Reading and Literacy.* Allyn and Bacon: Boston.

Chomsky, N. (1959). A review of verbal behavior by B.F. Skinner. *Language, 35*, 26-58.

Clark, B. (2010). *First and Second Language Acquisition in Early Childhood,* http://ceep.crc.illinois.edu/pubs/katzsym/clark-b.pdf.

Collier, V. P. (1995). *Acquiring a Second Language for School: Vol. 1, No. 4. Directions in language and education.* Washington, DC: National Clearinghouse for Bilingual Education. (ERIC Document No. ED394301).

Cox, C. (1999). *Teaching Language Arts: A Student and Response Centered Classroom.* Allyn and Bacon: Boston.

Cummins, J. (1979). Linguistic Interdependence and Educational Development in Bilingual Students. *Review of Educational Research.* 49:2, 222-251.

Cummins, J. (1981). The role of primary language development in promoting educational success for language minority students. In California State Department of Education (Ed.), *Schooling and Language Minority Students: A Theoretical Framework* (pp. 3-49). Los Angeles: National Dissemination and Assessment Center.

Cummins, J. (2008). BICS and CALP: Empirical and theoretical status of the distinction. In Street, B. & Hornberger, N. (Eds). *Encyclopedia of language and education* (2nd). Vol 2. Literacy, pp. 71-83. New York: Springer.

Dunn, K., and Dunn, R. (1978). *Teaching Students through their Individual Learning Styles.* Reston, VA: National Council of Principals.

Eggen, P & Kauchak, D. (2006). *Strategies and Models for Teachers.* Allyn and Bacon: Boston.

Emmitt, M, Pollock, J. & Komescaroff, J. (Eds.), (2003*). Language variation. Language and learning: An Introduction for Teaching,* 3rd Eds. Oxford University Press, Oxford.
Gersten, R. (1999). The changing face of bilingual education. *Educational Leadership, 56* (7), 41-45. (ERIC Journal No. EJ585637)

Grosjean, F. (1982). *Life with Two Languages.* Cambridge, MA: Harvard University Press.

Johnston, J. (2006). Factors that influence language development. *Encyclopedia of Language and Literacy Development* (pp. 1-6). London, ON: Canadian Language and Literacy Research Network.

Krashen, S.D. (1982). *Principles and Practice in Second Language acquisition*, Oxford: Pergamon.

Krashen, S. D. (1996). *Under Attack: The case against bilingual education.* Culver City, CA: Language Education Associates.

Krashen, S. D. & Terrell, T. (1983). *The Natural Approach: Language Acquisition in the Classroom.* San Francisco, CA. Alemany Press.

Pérez, B., & Torres-Guzmán, M. (1996). *Learning in Two Worlds* (2nd). New York: Longman.

Ramsey, P. G. (1987). *Teaching and Learning in a Diverse World.* New York: Teachers College Press. (ERIC Document ED388729)

Saville-Troike, M. (1982). The development of bilingual and bicultural competence in young students. In L. G. Katz (Ed.), *Current Topics in Early Childhood Education* (Vol. 4). Norwood, NJ: Ablex. (ERIC Document ED250100)

Scarcella, R. (1990). *Teaching Language Minority Students in the Multicultural Classroom.* Prentice Hall: Englewood Cliffs, NJ.

Tabors, P. (1997). *One Child, Two Languages.* Baltimore, MD. (ERIC Document No. ED405987)

Witkin, H.A., Moore, C.A., Goodenough, D.R., & Cox, R.W. (1977). Field-dependent and Field-independent Cognitive Styles and their Educational Implications. *Review of Educational Research,* 47, 1-64.

Wong F. L. (1991). Second language learning in students: A model of language learning in social context. In E. Bialystok (Ed.), *Language Processing in Bilingual Students.* Cambridge, England: Cambridge University Press.

Woolfolk, A. (1998). *Educational Psychology, 7th edition.* Allyn and Bacon: Boston.

Yokota, J. (1993). Issues in Selecting Multicultural Students' Literature. *Language Arts.* 70, 156-167.

Young, A. R., Beitchman, J. H., Johnson, C., Douglas, L., Atkinson, L., Escobar, M., et al. (2002). Young adult academic outcomes in a longitudinal sample of early identified language impaired and control students. *Journal of Child Psychology and Psychiatry and Allied Disciplines, 43*, 635-645.
http://www.essortment.com
http://www.literacyencyclopedia.com
http://www.sk.com.br/sk-krash.html
http://www.tea.state.tx.us
Http://www.utdanacenter.org

Practice Questions

1. Which of the following terms is NOT associated with Krashen's **Affective Filter Hypothesis**?

    a. motivation
    b. articulation
    c. self-confidence
    d. anxiety

B is correct; the term, articulation, is not associated with Krashen's Affective Filter hypothesis. Krashen's Affective Filter Hypothesis purports that a number of affective variables such as: student motivation, self-confidence and level of anxiety play a facilitative, but non-causal, role in second language acquisition.

2. The **two primary factors** that influence language development are:

    a. biological and environmental factors
    b. monolingual and bilingual factors
    c. cognitive and affective factors
    d. usage and application factors

A is correct.

3. Of the following factors, which has the MOST influence on the way a child uses language?

    a. a child's gender
    b. a child's region of birth
    c. a child's stature
    d. a child's social class

D is correct.

4. Which of the following definitions describes a **subtractive bilingual** student?

a. a student who speaks one language better than the other
b. a student who has successfully learned two languages
c. a student who speaks two languages equally well
d. a student who has lost his/ her first language

D is correct.

5. Which of the following groups of words best define the term, **receptive language**?

     a. speaking, representing, writing
     b. listening, reading, viewing
     c. reading, writing, drawing
     d. acting, speaking, writing

B is correct.

6. In general, how long does it take for an ELL student to achieve **cognitive academic language proficiency** (CALP) ?

     a. 1 to 2 years
     b. 2 to 3 years
     c. 2 to 4 years
     d. 5 years or longer

D is correct. Research supports that it takes 5 years or longer for ELL students to catch up to native English speakers and achieve cognitive academic language proficiency.

7. Many students in Mr. Holmes' 9th grade English class speak with a dialect using nonstandard, grammatically incorrect English. Which of the following is the BEST teaching method Mr. Holmes should use to promote the use of Standard English in his classroom?

    a. Mr. Holmes should continue to allow students a variety of opportunities to speak in class using their dialect of English to ensure that he does not correct or embarrass students in front of their peers.
    b. Mr. Holmes should model standard English at all times in his classroom. He does not tell students their form of English is incorrect, rather, he often says, "In Standard English, we say it this way," thereby ensuring students' exposure to Standard English.
    c. Mr. Holmes allows students to speak and write using their dialect; however, he does spend time writing corrections on their papers, this way ensuring that students are not embarrassed or demeaned in class.
    d. Mr. Holmes provides time during class for students to work in groups in order to compare the variations of their dialects with standard English.

B is correct. This is the best method the teacher can use to promote the use of Standard English.

8. Mr. Downs, a 10th grade language arts teacher, is teaching writing to a group of students whose native language is not English. He uses several teaching strategies with his ELL students which aid their understanding of the text and assignment. Of the following, which is the **best** instructional method Mr. Downs can use to aid his students' writing skills?

    A. Read aloud sample papers to students while speaking slowly and repeating words often.
    B. Have students write the assignment independently using a Standard English dictionary to aid spelling and grammar.
    C. Before writing the assignment, have students work with a partner or in a small group to read and discuss examples of student work written in Standard English.
    D. Have students write their assignment in their native language, then use a dictionary to translate the work into English.

C is correct. Working with other students to read and discuss works written in Standard English would best increase students' writing skills.

9. Mr. Garcia, a 7th grade language arts teacher, obtained state test scores for his ELL students from the previous year. Mr. Garcia can best utilize this knowledge to:

    A. to predict which students will need after school tutoring sessions.
    B. to discuss the results with other teachers on the planning team in order to determine which students will not do well academically.
    C. to determine how to group students for various classroom activities.
    D. to plan effective instruction that will address the strengths and weaknesses of his students.

D is correct. An effective use of the previous year's test scores would help teachers plan lessons which address students' current strengths and weaknesses. TEST TIP: Teachers must acknowledge the rapid physical, emotional, and psychological changes which can occur during the teen years. Students of this age group often grow and mature in "spurts," therefore, some test results may not provide an accurate picture of a student's current academic ability.

10. When planning an interdisciplinary unit on "Great American Authors" for her students, Mrs. Chen wants to ensure that the unit addresses the learning styles of her limited English speaking students. She can best ensure that this occurs by:

    A. having students work in cooperative groups as they complete the unit to ensure that students have opportunities to share their views and practice their oral language skills.
    B. planning a variety of lesson activities, which address a wide range of learning styles, for students to complete while working through the unit.
    C. creating a valid and reliable test for the end of the interdisciplinary unit.
    D. ensuring that the contents of the unit plan addresses student interests.

B is correct. Offering a variety of activities for the limited English speaking students will help ensure that Mrs. Chen has provided the best methods for optimizing student learning. TEST TIP: working in cooperative groups supports student learning; however, be sure to consider the members of each group carefully. Teachers must have knowledge of effective grouping practices. Placing lower achieving students exclusively together in a cooperative group is not generally effective. On the other hand, a group consisting exclusively of gifted and talented, high achieving students is often very effective. A small cooperative group consisting of students of varying academic achievement levels is also considered a very effective grouping practice.

Domain I: Chapter 3

Competency 3: The Study of English - *The teacher understands the structure and development of the English language and provides students with opportunities to develop related knowledge and skills in meaningful contexts.*

The beginning teacher

- Demonstrates knowledge of major historical, regional and cultural influences on the ongoing development of the English language (e.g., Anglo-Saxon migrations, emergence of dialects, changing technology).
- Understands and teaches how to research word origins and analyze word formation as an aid to understanding meanings, derivations and spellings.
- Understands and teaches relationships among words (e.g., homonyms, synonyms, antonyms) and issues related to word choice (e.g., connotative and denotative meanings, multiple-meaning words, idioms, figurative language).
- Knows and teaches rules of grammar, usage, sentence structure, punctuation and capitalization in Standard English and is able to identify and edit nonstandard usage in his or her own discourse and the discourse of others.
- Knows how to provide explicit and contextual instruction that enhances students' knowledge of and ability to use Standard English.
- Knows and teaches how purpose, audience and register affect discourse.
- Demonstrates an understanding of informal and formal procedures for monitoring and assessing students' ability to use the English language effectively.
- Uses assessment results to plan and adapt instruction that addresses students' strengths, needs and interests and that builds on students' current skills to increase their proficiency in using the English language effectively.

Key Terms

Active voice
Affective domain
Antonym
Assessment
Audience
Borrowed words
Capitalization
Chaucer
Clausal modifier
Cohesion
Coherence
Complex sentences
Compound – Complex
Compound sentences
Compound words
Confused / Misused words
Connotation
Content vocabulary
Context Clues
Conventional (forms of spelling)
Coordinating conjunction
Decode
Denotation
Derivation
Derivational morphology
Environmental stimuli
Epic
Etymology
Etymological knowledge
etymonline
Generativist
Generative grammar
Great Vowel Shift
Homonyms
Homophone
Industrial Revolution
Inflectional endings
Language development
Lexicon
Linguistics
Middle English

Modern English
Modifiers
Morphemes
Morphology
Morphemic analysis
Morphemic Knowledge
Morphological system
Noam Chomsky
Norman Conquest of 1066
Old English
Orthography
Philology
Phoneme
Phonology
Phono-semantic matching
Pragmatics
Passive voice
Phonological knowledge
Phrasal modifier
Predicate
Prefix
Punctuation
Purpose
Renaissance
Register
Semicolon
Semantics
Sentence structure
Simple sentences
Shakespeare
Statute of Pleading
Subject
Synonym
Syntax
Sight words
Suffix
Take Our Word For It
Universal Grammar
Visual knowledge
Word analysis
Word families

Historical, Regional, and Cultural Influences on the English language

The **historical** development of English is conventionally divided into three periods usually called **Old English** (or Anglo-Saxon), **Middle English**, and **Modern English**. However, the historical aspect of English really encompasses more than the three stages of development; English has a prehistory as well. Historically, English is a member of the Indo-European family of languages that includes:

- Latin and the modern Romance languages
- Germanic languages
- Indo-Iranian languages (including Hindi and Sanskrit)
- Slavic languages
- Baltic languages of Latvian and Lithuanian
- Celtic languages
- Greek language

Similarities have been found among early languages. However, examination of some of the languages has been difficult because early tribes had no written language and left no records. However, research reveals that ancient languages like Old Norse and Gothic, and modern languages like Icelandic and Norwegian have common characteristics with Old English and Old High German or Dutch that they do not share with French or Russian. Thus, it is clear that an earlier unrecorded language existed that has been labeled Germanic (Pyles & Algeo, 1993).

The origins of this Germanic language emerged in the Elbe river region over 3,000 years ago. This language was brought to the British Isles from the European continent by Germanic invaders during the 5th and 6th centuries (Pyles & Algeo, 1993).

Old English
The language that evolved from this Germanic settlement in the British Isles is known as Old English or Anglo-Saxon. The language developed further as four dialects of Old English emerged from this settlement:

- Northumbrian in the north of England
- Mercian in the Midlands
- West Saxon in the south and west
- Kentish in the southeast

the dialect of Wessex, is referred to as Standard Old English. About
used words in modern English have roots in Old English. It is the
as *Beowulf,* an **epic** poem that describes the adventures of the great
of the 6th century. *Beowulf* is the oldest surviving epic in British literature
). The first line and a half of *Beowulf* from the manuscript reads as follows:

sh	Modern English
RDE na ... eardagum peodcyninga	Lo! we [have heard] about the might of the Spear-Danes' kings in the early days ...

A few centuries later, the Viking invaders in the 9th century left their mark on the English
language in the form of numerous Scandinavian (North Germanic) words. During the 10th
century, Latin, Old Norse (the language of the Viking invaders), and especially the Anglo-
Norman French of the dominant class (after the **Norman Conquest** in 1066) also had a
substantial impact on the language, and the well-developed inflectional system that typifies the
grammar of Old English had begun to break down (Pyles & Algeo, 1993).

Middle English
Middle English begins with the **Norman Conquest** of 1066 and extends to the 15th century with
the death of Chaucer in 1400. The Norman conquerors spoke a dialect of Old French known as
Anglo-Norman. This dialect emerged from a Latin base but had considerable Germanic
influences. Influence of French (and Latin) upon the English language continued throughout this
period as many changes (phonological and grammatical) took place.

The influence of the **Norman Conquest** can be illustrated with the words *cow* and *beef. Beef,*
commonly eaten by the aristocracy, derives from the Anglo-Norman dialect, while the Anglo-
Saxon commoners who tended cattle, retained the Germanic word *cow.* French words such as
champagne, chandelier, bouquet, and *mayonnaise* are but a few of the many words instilled in
the English language from the Norman invaders. Politics and geography influenced the
increasing estrangement of the Norman noble classes of England from France and the nobility
adopted English as their native tongue.

During this time, there were significant social changes; the merchant classes grew in economic
and social importance and this growth increased the importance of English compared to Anglo
Norman. Moreover, the Black Plague (1348-50) caused the death of nearly one-third of the
English population. Two additional factors very influential during this period include: (l) the
Statue of Pleading, (c. 1362) the law stating that all court proceedings be conducted in English;
(2) and the fact that Chaucer chose to write his major works in East Midlands English dialect, the
dialect spoken in London at the time. The example below from Chaucer's *Knight's Tale*
illustrates the language of this time (Pyles & Algeo, 1993):

She gadereth floures, party white and rede,

To make a subtil gerland for hire hede;
And as an aungel hevenysshly she soong.

Modern English

Modern English extends from the 16th century until present time. With the Renaissance era, a vast array of Latin and Greek words expanded the existing vocabulary and had great influence upon the lexicon. The early part of this period saw the completion of a revolution in the phonology of English "**The Great Vowel Shift**" that had begun in late Middle English and that effectively redistributed the occurrence of the vowel phonemes to something approximating their present pattern. The **Great Vowel Shift** was a major change in the pronunciation of the English language that took place in the south of England between 1450 and 1750. The values of the long vowels form the main difference between the pronunciation of Middle English and Modern English, and the **Great Vowel Shift** is one of the historical events marking the separation of Middle and Modern English. For example, the vowel in the English word *date* was in Middle English pronounced [aː] (similar to modern *dart*); the vowel in *feet* was [eː] (similar to modern *fate*); the vowel in *wipe* was [iː] (similar to modern *weep*); the vowel in *boot* was [oː] (similar to modern *boat*); and the vowel in *house* was [uː] (similar to modern *whose*).

By the time of Shakespeare, the language was only a bit more inflected than it is today (Pyles & Algeo, 1993). Other important developments during this time period include the stabilizing effect of the printing press upon spelling, the first English dictionary published in 1604, and the publication of the King James Bible in 1611. London speech became established as the English language experienced a process of standardization, aided by the printing press. Late-Modern English (1800-present) is a distinctive period because of the introduction of a vast amount of new vocabulary. The rise of the British Empire and the growth of global trade and colonization introduced English to the world.

As the British conquered countries around the world, dialects of English in the many colonized areas resulted. These languages made small but interesting contributions to the English word-stock (i.e. French: *au gratin, garage*; India: *bandana, madras*) (Pyles & Algeo, 1993).

American-English dates from the 17th century and diverts in spelling and also idiomatically from British English. American-English influence on the language has been considerable within the sphere of new coinages and scientific words.

An important factor contributing to the increase in vocabulary was the technological influences which occurred during the Industrial Revolution. The industrial, political, and scientific upsurge during this time period resulted in the need for neologisms to describe the many inventions and discoveries. Terms such as *horsepower, airplane, radio, television, teletype, telephone,* and *typewriter* are new words created during this time.

In addition, many Native American words were integrated into English: *Mississippi, Roanoke, hickory, canoe,* and *raccoon* are a few examples (Pyles & Algeo, 1993).

More recent scientific, political, and social influences have produced terms such as: *DNA, login, website, web master, twitter, Facebook, Pilates, Cross-training, HOV lane, black hole, Space Shuttle, women's lib, gender wars, Cloud technology, digital divide, ipad, iphone, ebook, etc.*

Etymology: The Study of Word Origin

Etymology is the study of the history of words. The word **etymolog***y* comes from the Ancient Greek language and is composed of two parts: the Greek word *etymon,* which means "the true sense of a word," combined with the Greek element *logia,* which means "doctrine, study." Combining these two parts gives us "the study of the true sense of words" (www.behindthename.com/etymology.html).

A word may enter a language as a loanword or **borrowed word** (i.e., as a word from one language adopted by speakers of another language), through **derivational morphology** by combining pre-existing elements in the language, or by a hybrid of these two processes called **phono-semantic matching** (www.behindthename.com/etymology.html).

Teaching Word Origins: Meanings and Derivatives

In the dictionary, etymologies, or word origins, appear in square brackets following the entry definitions. (Hopper & Carter-Wells, 1994). When teaching etymologies, teachers need to emphasize "word families" so that students will recognize additional words that share a common etymology. For example, the etymology of the word "perceive" is illustrated in the following dictionary entry:

> Perceive (per' sev). V, -ceived, -ceiving. -v.1. to be aware of through the senses; see, hear, taste, smell, or feel: *Did you perceive the colors of that bird? We perceived a little girl coming toward us.* syn: see syn, under see. 2. to take in with the mind; observe: *I soon perceived that I could not make him change his mind. I plainly perceived some objections remain.* syn: understand, comprehend. -v.. to grasp or take in something with the senses or mind. [< Old North French *perceivre* < Latin *percipere* < per thoroughly + *capere* to grasp] -perceiver, n.

The teacher should emphasize that the word "perceive" originated from Latin *per* (thoroughly) plus *capere* (to grasp).

There are numerous specialized etymology dictionaries (i.e. Oxford Guide to Etymology). Online resources for researching entomologies include:

etymonline [etymonline.com] - a great resource for looking up the origins of specific words.

Take Our Word For It - a fun website for browsing through and learning about etymologies in a more entertaining, less structured way (*www.takeourword.com).*

Relationships among Words

Words, like people, have families that share the same names and words can be related in regard to their parts. A basic knowledge of word parts can help students unlock the meaning to thousands of related words. For example, the prefix *ambi* means both; the word *ambivert* refers to a person who is both an introvert and an extrovert. Other words containing the same word part can also be defined easily based on this knowledge. Therefore, the transfer of basic word part knowledge can unlock the meaning to words such as: *ambidextrous, ambiguous,* and *ambivalence.*

A word's **derivation** occurs when an affix is attached to the root or base word part. An affix that is attached to the front of the base word is called a **prefix**; whereas, an affix attached to the end of a base word is called a **suffix.** Some common English derivational affixes (prefixes and suffixes) include:

anti- anti-abortion	-able understand-able
de- de-activate	-(at)ion realiz-ation
mis- mis-identify	-ing sleep-ing
re- re-iterate	-ous lecher-ous
ex- ex-president	-ate captiv-ate

Homonym - one of two or more words spelled and pronounced alike but different in meaning. Example: quail(n) = a small bird / quail (v) = to cower, to falter, to recoil in dread or terror.

Homophone - one of two or more words pronounced alike but different in meaning, derivation or spelling. Example: to, too, two

Synonym - two or more words or expressions that have the same or nearly the same meaning. Example: profusion, abundance

Antonym - two or more words with the opposite meaning. Example: dearth, abundance

Connotation - a meaning that is associated with a word but not a part of the "official" meaning; many times the meanings are either positive or negative. Example: the connotation of the word skinny is negative; however, the connotation of the word slim is positive.

Denotation - the "official" dictionary definition attached to a word.

Word families - clusters of words sharing the same base or root. Example: biology, biochemistry, biosphere, biodegradable.

Pronunciation Overview

Modern English displays a vast inconsistency between sound and spelling, and so a dictionary of English must devote considerable attention to the pronunciation of the language. The English lexicon contains numerous eye rhymes (sight rhymes) such as *love, move,* and *rove,* words which do not sound alike despite their similar spellings. On the other hand, English also contains rhyming words such as *breeze, cheese, ease, frieze,* and *sleaze* whose rhymes are all spelled differently (http://www.merriam-webster.com).

English Vowels

English vowels present different complexities of sound and spelling partly due to the fact that William Caxton introduced printing to England in 1476, many decades before the sound change known as the Great Vowel Shift had run its course. With the rise of printing came an increasingly fixed set of spelling conventions, but the conventionalized spellings soon lost the connection to pronunciation as the vowel shift continued. The stressed vowels of *sane* and *sanity* are therefore identical in spelling though now quite different in quality. For the trained observer the vagaries of English orthography (spelling) contain a wealth of linguistic history; for most others, however, this disparity between sound and spelling is just a continual nuisance at school or work (http://www.merriam-webster.com).

Variant Pronunciations

Readers often turn to the dictionary when wanting to learn the exact pronunciation of a word, only to discover that the word may have several pronunciations, as is the case for *deity, economic, envelope*, and *greasy*, among many others. The inclusion of variant pronunciations disappoints those who want their dictionary to list one "correct" pronunciation (http://www.merriam-webster.com).

Structure, Acquisition, Use and Analysis of Language

Linguistics is the systematic study of language. Academics classify its study into a number of sub-fields - an important topical division being between the study of language structure (grammar) and the study of meaning (semantics).

Grammar encompasses **morphology** (the formation and composition of words), **syntax** (the rules that determine how words combine into phrases and sentences), and **phonology** (the study of sound systems and abstract sound units) (http://www.lingvotech.com/en/linguistics).

Morphology

Morphology refers to the rules that govern the use of **morphemes** (the smallest unit of meaning) within language. The morphology of English requires that plural endings vary according to the last sound of the word stem (Gleason, 2001). When a new word like "glitch" comes into the English language, adult speakers can immediately tell what its plural is; they do not need to consult a dictionary. They are able to pluralize a word that they have never heard before because they know the English inflectional **morphological system** (GLEASON, 2001).

The rules understood by the speaker reflect specific patterns (or regularities) in the way words are formed from smaller units (prefix, root words, suffix). For example, the word "unfaithful" contains three morphemes: *un* = not; *faith* = a belief that does not rest on logical proof or material evidence; and *full* = having a great deal or many (McMahon, 1994).

Syntax

Within the field of linguistics, **syntax** is the study of the principles and rules for constructing sentences in natural languages (the order of language). Modern researchers in syntax attempt to describe languages in terms of such rules (McMahon, 1994).

Phonology

Phonology is the study of the sound system of language, the sounds the language uses, as well as the rules for their combination. A phoneme is a speech sound that can signal a difference of meaning; two similar speech sounds /p/ and /b/ represent different phonemes in English because there are pairs of words with different meanings that have the same phonetic form, except that one contains b where the other contains p. For example: pet and bet (Gleason, 2001).

An important part of phonology is studying which sounds are distinctive units within a language. For example, the "p" in "pin" is aspirated while the same phoneme in "spin" is not. In addition to the minimal meaningful sounds (the **phonemes**), phonology studies how sounds alternate, such as the /p/ in English, and topics such as syllable structure, stress, accent, and intonation (McMahon, 1994).

Cognitive, Affective, and Socio-cultural Influences on Language Development

Language acquisition is the process by which humans acquire the capacity to perceive, produce, and use words to understand and communicate. Learning to talk is one of the most visible and important achievements of early childhood. In a matter of months, toddlers move from hesitant single words to fluent sentences (Johnston, 2006).

In very general terms, the two primary factors that influence **language development** are biological and environmental. However, a major challenge to understanding language acquisition is to understand how language capacities (syntax, phonetics, and vocabulary) are learned by infants from what appears to be very little external input. Opposing theorists try to explain this dilemma; one side purports the concept of **innatism**, explaining that a child is genetically born with innate language capacities, the opposing theorist explain language acquisition as a response to **environmental stimuli.**

Theoretical Debate

The nature of the mental activity that underlies **language development** as a child grows is widely debated among child language experts. However, in broad strokes, the observable "facts" of language development are not in dispute. Most children begin speaking during their second year and by age two are likely to know at least 50 words and begin combining them into short phrases. Once vocabulary size reaches about 200 words, the rate of word learning increases dramatically and grammatical function words such as articles and prepositions begin to appear with some consistency. During the preschool years, sentence patterns become increasingly complex and vocabulary diversifies to include relational terms that express notions of size, location, quantity, and time. From the age of four to six, most students have acquired the basic grammar of the sentence. From that point onward, students learn to use language efficiently and effectively. They also learn how to create, and maintain, larger language units such as conversation or narrative. Although there are individual differences in rate of development, the sequence in which various forms appear is highly predictable both within and across stages (Johnston, 2006).

The Nature of Language Knowledge

Noam Chomsky (1959) theorized that verbal communication requires productivity, i.e. the ability to create an infinite number of utterances never heard before. This endless novelty requires an understanding of abstract language knowledge. Ultimately, "rules" for combining words cannot be rules about particular words, but must be rules about classes of words such as nouns, verbs, or prepositions. Once these abstract blueprints are available, the speaker can fill the "slots" in a sentence with the words that best convey the message of the moment. Chomsky's (1959) key point was that since language abstractions can never be directly experienced, they must emerge from the child's own mental activity while listening to speech (Johnston, 2006).

Factors Affecting Language Acquisition and Development

As the debate between nurture vs. nature continues in many academic circles, several factors in each have been identified as contributing to language development (Johnston, 2006):

Basic Biological / Genetic Makeup

In the nature category, some researchers contend that students are born with an innate biological device for understanding the principles and organization common to all languages. This is to say that language development is programmed into the human design. Language development then simply happens innately and is not necessarily shaped by other outside influences. Many scientists believe that the human brain comes with a **universal grammar** that interacts with the rest of the brain in early development that forms the foundation of language fluency (Johnston, 2006).

Social Interaction

An active and communicative social environment influences language development because this provides ample input for children to process. Some linguists argue that adults play an important role in language development by providing children with repetitious exposure to correct language usage. In addition, social interaction offers opportunities for children to experiment with language – try out new words in new contexts, verbalize complicated and abstract thoughts, and more (Johnston, 2006).

Opportunities for Usage

Some researchers place more emphasis on the usage of language as an influential factor than biological make up or exposure. Children who are listened to and prompted with stimulating questions to speak often develop their language skills more quickly than those who do not use language as often. A good example is the baby of the family who seldom needs to speak because older siblings speak for them. This influences language development and often delays the natural development (Johnston, 2006).

Sociocultural Factors

There are **sociocultural** factors that influence language variation. Social class has a major bearing on the way a child uses language. Emmitt, Pollock & Komescaroff (2003) describe how different classes use different codes of language. A child's sociocultural circumstance dominates a child's use and development of language. In some sociocultural situations, language usage may inadvertently discriminate against **gender** groups and can therefore be considered discriminatory. **Ethnicity** can also be seen as a major factor in language variation. Students who do not speak English as their first language must understand the language conventions of English as they learn (Johnston, 2006).

Affective Considerations

The **affective** domain includes factors such as: empathy, self-esteem, extroversion, inhibition, imitation, anxiety, and attitudes. Some affective variables may seem at first rather far removed from language learning, but when one considers the pervasive nature of language, any affective factor can conceivably become relevant to language learning (Johnston, 2006).

However, the course of language acquisition is not driven exclusively from within. The structure of the language to be learned, and the frequency with which various forms are heard, will also have an effect. Despite the theoretical debates, it seems clear that language skills reflect knowledge and capabilities in virtually every domain (Johnston, 2006).

Analyzing Unknown Words:

Teachers should encourage students to try to unlock the meaning to unknown words by taking the following steps:

- **Use context clues**: read the words surrounding the unknown word; these words may help define the unknown word.

- **Decode the word**: look for roots, suffixes, prefixes. These word parts may provide clues to the word's meaning.

- **Try to pronounce the word:** use of letters and sounds (phonics) should help the reader pronounce the word.

- **Ask a friend** or teacher the meaning of the word, or look up the word in the dictionary. Reread the sentence and paragraph once the meaning of the unknown word is known.

Conventions of Oral and Written Language

The following outline serves to review the teacher candidate on basic grammar and usage terms needed for the certification exam. A secondary English teacher must know the rules of grammar, usage, sentence structure, punctuation, and capitalization in Standard English and be able to edit non-standard usage in student writing.

Parts of Speech

Noun - names a person, place, thing, or idea. Example: golf, freedom, theater. *Note:* Proper nouns name a particular place or person and are capitalized. Example: Don, Austin, Alley Theater.

Pronoun - used in place of a noun. Example: he, she, it, they, someone. A pronoun identifies people, places, things or ideas without renaming them. The noun that a pronoun replaces is the antecedent of the pronoun. If a pronoun is placed too far away from its antecedent it is considered unclear or vague in reference. The three types of pronouns include: simple (I, you, he, she, it, we, they, who, what); compound, (itself, myself, anybody, someone, everything; and phrasal (each other, one another).

Verb - expresses action or state of being. Types of verbs include: action verbs (run, jump, memorize, crawl), linking / helping verbs (be, is, was, were, may, might, shall) .

Adjective - a word that modifies a noun or a pronoun and answers the question: Which one? What kind? How many? Example: *western* civilization, *unorthodox* service, *twenty thousand* people.

Adverb - a word that modifies a verb, adjective, or another adverb and answers the question: How? When? Where? How often? To what extent? Example: Though injured, Joanna walked the last mile of the race *courageously.* Jonathan is rather *doubtful* about hiring the new assistant.

Preposition - expresses a relationship between a noun or pronoun and another word in a sentence. Example: The designer *from* Paris visited our showroom and restructured our display cases. *Note:* A preposition is usually followed by a noun or a pronoun, which is called the object of the preposition. Together, the preposition, the object, and the modifiers form a *prepositional phrase*.

Conjunction - a word that connects words or groups of words. Three types of conjunctions include:

> **Coordinating Conjunction** - Examples: and, but, for, nor, or, so and yet. The biologist, hoping to find a good specimen, *but* not expecting to find one, traveled to the rainforest.

> **Correlative Conjunction** - Example: either ... or; not only ... but also; neither ... nor; whether . .. or. Jon stated that he had *neither* watched the video *nor* read the novel before the English test.

> **Subordinating Conjunction** - introduces a subordinate clause that cannot stand by itself as a complete sentence. Example: *As* the weeks and months passed, the young woman's health problems began to diminish.

Gerund - is made up of a present participle (a verb ending in –ing) and always functions as a noun. Example: ***Snorkeling*** *is Michael's hobby.*

Infinitive - is made up of the word "*to*" and the base form of a verb, such as *to show* or *to love.* An infinitive can function as an adjective, adverb, or noun.

Interjection - an exclamatory word or phrase that usually expresses strong emotion. Example: *Wow!* I love this Italian food.

Participle - is a verb form that usually ends in –ing or –ed. Participles operate as adjectives but also maintain the characteristics of verbs. Examples: the *dancing bear* or *baked goods*.

Parts of Sentences

Subject - tells who or what the sentence is about. Subject complement-follows the linking verb and describes or identifies the subject. Example: **Dr. Bhattacharjee** is a *professor*. **Dr. Bhattacharjee** is *efficient*.

Predicate - the verb or verb phrase that describes the action or state of being of the subject.

Direct Object - a noun or pronoun that follows a verb and answers the question: what? or whom?

Indirect Object -a noun or pronoun that follows a verb and answers the question: to whom? For whom? to what? for what?

Phrase - a group of related words that functions as a single part of speech but lacks a subject, a predicate, or both.

Prepositional phrase - A phrase that consists of a preposition and its object and has adjectival or adverbial value, such as *under the house* or *over the hill.*

Appositive Phrase - explains the noun. Example: Joanna Williams, *vice-president of marketing,* presented the new business plan to the board of directors.

Participle Phrase - functions as an adjective in the sentence. Example: There is Jonathan *walking across the parking lot to his car.*

Gerund Phrase - a verb that ends in "ing" and functions as a noun in the sentence. Example: *According to Joanna,* shopping at the mall eases her stress level.

Infinitive Phrase - a verb usually proceeded by "to" that functions as a noun, adjective, or adverb in the sentence. Example: The best way *to prepare for a career* is to attend college.

Clause-a group of related words that contains both a subject and a predicate.

Independent Clause - can stand alone as a complete sentence. Example: *I love this beautiful day.* Connect two independent clauses with a coordinating conjunction (and, or, but) or a semi-colon. Example: *I love this beautiful day; I am going to play outside.*

Subordinate Clause (Dependent Clause) - is not a complete sentence and is connected to an independent clause by a comma. Example: *Although the day was cold,* Don played a complete round of golf.

Adjective Clause - functions as an adjective and usually begins with a relative pronoun: that, which, who, whom or whose. Example: Jon often dresses in jeans and a western shirt, *which is typical attire for a Texas man.*

Adverb Clause-functions as an adjective in the sentence. Example: *After twelve weeks of exercise in the gym,* I began to see a difference in the muscle tone of my body.

Noun Clause-functions as a noun in the sentence. Example: *Whether or not to sell the house* was a concern for all of us.

Writing Complete Sentences

A complete sentence is a group of words that has a subject and a predicate and expresses a complete thought.

Fragment - a group of words that is not a complete sentence. Example: *Planning to graduate from college.*

Run-on Sentence - consists of two or more sentences written as one sentence. Several ways exists to correct run-on sentences: (1) separate the run-on sentence into two sentences, (2) use a coordinating conjunction, (3) use a semicolon, (4) turn one of the independent clauses into a subordinate clause, or (5) use a semicolon and a conjunctive adverb (however, therefore).

Parallel Structure - similarity of structure in a pair or series of related words, phrases, or clauses. By convention, items in a series should appear in parallel grammatical form: a noun is listed with other like nouns, For example: an *-ing* form with other *-ing* forms. She spent time *combing* her hair, *brushing* her teeth and *washing* her face.) Failure to express such items in similar grammatical form is called **faulty parallelism.**

Idioms - A set expression of two or more words that means something other than the literal meanings of its individual words.
Examples:
If we *play our cards right*, we may be able to find out when the men will return.
He's *true blue*.
He really *went to town* on that issue.

Usage and Agreement in Sentences
Subject-Verb Agreement - a subject and verb must agree in number; that is, if a subject is singular, the verb should also be singular. Likewise, if the subject is plural, the verb should also be plural. Example: *Joanna has* traveled all over the world. *Joanna and Jonathan have* traveled all over the world.

Count nouns refer to items which can be counted, meaning that there can be more than one of them. Also, when a count noun is singular and indefinite, the article "a/an" is often used with it. Thus, the real meaning of "a/an" is "one." Examples: "There is a book on the table." "There is an odor in my car."

Non-count Nouns (or uncounted nouns) name items which cannot be counted, such as rice or water. **Non-count nouns** are treated as grammatically singular, but when they are indefinite, the writer should use the word "some" (or nothing at all) instead of an article.
Example: "May I have some water please?" "I would like rice with my steak."

Pronoun-Antecedent Agreement - a pronoun must agree with its antecedent in number (singular or plural), gender (masculine or feminine), and person (first person, second person, or third person).

Consistency in Verb Tense - use of verb tense by the writer indicates whether an action or condition takes place in the present, past or future. The writer should stay consistent with verb tense. Example: Jonathan *lifted* the box while his mother *swept* the floor under it. If a shift is needed, the writer must indicate to the reader that the change took place.

Correct Use of Modifiers - misplacement of modifiers (subordinate clauses) can create misunderstanding. Faulty sentence example: *Hanging on the museum wall, Joanna examined the beautiful paintings by Remington.* Correct the faulty structure of this sentence by moving the modifier closer to the noun that it modifies. Example: *Joanna examined the beautiful paintings by Remington hanging on the museum wall.*

Capitalization - a writer should capitalize the following:
- first word in a sentence
- first word of a direct quote
- proper nouns
- official titles (Dr., Dean, Mr.)
- gods of mythology
- heavenly bodies
- names of peoples and nationalities
- titles of books, newspapers, poems, etc.
- names of academic subjects and languages
- names of organizations, government bodies, clubs, schools
- proper adjectives (Example: Russian wolfhound)
- both letters in abbreviations
- states, cities, counties

Conventional Forms of Spelling

The value of correct spelling is that it gives writing credibility and therefore helps writers communicate effectively. Recent developments in technology, such as spell-check software, have not replaced the need for writers to understand how to spell words correctly. Such technology assists in proofreading, but is not a substitute for spelling knowledge (McCrum, et al, 2002).

In the early stages of their language and spelling development, students often use spellings that approximate conventional forms. Students typically move from inventive spelling to approximation to correct spelling during their education. During these stages, in particular, it is important that teachers give students support and encouragement about how to spell unfamiliar words correctly.

The early form of English (or Anglo-Saxon) was more phonetically regular than Modern English. In the original English, grammatical meaning was heavily dependent on word endings and word order was less important. Some of these original features still remain (e.g. *ox–oxen, man–men; mouse– mice*). Over time, as word order assumed greater importance, many of the word endings dropped off. The silent *e* at the end of many English words is due to this change (McCrum, et al, 2002).

After the introduction of Christianity and the Norman invasion, large numbers of Latin and French words entered the language. Because the Anglo-Saxon language had many sounds that were not found in French, and also because French handwriting was different from that used by the Anglo-Saxons, some spelling compromises had to be made when writing the language.
For example, the latter phenomenon led to the introduction of the letter *o* in words like *love, son,* and *women*.

Consistency in spelling is a comparatively recent phenomenon. For example, as Anglo-Saxon moved towards Middle English and into Elizabethan times, many words with *i* and *e* vowels and the *ae* diphthongs changed.

In Shakespeare's time, for example, the word *reason* was pronounced "raisin" (as it still is in parts of the United Kingdom today), which is why Shakespeare indulges in a "play on words" with *reasons* and *blackberries* in *Henry IV* (McCrum, et al, 2002).

Since medieval times, English has acquired thousands of new words from a variety of sources. Many of these were derived from Latin and Greek during the Renaissance. Other words were derived from the languages of communities colonized by Britain. Following the industrial revolution, additional words had to be invented. Moreover, when scientific knowledge was growing in the early modern age, Greek words were used as the basis for coining new scientific words. The Greek alphabet has some letter sounds that the English alphabet does not have, such as *phi, chi,* and *psi*. This accounts for the non-phonetic spelling of a host of English words, such as *telephone, trachea,* and *psychology* (McCrum, et al, 2002).

Understanding English Spelling

Within the context of meaningful written language experiences, students need explicit teaching about the phonological, visual, morphemic, and etymological aspects of spelling that are relevant to their stage of spelling development. When they have access to this knowledge, students will be better able to spell unfamiliar words accurately for a variety of social and academic purposes (McCrum, et al, 2002).

Basic Spelling Rules

One of the most common spelling rules is "I before E, except after C, unless it says A as in neighbor and weigh." However, there are a number of other rules students can use to help decode the spelling of an unfamiliar word (http://grammar.about.com/od/words/tp/spellrules.htm).

For example:

- The letter Q is always followed by U. In this case, the U is not considered to be a vowel.

- The letter S never follows X.

- The letter Y, not I, is used at the end of English words. Examples of this rule include my, by, shy, and why.

- To spell a short vowel sound, only one letter is needed. Examples of this rule include at, red, it, hot, and up.

- When a word ends with a silent final E, it should be written without the E when adding an ending that begins with a vowel. In this way, come becomes coming and hope becomes hoping.

- When adding an ending to a word that ends with Y, change the Y to I if it is preceded by a consonant. In this way, supply becomes supplies and worry becomes worried.

- All, written alone, has two L's. When used as a prefix, however, only one L is written. Examples of this rule include always and almost.

- Generally, adding a prefix to a word does not change the correct spelling.

- Words ending in a vowel and Y can add the suffix -ed or -ing without making any other change.

Morphemes are the smallest units of language that carry meaning. The **phonemes** (sounds) /b/, /a/ and /t/ blend together to form the morpheme /bat/. While the word *bat* carries some meaning, its particular meaning depends on the context of its use. For example, its meaning is different in each of the following sentences:

> I bought a baseball bat.
> She went to bat for him.
> The bat spread its wings.

The ending *-ing* is also a morpheme, even though it carries meaning only when it is bound to a word like *bat*, to make *batting*. Therefore, adding the *-ing* morpheme causes a change to the other morpheme, in this case the doubling of the end consonant. Fortunately, such morphemic changes are fairly regular in English, which is why understanding morphemic patterns is another important aspect of spelling knowledge. This is often the point of spelling "rules" (McCrum, et al, 2002)).

Understanding these features of the English language helps writers spell, because it is useful to remember that many of the words that are difficult to spell have non-phonetic spellings for a variety of reasons: their present spelling might reflect the way they were pronounced many years ago (the word *knight*), or they might be borrowed from a foreign language (the French word *charade*).

Most of these features must be learned as individual cases. There is no consistent approach to what the English language does with words borrowed from other languages. Either **visual knowledge** or **etymological knowledge** is used in these instances.

The best way to learn how to spell the common word *two* correctly is simply to rely on visual knowledge. On the other hand, the best way to learn how to spell *psychology* correctly is to learn that it starts with the Greek letter *psi* and has within it the other Greek letter *chi*, the same letter as in *Christmas*. This demonstrates the importance of **etymological knowledge** (a word's origin), not only for older students, but also for students at any stage of learning when they need to learn the spelling of a particular word (http://grammar.about.com/od/words/tp/spellrules.htm).

Proficient Spellers
The knowledge that students need if they are to become proficient spellers takes four different forms:
>   **Phonological Knowledge** - how words and letter combinations sound
>   **Visual Knowledge** - the way words and letter combinations look
>   **Morphemic Knowledge** - the meaning of words (or word parts) and the way words take different spellings when they change form
>   **Etymological Knowledge** - word origin; the derivations of words

Phonological knowledge focuses on how sounds correspond to letters. This includes teaching students:

- **the names of letters**, the sounds they represent and the ways in which letters can be grouped to make different sounds e.g. vowels, consonants, consonant blends, and word families like *ound, itch, ock*
- **the concept of onset and rime** e.g. in the word *pink*, *p* is onset and *ink* is rime
- **how to segment the sounds** in words into "chunks" of sound (phonemic awareness): the word *that*, has three phonemes or sounds

Visual knowledge focuses on how words look. This includes teaching students:

- **to recall and compare the appearance** of words, particularly those which they have seen or learned before or those which are commonly used
- **to recognize letters** and how to write them
- **to recognize** that **letters can be grouped** in particular ways, e.g. endings that frequently occur in words

Morphemic Knowledge focuses on the meaning of words and how they change when they take on different grammatical forms. This includes teaching students:

- how to use **morphemes** to assist them to spell words
- how **compound words** are constructed (examples: hotdog, bathroom, football)
- knowledge of **suffixes** and **prefixes,** generalizations that can be made, and the rules that can be generated about adding them to words

Etymological Knowledge focuses on the origins and meaning of non-phonetic words. This includes teaching students:

- about the roots of words and word meanings
- particular clusters of letters that appear in words not only look the same, but also are related in meaning, often because of their root, e.g. *aquatic, aquatint, aquarium.*

Punctuation

Commas

- Separate three or more words or phrases in a series.

- After introductory phrases. Example: *After the trip to Hawaii, Joanna felt rested and ready to return to work.*

- Separate sentence parts that may be misread or confused. Example: *Whenever possible, alternative ideas should be offered by each member of the group.*

- Distinguish non-essential phrases. Example: *The new employees, who did not understand the insurance benefits, attended an additional information meeting.*

Types of Sentences

Simple Sentence - A complete sentence that expresses a single thought and contains a subject and a verb.

Independent Clause - A simple sentence which can be combined with another simple sentence or a dependent clause to form either a compound or complex sentence.

Dependent Clause - A group of words that adds information to or modifies an independent clause. It is not a complete sentence and cannot stand by itself as a sentence.

Compound Sentence - A sentence formed by the joining of two independent clauses using a coordinating conjunction, a semicolon, or a conjunctive adverb.

Complex Sentence - A sentence composed of an independent clause and one or more dependent clauses joined by subordinating conjunctions.

Compound-Complex Sentences - A sentence containing two or more independent clauses and one or more dependent clauses. The methods of joining these clauses may include any of the options below.

Techniques for Creating Sentence Variety
The Coordinating Conjunction
The most common way to join two simple sentences (independent clauses) is with a coordinating conjunction (and, or, but, nor, for, yet, so)
Example: I went to China, *but* Michael went to Mexico.
I went to China **(independent clause), (comma)** *but* **(conjunction)** Michael went to Mexico **(independent clause)**.

The Semicolon
To join two closely related simple sentences (independent clauses), you may use a semicolon without a conjunction.
Example: I went to China**;** Michael went with me. I went to China **(independent clause);** **(semicolon)** Michael went with me **(independent clause)**.

The Semicolon and a Conjunctive Adverb
To combine two simple sentences (independent clauses), you may use a semicolon and a conjunctive adverb (however, therefore, indeed, moreover, consequently, etc.). Conjunctive adverbs carry the thought of the first independent clause to the related independent clause that follows it.
Example: I wanted to become a professor; **therefore**, I completed a doctorate degree.
I wanted to become a professor **(independent clause); (semicolon)** therefore **(conjunctive adverb), (comma)** I completed a doctorate degree **(independent clause)**.

Subordinate Conjunction

Another method of joining two simple sentences is the use of subordinating conjunctions (after, although, as, as if, before, because, if, since, unless, when, whenever, until, while, etc.). The example below contains a common subordinating conjunction. The main point of the sentence is an independent clause and the dependent clause contains the subordinate conjunction.

Example: *Although* I recently recovered from a bad cold, I continued with my vacation plans.
Although **(subordinating conjunction)** I recently recovered from a bad cold **(dependent clause),** I continued with my vacation plans **(independent clause)**.

Clausal and Phrasal Modifiers

Clausal modifier - a phrase with an adjective or adverb that adds detail to the sentence.
Examples: *The dog ran after the ball **that bounced across the road**.* I love broccoli, **which is a very healthy vegetable**. The little boy, **who wanted his Mom to buy him a toy,** was throwing a tantrum in the store.

Phrasal Modifier - a phrase, joined by hyphens, that is used to modify a noun; the noun is singular. Examples: We have a **three-day weekend** coming up. My **ten-speed bicycle** broke down. I need a roommate for my **two-bedroom apartment**.

Devices to Control Focus in Sentences and Paragraphs

Concrete language refers to experiences related directly through the senses. Specific language refers directly to particular cases, not generalizations about many cases. For example, the name of an individual person, "Mr. Downs," is both specific and concrete. A larger group, "the teachers at Labay Middle School," is concrete but more general. "Teachers" is even more general. Whenever possible, a writer should use concrete, specific language.

Active and Passive Voice

In sentences using the active voice, the subject of the sentence does the action. In sentences using the passive voice, the object of the sentence does the action, which weakens the sentence's subject. Active sentences are more emphatic and vigorous, although there are instances in which the passive voice may be preferred.

Active construction: (Who) (did what) (to whom) or (actor) (performed action) (on recipient)
Passive construction: (Who) (had what done) (by whom) or (recipient) (acted upon) (by actor)
Below are easy steps to follow in order to change passive voice to active voice:
    1. Find the verb in the sentence.
    2. Ask who or what is performing the action in order to identify the actor in the sentence.
    3. Construct the sentence so the actor performs the action.

Examples:

Passive The poisonous spider *was caught* by Cooper.
Active   Cooper *caught* the poisonous spider.

Passive The house *was struck* by lightning, plunging us into darkness.
Active   Lightning *struck* the house, plunging us into darkness.

Passive The apartment building *was destroyed* by years of neglect.
Active   Years of neglect *destroyed* the apartment building.

Transitional Words and Phrases

Transitions are words or phrases that specify a relationship between sentences (or paragraphs) which help direct the reader from one idea to another.

Common transitions include:

1. **To specify sequence** - again, also, and, and then, besides, finally, first, second, third, furthermore, last, moreover, next, still, too

2. **To specify time** - after a few days, after a while, afterward, as long as, as soon as, at last, at that time, before, earlier, immediately, in the meantime, in the past, lately, later, meanwhile, now, presently, simultaneously, since, so far, soon, then, thereafter, until, when

3. **To specify comparison** - again, also, in the same way, likewise, once more, similarly

4. **To specify contrast** - although, but, despite, even though, however, in contrast, in spite of, instead, nevertheless, nonetheless, on the contrary, on the one hand, on the other hand, regardless, still, though, yet

5. **To specify examples** - after all, for example, for instance, indeed, in fact, of course, specifically, such as, the following example, to illustrate

6. **To specify cause and effect** - accordingly, as a result, because, consequently, for this reason, hence, if, then, since, so, then, therefore, thereupon, thus, to this end

7. **To specify place** - above, adjacent to, below, beyond, closer to elsewhere, far, farther on, here, near, nearby, opposite to, there, to the left, to the right

8. **To specify concession** - although it is true that, granted that, I admit that, it may appear that, naturally, of course

9. **To specify summary, repetition, or conclusion** - as a result, as has been noted, as I have said, as mentioned earlier, as we have seen, in any event, in conclusion, in other words, in short, on the whole, therefore, to summarize

Cohesion and Coherence

Cohesion and **coherence** are terms used in discourse analysis and text linguistics to describe the properties of written texts. A text may be cohesive without necessarily being coherent. Cohesion is determined by lexically and grammatically overt relationships, whereas coherence is based on semantic relationships.

Cohesive Devices
Linking Adverbials

The writer may use linking adverbials to explicitly state relationships between sentences, paragraphs, and ideas. The result is increased cohesion of text *(www.webenglishteacher.com)*. Linking adverbials can show six different categories of relationships:

- Enumeration and addition
- Summation
- Apposition
- Result/inference
- Contrast/concession
- Transition

Enumerative Linking Adverbials

Enumerative linking adverbials can be used to show the order of pieces of information. Enumeration can follow logical or time sequences, or can be used to move to the next point:
- ordinal numbers - first, second, third, etc.
- adverbs - finally, lastly
- phrases - for one thing, to begin with, next

Additive Linking Adverbials

Similar to enumerative linking adverbials, additive linking adverbials link items together. Additive linking adverbials state explicitly that two items are similar to each other:

- also
- similarly
- by the same token
- further(more)
- likewise
- moreover

Summative Linking Adverbials

Summative linking adverbials explicitly state that the text is concluding. They signal that the author is summarizing the information already presented:

- in sum
- in conclusion
- to conclude
- all in all
- overall
- to summarize

Appositive Linking Adverbials

Appositive linking adverbials signal a restatement of the previous information which will be expressed in a slightly different manner to make it more explicit:

- which is to say
- in other words
- that is

In addition, appositives may introduce an example that is the equivalent of the first piece of information:

- for example
- for instance
- namely
- specifically

Result/Inference Linking Adverbials

Result/inference linking adverbials demonstrate to readers that the following textual element is the result or consequence of the previous information:

- consequently
- thus
- as a result
- hence
- so
- therefore

Contrast/Concession Linking Adverbials

Contrast linking adverbials signal differences or alternatives between two pieces of information:
- on the other hand
- in contrast
- alternatively
- conversely
- by comparison
- instead

Linking adverbs of concession demonstrate that the following information signals a reservation concerning the previous information:
- though
- anyway
- however

Cohesive Devices: Coordinating Conjunctions

Writers use coordinators (also called coordinating conjunctions) to add elements to a sentence. These coordinators indicate that the elements have the same syntactic role, meaning that they are on an equal level. The three main coordinators are:

- and
- but
- or (and negative nor)

Cohesive Devices: Subordinating Conjunctions

The use of subordinators (also called subordinating conjunctions) contributes greatly to the cohesion of a text. Unlike coordinators, these words and phrases introduce ideas that are dependent to the main clause in a sentence. Three types of subordinators include:

- simple
- complex
- correlative

Simple Subordinating Conjunctions

Simple subordinators consist of single words that introduce dependent clauses.

Simple subordinators can belong to three classes:

- adverbial clauses: after, as, because, if, since, although, whether, while
- degree clauses: as, than, that
- complement clauses: if, that, whether

Adverbial and degree clauses signal a particular relationship between the clauses. On the other hand, complement clauses signal structural dependency.

Complex Subordinating Conjunctions

Complex subordinators are phrases of two or more words. Complex subordinators perform the same function as simple subordinators.

- as far as
- as long as
- given that
- on condition that
- provided that
- supposing that
- now that
- except that
- so that
- even though
- in case
- even if

Purpose, Audience, and Register

Students must acknowledge the myriad purposes for communication. Thus, students must consider **purpose, audience, subject matter,** and **register** (**formality of language**) and how each of these affects discourse.

An important feature of writing is the major purpose or aim of the writer. The four basic purposes of writing can be categorized as follows:

- **convey information** (to convey knowledge, to describe a scene, to give instructions, etc.)
- **persuade** (to inspire, to express a desire or need, to prove a point, etc.)
- **express the self** (to express beliefs, to express emotions, to react to an event, etc.)
- **create literature** (to tell a story, to amuse, to reveal the human condition, etc.)

The strategies a writer uses for **informing** the reader about a subject are vastly different from those a writer uses when trying to persuade the reader. The writer who is trying to **inform** conveys his or her message while providing subject knowledge, while the writer who is trying to **persuade** concentrates on having an effect on the reader (Hunt, 1991).

Moreover, the strategies and skills for writing literature are equally specialized from those used when writing for **self-expression**. The writer who is creating literature places emphasis on literary characteristics such as plot, characterization, rhythm, symbolism, and dialogue, while the writer who writes for **self-expression** focuses on his or her inner feelings and expressions. Most writing does not attempt to achieve all of these aims, but rather conveys a single, dominant purpose while subordinating the others (Hunt, 1991).

A writer must also consider **register**, the formality or informality of language, when writing. **Formal** English utilizes words, expressions, grammar, and standards of usage used for serious occasions when writing essays, research papers, scholarly works, literary criticism, and speeches. The syntax of **formal** language is precisely structured with extensive use of vocabulary, few contractions, and little or no use of slang or colloquial expression (Hunt, 1991). Conversely, **informal** English is the Standard English used in oral conversations and broadcasting as well as in newspapers, magazines, and trade books. The syntax and vocabulary of **informal** English reflect more relaxed standards than those used in formal English and also include the use of contractions, colloquial expressions, and slang (Hunt, 1991).

Methods for Assessing English Language Arts Literacy Skills

The most important tool for assessment is the teacher. The teacher is constantly monitoring and observing students and their work in an informal way. Teachers can observe firsthand the growth and development of their students' progress. There are multiple ways that teachers can informally assess students' progress including: checklists, informal conversations, questionnaires, journal entries, and portfolio assignments. The advantage of informal assessment is that it is a quick, efficient method whereby a teacher can obtain valuable information on students that is not provided by formal tests. The teacher can then use this information to diagnose and correct problem areas quickly and efficiently. (Cox, 1999)

When assessing students, teachers need to make every effort to implement authentic assessment procedures that allow students to demonstrate their abilities to perform tasks with real-world application. Authentic assessment allows students to demonstrate their own understanding and may involve the following activities:

- Teacher observation
- Reading logs, learning logs, diary, personal journal entries
- Teacher / student conferences
- Anecdotal records of student performance
- Teacher checklist
- Writing samples, grading rubrics
- Group and individual projects
- Oral presentations
- Self-evaluations
- Student portfolio

Summative Assessments are given periodically to determine at a particular point in time what students know and do not know. Summative assessments include:

- State assessments

- District benchmark or interim assessments

- End-of-unit or chapter tests

- End-of-term or semester exams

- Scores that are used for accountability for schools

The key is to think of **summative assessment** as a means to gauge, at a particular point in time, student learning relative to content standards. Although the information that is gained from this type of assessment is important, it can only help in evaluating certain aspects of the learning process. Because they are spread out and occur *after* instruction every few weeks, months, or once a year, summative assessments are tools to help evaluate the effectiveness of programs, school improvement goals, alignment of curriculum, or student placement in specific programs. Summative assessments happen too far down the learning path to provide information at the classroom level and to make instructional adjustments and interventions *during* the learning process.

Formative Assessment is part of the instructional process. When incorporated into classroom practice, it provides the information needed to adjust teaching and learning while they are happening. In this sense, formative assessment informs both teachers and students about student understanding at a point when timely adjustments can be made (Garrison & Ehringhaus, 2011).

Formative assessment can be thought of as a "practice" grade. Formative assessment helps teachers determine next steps during the learning process as the instruction approaches the summative assessment of student learning.

Another distinction that underpins formative assessment is student involvement. If students are not involved in the assessment process, formative assessment is not practiced or implemented to its full effectiveness. Students need to be involved both as assessors of their own learning and as resources to other students.

One of the key components of engaging students in the assessment of their own learning is providing them with descriptive feedback as they learn. Descriptive feedback provides students with an understanding of what they are doing well, links to classroom learning, and gives specific input on how to reach the next step in the learning progression (Garrison & Ehringhaus, 2011). Instructional strategies that can be used formatively include:

- **Criteria and goal setting** with students engages them in instruction and the learning process by creating clear expectations. In order to be successful, students need to understand and know the learning target/goal and the criteria for reaching it. Establishing and defining quality work together, asking students to participate in establishing norm behaviors for classroom culture, and determining what should be included in criteria for success are all examples of this strategy.

- **Observations** go beyond walking around the room to see if students are on task or need clarification. Observations assist teachers in gathering evidence of student learning to inform instructional planning. This evidence can be recorded and used as feedback for students about their learning or as anecdotal data shared with them during conferences.

- **Questioning strategies** should be embedded in lesson/unit planning. Asking better questions allows an opportunity for deeper thinking and provides teachers with significant insight into the degree and depth of understanding. Questions of this nature engage students in classroom dialogue that both uncovers and expands learning. An "exit slip" at the end of a class period to determine students' understanding of the day's lesson or quick checks during instruction such as "thumbs up/down" or "red/green" (stop/go) cards are also examples of questioning strategies that elicit immediate information about student learning.

- **Self and peer assessment** helps to create a learning community within a classroom. Students who can reflect while engaged in metacognitive thinking are involved in their learning. When students have been involved in criteria and goal setting, self-evaluation is a logical step in the learning process. With peer evaluation, students see each other as resources for understanding and checking for quality work against previously established criteria.

- **Student record keeping** helps students better understand their own learning as evidenced by their classroom work. This process of students keeping ongoing records of their work not only engages students, it also helps them, beyond a "grade," to see where they started and the progress they are making toward the learning goal (Garrison & Ehringhaus, 2011).

Portfolio Assessment

Portfolio assessments has grown in popularity in the United States as part of a widespread interest in **alternative assessment**. Because of high-stakes accountability, public schools experienced an increase in the use of norm-referenced, multiple-choice tests designed to measure academic achievement. The current climate, however, reveals increased criticisms over the reliance on these tests, which opponents believed assess only a very limited range of knowledge and encourage a "drill and kill" multiple-choice curriculum.

Advocates of **alternative assessment** argue that teachers and public schools have limited their educational impact by modeling their curriculum to match the limited norm-referenced tests in trying to assure that their students do well. Thereby, "teaching to the test" rather than teaching content relevant to the subject matter.

The use of alternative assessments, involving a wide variety of learning products and artifacts, would enable teachers and researchers to examine the wide array of complex thinking and problem-solving skills required for subject-matter accomplishment. More likely than traditional assessments to be **multidimensional**, these **assessments** also may reveal various aspects of the learning process, including the development of cognitive skills, strategies, and decision-making processes.

Types of Portfolios

While portfolios have broad potential and can be useful for the assessments of students' performance for a variety of purposes in core curriculum areas, the contents and criteria used to assess portfolios must be designed to serve those purposes. For example, **showcase portfolios** exhibit the best of student performance, while **working portfolios** may contain drafts that students and teachers use to reflect on process. **Progress portfolios** contain multiple examples of the same type of work done over time and are used to assess progress. If cognitive processes are intended for assessment, content and rubrics must be designed to capture those processes.

Portfolio assessments can provide both **formative and summative** opportunities for monitoring progress toward reaching identified outcomes. By setting criteria for content and outcomes, portfolios can communicate concrete information about what is expected of students in terms of the content and quality of performance in specific curriculum areas, while also providing a way of assessing their progress along the way. Depending on content and criteria, portfolios can provide teachers and researchers with information relevant to the cognitive processes that students use to achieve academic outcomes (http://www.answers.com/topic/portfolio).

Uses of Portfolios

Student portfolios work well for evaluation and assessment of student writing. Periodic conferences should be held between teachers and students to review the portfolio's contents. Portfolios can be very effective for teacher-parent conferences as well. The portfolio should contain a balance of assignments. Specifically, there should be a collection of work in the portfolio reflecting both **aesthetic** and **efferent** assignments.

Moreover, teachers can use student portfolios to discover consistent patterns in the work that reflect strengths or weaknesses. English / language arts teachers should use assessment results to plan and adapt instruction that addresses students' strengths, needs, and interests.

During periodic conferences, the teacher and student can discuss the goals that need to be met to improve reading and writing skills. Portfolios can also be used by students to **self-evaluate** their growth and set their own goals for learning. **Self-evaluation** activities help students reflect upon their own writing and take ownership of the learning process.

Holistic Evaluation vs. Analytical Evaluation

Holistic evaluation assesses a student's writing as a whole instead of examining each part. When grading a writing assignment **holistically**, teachers should read the paper once to get an impression of the work as a whole. The writing is then graded according to the impression of the whole work rather than in parts. The use of a **grading rubric**, that establishes the overall criteria for a certain score, is very effective when grading work holistically. The disadvantage of **holistic scoring** is that it is very subjective.

On the other hand, **analytical evaluation** is a more objective method of evaluating student work. **Analytical evaluation** specifies the criteria and quality for success and provides a point value for each criterion. Some students prefer this type of evaluation system since it is objective and outlines specific strengths and weaknesses. The disadvantage of **analytical evaluation** is that it places great emphasis on the parts of a writing assignment rather than the whole.

References

Alverman, D. & Phelps, S. E. (1994). *Content Reading and Literacy.* Allyn and Bacon: Boston.

Cox, C. (1999). *Teaching Language Arts: A Student and Response Centered Classroom.* Allyn and Bacon: Boston.

Garrison, C. & Ehringhaus, M. (2011). Formative and Summative Assessments in the Classroom. National Middle School Association Publication. (http://www.nmsa.org/portals/0/pdf/publications/Web)

Gleason, J.B. (2001). *The Development of Language*, 5th edition. Allyn and Bacon: Boston. Hopper, J. & Carter-Wells, J. (1994). *The Language of Learning*. 2nd Edition. Wadsworth Publishing Company, Belmont, CA.

Hunt, D. (1991). The *Riverside Guide to Writing.* Houghton Mifflin Company: Boston.

Johnston, J. (2006). Factors that influence language development. *Encyclopedia of Language and Literacy Development* (pp. 1-6). London, ON: Canadian Language and Literacy Research Network. Retrieved 1/30/2011.

McCrum, R., MacNeil, R., & Cran, W. (2002). *The Story of English*. Penguin: NY.

McMahon, A. (1994). *Understanding Language Change*, Cambridge University Press.

Pyles, T. and Algeo, J. (1993). *The Origins and Development of the English Language.* Harcourt Brace Jovanovich: New York.

Rosenblatt, L. M. (1983). *The Literary Transaction: Evocation and Response Theory into Practice,* V. 21: 268-277.

http://www.behindthename.com
http://merriam-webster.com

Practice Questions

1. The students in Mr. Hockley's 10th grade English class often have difficulty when reading new words. Mr. Hockley has taught the students to use structural analysis when trying to determine the meaning of a word. Structural analysis would be most effective with which of the following words?

    a. au pair
    b. détente
    c. audiophile
    d. vilify

C is correct. Audio = sound or hearing; phile = lover of

2. Of the following words, which are considered compound words?
    a. high school, sailboat, can't
    b. sailboat, sunflower, wouldn't
    c. meantime, grandmother, cannot
    d. ungrateful, unclean, redo

C is correct.

3. Which of the following is a good online resource for researching etymology?
    a. Wikipedia
    b. etymonline
    c. whatsthatword.com
    d. Google

B is correct.

4. Which of the following words does not follow a common spelling rule?

    a. ceiling
    b. receive
    c. conceit
    d. height

D is correct. This word is an exception to the spelling rule "i before e, except after c."

5. All of the following statements are attributed to Noam Chomsky's theory of linguistic theory of generative grammar EXCEPT:

    a. A human being or any complex organism has a system of cognitive structures (for language) that develop much in the way the physical organs of the body develop. That is, in their fundamental character they are innate.
    b. The basic form of cognitive structures for language are determined by the genetic structure of the organism. Of course, they grow under particular environmental conditions.
    c. Much of what is distinctive among human beings is a specific manner in which a variety of shared cognitive structures develop. Perhaps the most intricate of these structures is language.
    d. Language is a special case of behavior because it is reinforced exclusively by other organisms. Apart from the effect that language has on someone else, verbal behavior does not produce any reinforcement in and of itself.

D is correct. This statement is purported by behaviorist theorists and explains language through a stimulus response relationship.

6. What is the word origin of the word below?

Bandana, bandanna, ban-dan'-a, n. [Hind.bandhnu, to tie.] A handkerchief having a pattern formed by tying little bits so as to keep them from being dyed; hence, a cotton handkerchief, having a somewhat similar patter, that is, a uniform ground, usually of bright red or blue, with white or yellow figures of simple form.

    a. noun
    b. a handkerchief
    c. Hindustani or Hindi
    d. to tie

C is correct.

7. **Pragmatics** refers to:

    a. the context-dependent features of language
    b. the study of the sounds of language
    c. the smallest unit of meaning in a word
    d. the study of word origin

A is correct.

8. A morpheme is:
    a. the graphic – phonemic relationship of a sound within a word
    b. the smallest unit of meaning in a word
    c. the context dependent features of language
    d. the units of sound in a word

B is correct.

9. Which of the following describes the early origins of the English language in Great Britain during the 5th and 6th centuries?

a. The French brought about the development of the language during The Norman Conquest.

b. The English language was brought from the European continent by Germanic tribes.

c. The early dialect established in the now present London area spread throughout the region.

d. Latin and, to a lesser extent, Greek influenced the early development of the language in Rome.

B is correct. The origins of this Germanic language emerged in the Elbe river region about 3,000 years ago. This language was brought to the British Isles from the European continent by Germanic invaders during the 5th and 6th centuries.

10. The Great Vowel Shift on English pronunciation took place:

a. before the Middle Ages

b. between Middle and Modern English

c. during the time of Old English

d. during the Germanic invasion during the 5th and 6th centuries

C is correct. The **Great Vowel Shift** was a major change in the pronunciation of the English language that took place in the south of England between 1450 and 1750. The values of the long vowels form the main difference between the pronunciation of Middle English and Modern English, and the **Great Vowel Shift** is one of the historical events marking the separation of Middle and Modern English.

11. All of the following are approaches to grammar instructions EXCEPT:

a. transformational

b. traditional

c. structural

d. etymological

D is the exception.

DOMAIN II:

Chapter 4: Reading Processes

Chapter 5: Reading Literary & Nonliterary Text

Chapter 6: Literature

Chapter 7: Responses to Literature

DOMAIN II —READING PROCESSES, READING LITERARY / NONLITERARY TEXT, LITERATURE

Competency 4: Reading Processes

- Understands and promotes reading as an active process of constructing meaning (e.g., knows how readers' backgrounds and experiences influence meaning).
- Understands reader response and promotes students' responses to various types of text.
- Knows how text characteristics and purposes for reading determine the selection of reading strategies and teaches students to apply skills and strategies for reading various types of texts for a variety of purposes.
- Knows how to use, and teaches students to use, word analysis skills (e.g., graphophonics, semantics), word structure (e.g., affixes and roots), word order (syntax) and context for word identification and to confirm word meaning.
- Demonstrates an understanding of the role of reading fluency in reading comprehension and knows how to select and use instructional strategies and materials to enhance students' reading fluency.
- Knows and applies strategies for enhancing students' comprehension through vocabulary study.
- Understands and teaches students comprehension strategies to use before reading (e.g., predicting, recalling prior knowledge), during reading (e.g., note taking, mapping, paired reading) and after reading(e.g., retelling, summarizing, responding).
- Understands the role of visualization, metacognition, self-monitoring and social interaction in reading comprehension and promotes students' use of these processes.
- Understands levels of reading comprehension and strategies for teaching literal, inferential, creative and critical comprehension skills.
- Knows how to intervene in students' reading process to promote their comprehension and enhance their reading experience (e.g., using questioning, guiding students to make connections between their prior knowledge and texts).
- Knows how to provide students with reading experiences that enhance their understanding of and respect for diversity and guides students to increase knowledge of cultures through reading.
- Knows how to use technology to enhance reading instruction.
- Demonstrates an understanding of informal and formal procedures for monitoring and assessing students' reading, such as using reading-response journals.

- Uses assessment results to plan and adapt instruction that addresses students' strengths, needs and interests and that builds on students' current skills to increase their reading proficiency.

Competency 5: Reading literary / nonliterary texts

- Demonstrates knowledge of types of nonliterary texts (e.g., textbooks, newspapers, manuals, electronic texts, memoranda) and their characteristics.
- Understands purposes for reading nonliterary texts (e.g., for information, for pleasure), reading strategies associated with different purposes and ways to teach students to apply appropriate reading strategies for different purposes.
- Knows strategies for monitoring one's own understanding of nonliterary texts and for addressing comprehension difficulties that arise (e.g., by rereading, using other resources, questioning) and knows how to teach students to use these strategies.
- Demonstrates knowledge of skills for comprehending nonliterary texts (e.g., identifying main ideas and supporting details, summarizing, making inferences, drawing conclusions, analyzing historical and contemporary contexts) and knows how to provide students with opportunities to apply and refine these skills.
- Understands types of text organizers (e.g., overviews, headings, tables of contents, graphic features) and their use in locating and categorizing information.
- Demonstrates knowledge of types of text structure (e.g., chronological order, compare/contrast, cause/effect) and strategies for promoting students' ability to use text structure to facilitate comprehension of nonliterary texts.
- Knows strategies for helping students increase their knowledge of specialized vocabulary in nonliterary texts and for facilitating reading comprehension (e.g., creating graphic organizers, using study strategies such as skimming and scanning, note taking and outlining).
- Knows how to locate, retrieve and retain information from a range of texts, including interpreting information presented in various formats (e.g., maps, graphs) and uses effective instructional strategies to teach students these skills. I. Knows how to evaluate the credibility and accuracy of information in nonliterary texts, including electronic texts, and knows how to teach students to apply these critical-reading skills.
- Demonstrates an understanding of the characteristics and uses of various types of research tools and information sources and promotes students' understanding of and ability to use these resources.
- Understands steps and procedures for engaging in inquiry and research and provides students with learning experiences that promote their knowledge and skills in this area.

Competency 6: Literature

- Demonstrates knowledge of genres and their characteristics through analysis of literary texts.
- Demonstrates knowledge of literary elements and devices, including ways in which they contribute to meaning and style, through analysis of literary texts.
- Demonstrates knowledge of major literary movements in American, British and world literature, including their characteristics, the historical contexts from which they emerged, major authors and their impact on literature and representative works and their themes.
- Demonstrates knowledge of a substantial body of classic and contemporary American literature.
- Demonstrates knowledge of a substantial body of classic and contemporary British literature.
- Demonstrates knowledge of a substantial body of classic and contemporary world literature.
- Demonstrates knowledge of a substantial body of young adult literature.
- Demonstrates knowledge of various critical approaches to literature.

Competency 7: Responses to Literature.

- Demonstrates knowledge of various types of responses to literary texts (e.g., experiential, aesthetic, pragmatic) and encourages a variety of responses in students. B. Knows strategies for motivating students to read literature and for promoting their appreciation of the value of literature.
- Knows how to draw from wide reading in American, British, world and young adult literature to guide students to explore and select independent reading based on their individual needs and interests.
- Knows how to promote students' interest in literature and facilitate their reading and understanding.
- Uses technology to promote students' engagement in and comprehension of literature.
- Knows strategies for creating communities of readers and for promoting conversations about literature and ideas.
- Understands and teaches students strategies to use for analyzing and evaluating a variety of literary texts, both classic and contemporary.
- Applies effective strategies for helping students view literature as a source for exploring and interpreting human experience.
- Applies effective strategies for engaging students in exploring and discovering the personal and societal relevance of literature.
- Promotes students' understanding of relationships among literary works from various times and cultures.

- Promotes students' ability to analyze how literary elements and devices contribute to meaning and to synthesize and evaluate interpretations of literary texts.
- Knows effective strategies for teaching students to formulate, express and support responses to various types of literary texts.
- Demonstrates an understanding of informal and formal procedures for monitoring and assessing students' comprehension of literary texts.
- Knows how to use assessment results to plan and adapt instruction that addresses students' strengths, needs and interests and that builds on students' current skills to increase their proficiency in comprehending literary texts.

Domain II: Chapter 4

Competency 4: Reading Processes - *The teacher understands reading processes and teaches students to apply these processes.*
The beginning teacher:

- Understands and promotes reading as an active process of constructing meaning (e.g., knows how readers' backgrounds and experiences influence meaning).
- Understands reader response and promotes students' responses to various types of text.
- Knows how text characteristics and purposes for reading determine the selection of reading strategies and teaches students to apply skills and strategies for reading various types of texts for a variety of purposes.
- Knows how to use, and teaches students to use, word analysis skills (e.g., graphophonics, semantics), word structure (e.g., affixes and roots), word order (syntax) and context for word identification and to confirm word meaning.
- Demonstrates an understanding of the role of reading fluency in reading comprehension and knows how to select and use instructional strategies and materials to enhance students' reading fluency.
- Knows and applies strategies for enhancing students' comprehension through vocabulary study.
- Understands and teaches students comprehension strategies to use before reading (e.g., predicting, recalling prior knowledge), during reading (e.g., note taking, mapping, paired reading) and after reading (e.g., retelling, summarizing, responding).
- Understands the role of visualization, metacognition, self-monitoring and social interaction in reading comprehension and promotes students' use of these processes.
- Understands levels of reading comprehension and strategies for teaching literal, inferential, creative and critical comprehension skills.
- Knows how to intervene in students' reading process to promote their comprehension and enhance their reading experience (e.g., using questioning, guiding students to make connections between their prior knowledge and texts).
- Knows how to provide students with reading experiences that enhance their understanding of and respect for diversity and guides students to increase knowledge of cultures through reading.
- Knows how to use technology to enhance reading instruction.
- Demonstrates an understanding of informal and formal procedures for monitoring and assessing students' reading, such as using reading-response journals.
- Uses assessment results to plan and adapt instruction that addresses students' strengths, needs and interests and that builds on students' current skills to increase their reading proficiency.

Key Terms

After reading
Analysis
Application
Applied level of comprehension
Author's purpose
Before reading
Borrowed words
Cause / effect
Choral reading
Citing sources
Compare / contrast pattern
Concept mapping
Confused words
Content area
Context clues
Critiquing sources
Cultural accuracy
Cultural awareness
Decoding
Definition pattern
Directed Reading Thinking lesson
Discovery lessons
Drawing conclusions
During reading
Effective questioning
Electronic books
Expressive Reading
GH Player
Google scholar
Higher order thinking
Inferential level of comprehension
Inflection

Inquiry
Inquiry lessons
Intonation
iSEEK
Kurzweil 3000
Literal level of comprehension
Mapping
Metacognitive skills
Misused words
Morphemic analysis
Organizational patterns
Prosody
Purpose
Purpose for reading
Read & Write Gold
Read: Out Loud
Reader's theater
Reading fluency
Scan & Read Pro
Self-assessment
Sequential
Sight word vocabulary
Signal Words
Specialized vocabulary
SSR
Synthesis
Time order / Sequential pattern
Universal Reader
Visualize
Word families
WYNN: What You Need Now

Reading Processes

Middle and high school students are expected to read and interpret a wide variety of reading materials, not only literary works, but nonliterary texts as well. Students are expected to be able to see relationships between parts and wholes, place people and events into a historical context, and retain facts and figures. Students come into contact with myriad sources of information including: textbooks, newspapers, manuals, lectures, electronic texts, memoranda, diaries, business letters, and reports. For efficient readers, no one approach to the reading materials can be universally effective. Students must be taught to vary the method and rate of reading according to the purpose for reading and according to their prior knowledge of the material being read. Students must also be taught to monitor their own understanding of nonliterary texts and address comprehension difficulties that arise by rereading, using other resources, creating questions, or seeking help from outside sources (Smith, 1993).

Cognitive Elements of Reading and Writing
It is important for English, Language Arts and Reading teachers to understand the cognitive elements of reading and writing and how they support reading acquisition. It is also important for teachers to understand that these cognitive elements are all interdependent and interrelated in a student's acquisition of language and literacy.

Language Comprehension
An important cognitive element underlying reading comprehension is **language comprehension**. This generally refers to one's ability to understand speech. Students must understand that there are different **levels of language**. For example, adults do not speak to small children the way they speak to other adults; students do not speak to their parents in the same way that they speak to their younger brothers and sisters.

Language can be **formal or informal.** Informal language is most often influenced by the setting; informal conversation usually focuses on information that is immediately relevant and often concrete. Formal language, on the other hand, can be vague and abstract, requiring students to infer the meaning "read between the lines" or draw a conclusion.

Similarly, there are different types and levels of **language comprehension** as well. The most commonplace form is **explicit comprehension**—the listener literally understands what is clearly stated. The listener may not need to draw any inferences or elaborate on what is said.

A deeper form of language comprehension, **inferential comprehension,** builds upon explicit comprehension. In order to truly understand the message, the listener must consider the context in which communication is taking place. The listener needs to "**read between the lines**" and **draw inferences**. In many cases, the inferences are context dependent, meaning that it is necessary to consider the speaker, the setting, and the audience. In real communication, sometimes a true message is never explicitly stated—the listener must deduce the speaker's intent behind the message by analyzing tone, syntactical structure, or semantics. Sometimes, what is not said is as important as what is said.

Another important cognitive element underlying reading comprehension is determining the author's or speaker's **purpose of communication.** In order to determine the purpose, students must develop an understanding of varying **genres** (fiction, nonfiction, poetry, etc.), voices (1st person, 3rd person, omniscient, etc.), perspectives, and styles (humorous, narrative, informative, etc.). Students need to understand how these elements reflect the intent and underlying meaning of the speaker or writer.

Pragmatics involves the study of language in use; that is, how individuals produce and interpret language in social interaction and specific contexts. A teacher might need to conduct explicit lessons regarding the pragmatics of language. Young students typically do not have a well-developed appreciation of the **pragmatics** of speech.

It is important to note that failure to comprehend the written or spoken word is not just a concern of students who are learning English as a second language, or students who speak a **non-standard dialect** of English. Some English speaking students may live in an impoverished linguistic environment. Despite the fact that English is the native language of a student, the language comprehension skills of some students may be severely underdeveloped due to the effects of poverty.

Decoding
Another cognitive element underlying reading comprehension is **decoding**, a student's ability to recognize the symbols of language (letters and words) and process that written information into an understandable message.

Today's young readers should learn a variety of strategies to decode words. For example, students should be taught to recognize high-frequency words. This strategy is known as "**sight-word reading**." Reading sight words involves looking at a word as a whole unit. Sample sight words include: is, am, I, there, here, was, that, if, and, etc.). Having a strong sight word vocabulary can strengthen a reader's fluency and comprehension. Students should also be taught words that do not follow regular English pronunciation rules using the sight word method. For example, a word that contains the "schwa" sound (any vowel that sounds like "uh,") should be taught as an irregular word. *M**o**ther, penc**i**l,* and *<u>a</u>bout* are irregular words.

However, a student should also be taught to decode the sounds of language (phonics) and the meanings of small units of language (morphemes). If a student only relies on the sight word approach, the capacity for learning new words may diminish and some words that look alike may be confused (there, here, though, thought, etc.).

Even adult readers come across new words that are not pronounced the way they are spelled. However, it is reasonable to say that readers are decoding text appropriately if they are correctly recognizing irregular or exception words within their vocabulary and pronouncing unfamiliar words in a way consistent with the conventions of written English (Southwest Education Development Laboratory; http://www.sedl.org/reading/framework/elements.html).

Construction of Meaning: Background Knowledge

Another cognitive element underlying reading comprehension is the development of background knowledge. To have strong language comprehension skills, students must understand the world in which they live, and must possess prior knowledge that is relevant to new information. This knowledge should be more sophisticated than mere facts or word definitions. This knowledge comes from personal experiences and already exists in the brain as a "schema" – as an idea or understanding of a concept. A student's understanding grows as he/she draws upon that knowledge and builds upon it; thus, developing a more complex understanding of the concept.

Linguistic Knowledge

Another cognitive element underlying reading comprehension is knowledge of the structure and meaning of language. Fortunately, children are born with an innate readiness for language and begin to build linguistic skills at a very young age. Even a young preschool student knows the correct order for language. For example: if students are asked to complete the following sentence, "The man went to the _____." Most four year-old students will answer: the store, the zoo, etc. Students at a young age would know that the article "the" would never fit into the blank.

At a very young age children know that languages are composed of sounds that are assembled to form words, which are combined to form sentences, which are arranged to convey ideas. Each of these processes is constrained and governed by linguistic rules. An implicit knowledge of their structure and their integration is essential to language comprehension. Three basic elements come together to support linguistic knowledge:

- **Phonology**: to understand language, one must be able to hear, distinguish, and categorize the sounds in speech.

- **Syntax**: one needs to be implicitly familiar with the structure that constrains the way words fit together to make phrases and sentences.

- **Semantics**: one must be able to understand the meaning of individual words and sentences being spoken and the meaningful relations between them.

Linguistic knowledge depends upon all three elements being synthesized rapidly and fluently (http://www.sedl.org/reading/framework/elements.html).

Text Structure Knowledge

Another cognitive element underlying reading comprehension is knowledge of **text structure.** By identifying the organizational structure of texts, students can observe how authors arrange ideas and determine which kinds of structures are used to relate these ideas.

Authors usually have a definitive purpose for writing and choose a structure or pattern of organization to support that purpose. An author may wish to convey an opinion, explain an idea, describe an event, entertain, provide a sequence of events or steps, provide reasons or rational for an idea, etc. English / Language Arts teachers must be able to demonstrate knowledge of types of text structures and provide students with strategies to facilitate comprehension. Numerous patterns exist for organizing and structuring nonliterary material. For example, if a history writer wanted to explain the reasons and consequences for the American Civil War, the writer would probably choose a cause and effect pattern of organization.

A student might wish to think of organizational patterns as the backbone or skeleton of a reading selection. The following are examples of the patterns of organization that are found most frequently in textbooks (Smith, 1993):

- **Time order** or sequence-the selection usually contains signal words such as *first, second, third, next, after, finally,* etc.

- **Compare / contrast**-the selection usually contains signal words such as *on the other hand, similarly, however, in the same way,* etc.

- **Definition**-the entire selection is devoted to explaining a concept such as *beauty, freedom, democracy, terrorism, nuclear fission,* etc.

- **Cause/effect**-the selection usually contains signal words such as *because, consequently,* etc.

Setting the Purpose for Reading
The purposes for reading a selection are endless; students can read to solve a problem, search for answers, verify predictions, etc. Some students may think that recalling, or memorizing text in order to answer questions correctly or prove that they know exactly what someone wanted them to know may be the ultimate proof that learning has occurred. However, secondary English teachers must understand that how a student responds to a text and what meaning the student constructs from a text is influenced greatly by the purpose the student has for reading. Students should be made aware that text characteristics and purposes for reading will determine the strategies and skills they need to use to increase their understanding of a selection (Cox, 1999).

Effective Strategies to Analyze Text
When defining a competent reader, most teachers would allude to the student's knowledge of vocabulary, reading fluency, and reading comprehension. In order to increase a reader's competency in these three areas, teachers must begin by increasing students' word attack and vocabulary skills (Cox, 1999).

Word Analysis
English / Language Arts teachers should know strategies for helping students increase their knowledge of specialized vocabulary in nonliterary texts and for facilitating reading comprehension. Every content area has a large collection of specialized vocabulary that students may or may not be able to understand. Research on vocabulary instruction suggests that teachers should build student vocabulary by starting with what students already know, providing students with multiple exposures to new terms and concepts, and aiding students' transfer of new vocabulary knowledge to other subjects and reading situations (Alverman & Phelps, 1994).

When a student encounters an unknown word he or she must be aware that several effective methods can be applied to gain meaning of the word. The first method is to use **context clues** to unlock the word's meaning. **Context clues** are the words and ideas surrounding the unknown word that may give clues to its meaning. This method of vocabulary instruction is very effective because it is useful in building vocabulary by starting with what the student already knows.

However, context is not always helpful and students must be taught other means of unlocking the meaning of unknown words. Students usually then apply **structural or morphemic analysis**. Teachers should encourage students to try to unlock the meaning to unknown words by taking the following steps:

> **Use context clues** - read the words surrounding the unknown word; these words may help define the unknown word.
> **Decode the word** - look for roots, suffixes, prefixes. These word parts may provide clues to the word's meaning.

Try to pronounce the word - use of letters and sounds (phonics) should help the reader pronounce the word.
Ask a friend or teacher the meaning of the word, or look up the word in the dictionary. Reread the sentence and paragraph once the meaning of the unknown word is known.

Developing a Reader's Fluency

Teachers should understand the role of reading fluency in aiding reading comprehension. Secondary English / Language Arts teachers should use instructional strategies and materials to enhance students' reading fluency. Cox (1999) describes several effective strategies to develop a reader's fluency. These include:

- Read young adult novels or other high interest selections
- Reread favorite reading selections
- Participate in Reader's Theater-students write stories, then read them aloud while "on stage"
- Choral-read aloud with a friend or a group
- Read aloud to friends and family members
- Allow the student time to recognize and correct a mistake
- Allow for discussion time about errors after the reading

Oral Reading Strategies for Increasing Fluency

Guided Oral Reading

Guided oral reading is an excellent tool for improving fluency that benefits students in developing accuracy and word recognition skills, two of the components of fluency. Sometimes, the teacher may wish to work with students one-on-one. The student reads a text that is at or slightly above the established independent reading level aloud with the teacher guiding. The role of the teacher is not to constantly correct the student's oral reading, but to guide the students in applying appropriate strategies for comprehending the text http://www.k12reader.com/reading-fluency-and-instruction/.

Repetitive Oral Reading

Repetitive oral reading is a strategy for improving a reader's fluency and vocabulary. Like guided oral reading, repetitive reading is conducted one-on-one. The teacher should select a text that is at least 50 words long and is at or slightly above the student's independent reading level. The student reads the selection aloud several times with the teacher providing guiding feedback focusing on different elements of fluency each time the text is read. Each time the student reads the piece, fluency should increase. If using student pairs for the activity, teachers should consider student personalities as well as reading abilities. Generally, students with low fluency rates should be paired with compassionate students who are at or above grade level in their fluency.

Choral Reading

Choral reading is a beneficial one-on-one oral reading activity for students. For this activity paired readers sit close together with a single copy of the text. The two read the text aloud with the teacher (or stronger student reader) reading it at a slightly faster rate than the other. As the pair reads, the teacher (or stronger student reader) tracks the words on the page with a finger to help the other reader follow along.

Readers' Theatre

Readers' theatre is a whole class or small group activity for improving fluency. In readers' theatre the readers "perform" a dramatic script using only their voices. While there are many texts specifically designed to be used for readers' theatre (see list below) any piece of drama may be used. Students are assigned roles in the play and are given an opportunity to silently read over the script. Then they read it aloud focusing on fluency. The teacher should guide students in using appropriate pacing, expression and phrasing. **Readers' Theatre** is most beneficial when the script is read aloud several times because this gives the readers multiple opportunities to practice reading it fluently. This strategy is particularly useful in developing prosody http://www.k12reader.com/reading-fluency-and-instruction/.

Silent Reading Strategies for Increasing Fluency
Silent Sustained Reading (SSR)

In silent sustained reading (SSR) students spend a pre-selected amount of time silently reading texts that they have chosen. The goal of this activity is to give students opportunities to engage in pleasurable, sustained reading. It is important that students are able to select what they read during this activity because choice increases motivation and ability to focus. It is also essential that the SSR period be uninterrupted. Fluency increases when a reader is given the time to "get into" a text.

Audiobooks

Audiobooks provide an excellent bridge between decoding and comprehension for struggling readers. Students who are reluctant to read (or have low rates of fluency) benefit from hearing a text read aloud while following along using a print version http://www.k12reader.com/reading-fluency-and-instruction/.

Vocabulary Study
Words can only be mastered through repeated experiences within meaningful context; therefore, it is vital that English / Language Arts teachers provide students with strategies for enhancing their vocabulary skill. There are a variety of effective and meaningful strategies for introducing and teaching vocabulary (Cox, 1999).

Structural Analysis -The number of words in content subject areas that are built with common roots, prefixes and suffixes increases dramatically during middle and high school. Therefore, the study of Latin and Greek derivatives is an effective means for building vocabulary.

Word families - Students can categorize groups of words into word families. Example: in Latin the word part "ped" means foot; in Greek the word part "ped" means child; to enhance vocabulary, students should learn words within the same family: pedestrian, pedal, pediatrician, pediatrics, orthopedics.

Morphemic analysis - **(morphemes)** – the smallest unit of meaning. Students should study the meaning of prefixes, roots, and suffixes. For example: have students analyze one of the longest words in the English language below to see if they can determine the word's meaning through morphemic analysis.

pneumonoultramicroscopicsilicovolcanokoniosis

pnuemono-pertaining to the lungs, as in pneumonia
ultra-very, beyond, as in ultraviolet light
micro-small, as in microscope
scopic-to view or examine, as in microscope
silico-from the element of silicon, as found in the particles of sand or ash
volcano-from a volcano
koni-Greek work for dust
osis-a suffix meaning illness or infection

Borrowed words or phrases - Students can study words that have been adopted from other languages. Example: *ad hoc* in Latin means, for one purpose; *avant-garde* in French means a leading idea, incident, or person of an artistic movement; *sine qua non:* in Latin means something essential.

Content area vocabulary - Students can study words from specific content areas. For example: social studies: *geocentric;* science: *congenital;* computers: *modem*; psychology: *psychopathology.*

Confused / misused words - Students can study words that are commonly confused or misused *(affect vs effect; who's vs whose).*

Develop sight vocabulary - Students should develop their sight vocabulary (frequently occurring words that they should know instantly without hesitation) by applying the following strategies:

- Reread favorite reading selections
- Echo-reading and choral-reading in partners or groups
- Read aloud often with a friend or family member
- Create a personal word bank or word notebook

Word Wall-Students can place specific words on the wall of the classroom; teachers can frequently make reference and point to the words as they are used in lessons.

Direct Teaching Strategies to Develop and Enhance Reading Comprehension.

Developing Metacognitive Skills

English / Language Arts teachers should understand the role of visualization, **metacognition**, self-monitoring, and social interaction in reading comprehension. The term **metacognition** refers to a student's self-awareness as they read. A student with well-developed metacognitive skills is aware of whether or not his mind is engaged when he is reading, whether or not he understands what is being read, and what further strategies are needed to gain meaning from the page.

Students must become independent, self-directed readers. To support students as they grow in independence and self-direction, teachers need to model specific **metacognitive strategies** for students to use while reading (Alverman & Phelps, 1994).

Before Reading

Teachers must help build the prior knowledge of their students so they are ready to connect background information to new information. Because of the vast diversity among students' cultural and experiential backgrounds, teachers must lead classroom discussions to ensure students possess the background knowledge needed for learning. Classroom discussions, viewing films, observing photographs, listening to guest speakers, or taking virtual field trips are all activities that teachers can employ to build student background before reading (Alverman & Phelps, 1994).

Before reading, students must learn to preview the material (read the headings and subheadings, and look at photos and graphics) and ask questions about the material's content. Teachers may ask that students use the SQ3R reading and study method while reading content area reading selections (Preview or **Survey** the test titles and subtitles, turn the titles and subtitles into **Questions**, **Read** to answer the questions, **Recite** and **Review** to ensure retention of the material)
.

During Reading

During reading, teachers need to help or scaffold students as they develop strategies for interacting effectively with various texts. Students must learn to ask questions, make predictions, read and comprehend the selection, make connections among important ideas, decide "what is important," take notes, and write summaries. In order to do this, students must learn to develop their own metacognitive awareness as they read and learn. **Metacognition** involves awareness of, knowledge about, regulation of, and ability to control one's own cognitive processes when reading and learning. Quite simply, **metacognitive awareness** is the ability to think about and control one's own learning (Alverman & Phelps, 1994). An effective guide for teaching students to think and interact with the text as they read is to conduct a (DRT) directed reading and thinking lesson.

Directed Reading-Thinking lesson guidelines

- Choose a story with clear episodes and action. Plan times during the story to stop and discuss the action.
- During each stopping time, ask students to summarize the events so far, and make predictions of what will happen next. Use terms such as "what might happen," "what could possibly happen," or "what is most likely to happen." Avoid definitive terms such as "right" or "wrong."
- Ask the student to explain how he or she made the prediction (based on what information in the story).
- Ask students to keep reading the story to determine if predictions were favorable; then let the students change their predictions or ideas as they learn more from the text.
- Keep up the pace of the story; get back to the story quickly (Temple & Gillet, 1999).

Additional reading strategies that support metacognitive awareness may involve:

- Asking students to **visualize** the setting, specific events, or character actions of the story.
- Teaching students to recognize common **organizational patterns** found in reading selections: sequential, cause / effect, problem / solution, definition, etc.
- Teaching students to take notes as they read, map the story, create a plot graph of the story's events, or create a map or graph of a character's development.

After Reading

A number of effective reading strategies exist which teachers can use to promote reflective thinking, student interactions, and the application and extension of ideas. Teachers can ask students to retell the story, create a graphic organizer, summarize the selection, or give a personal response to the selection.

Other effective strategies include: completing reaction guides that have been designed for lesson extension, creating a discussion web or concept map, or composing a written response to the reading selection. These strategies can be applied to increase reading comprehension and understanding in order to: generate ideas (brain storming, etc.); design a complex structure (long texts, hypermedia, large web sites, etc.); communicate complex ideas; aid learning by explicitly integrating new and old knowledge; and assess understanding or diagnose misunderstanding (Alverman & Phelps, 1994).

Effective Questioning Strategies
Students of all ages should have experience with answering thought-provoking questions. In order to master critical thinking and problem solving, students must gain experience in this type of thinking. A teacher's choice of questions can guide a student into higher order thinking. Questions can be posed that encourage thinking at every level of the cognitive domain.

Both high and low-level questions can be effective; the teacher should use a variety of questions in order to meet the wide variety of student abilities found within the class. The list below presents questions that encourage higher order thinking. English / Language Arts teachers need to be able to identify and compose questions that promote higher order thinking in their students (http://eprentice.sdsu.edu/J03OJ/miles/Bloomtaxonomy(revised)1.htm.).

Higher order thinking questions based on Bloom's Revised Taxonomy:
Application Level - using information to solve a problem (usually the question has one correct answer)
- How is the story like a real-world situation?
- Create a timeline of the story events.
- Write a letter to the main character in the story.
- Which principle is demonstrated in __?

Analysis Level - applying critical thinking, identify reasons and motives, making inferences based on data, analyzing conclusions to determine if supported by evidence
- Can you find a mistake in usage or grammar in this selection?
- Compare / contrast two characters of the story.
- Compare the main character of the story to yourself.
- How would you solve the problem in the story?
- Which of the following are facts and which are opinions?
- What or who influenced the writings of___?

Evaluation Level - offering opinions, judging the merit of something
- What fallacies, consistencies, inconsistencies appear?
- Which is more important, moral, better, logical, valid, appropriate?
- Find the errors.

- Is there a better solution to …?
- Judge the value of …
- What do you think about …?
- Can you defend your position
- about …?

Create Level

- Can you design a … to …?
- Can you see a possible
- solution to …?
- If you had access to all
- resources, how would
- you deal with …?
- Why don't you devise
- your own way to …?
- What would happen if?

Understanding and Enhancing Reading Comprehension

As previously stated, students can monitor their own understanding of nonliterary texts by using their **metacognitive** skills while reading. In order to support student reading and comprehension of nonliterary text, teachers need to conduct explicit lessons to explain the thinking processes used with **metacognitive** skills. Explicit instruction on setting a purpose for reading the text, recognizing the author's main idea and supporting details, and using context clues to unlock the meaning of specialized vocabulary are all effective strategies that can be modeled by the teacher.

Students must also be made aware that they may need to further enhance their reading comprehension by rereading the assignment, creating questions, or seeking help from outside resources (Smith, 1993). Skills needed by effective readers in order to comprehend nonliterary texts include:

- identifying main ideas and supporting details
- summarizing
- making inferences
- drawing conclusions
- analyzing historical and contemporary contexts

Levels of Reading Comprehension

English / language arts teachers must understand the different levels of reading comprehension (literal, inferential, and applied) and learn to promote students' interactions with texts at every level. Students can comprehend reading selections on three levels (Vaca & Vaca, 1999):

Literal level of comprehension - the student is able to obtain the facts of the story.

Inferential level of comprehension - the student is able to draw conclusions, make inferences, connections, and interpretations of the material.

Applied level of comprehension - the student is able to move beyond the material in order to think creatively and critically about the selection's content.

Teaching Study Skill Strategies for Increasing Reading Comprehension:

The **Observation/Proof Note-Taking System** has proven to be a very effective method of teaching students to organize nonliterary text and apply metacognitive skills to monitor their own comprehension (Vacca & Vacca, 1999). [This strategy is similar to the Cornell Note taking Method]. This strategy allows students to make observations and support these observations with evidence. Steps for this method of note taking include:

1. The student reads an assigned chapter or pages of text.
2. The student develops observations about what has been read. The student draws a vertical line down the paper about two inches from the left side. The student's observations are written on the left-hand column.
3. The student writes supporting evidence for the observations in the right-hand column. The evidence must be derived from the text along with the page number for reference. The student should then be able to use this information when completing additional assignments such as writing a summary or studying for an exam.
4. The student shares his/her observation/proof notes with the class.
5. Extension- The student may use his/her observation/proof notes to create a written report.

Question/Answer Relationship (QAR) Strategy - QAR is a questioning strategy that emphasizes that a relationship exists between the question, the text, and the background of the reader. In this strategy, students are taught to use four question/answer relationships (QAR's) to find the information they need to answer questions and determine the category of their answer: (Raphael, 1982).
1. The teacher introduces QAR and explains the four types of question/answer relationships (QAR's).

Think & Search - The answer is in the selection, but students need to put together different pieces of information. The answer is found in more than one place.

Right There - The answer is in the text and is usually easy to find. The information is found in one place.

Author & You - The answer is not explicitly stated in the text. Students need to think about what they already know, what the author tells them in the text, and how it fits together.

On My Own - The answer is not text-based. Students may be able to answer the question without reading the selection by using their own experiences and background knowledge

2. The teacher models the QAR process with a short reading passage. First, the teacher reads the story and questions to the student, and then identifies the QAR's which are evidenced. Finally, the questions are answered and discussed.
3. The teacher practices identifying the QAR's with the class.
4. The teacher provides independent practice.
5. The teacher gradually increases the length and complexity of the texts used with QAR.
6. The students continue to use QAR throughout the year, especially when reading content area information.

Annotating and Underlining to Increase Reading Comprehension
Students must learn to reduce lengthy passages to more comprehensible and manageable sizes by marking the text using a systematic technique. Research reveals that students who are knowledgeable about underlining and summarizing have increased reading comprehension skills. The following steps should be taken to teach students this strategy:
    1. Introduce the strategy by giving the students key points
        • read the entire text before marking
        • be very selective about what and how is marked
        • work quickly and neatly

    2. Teach the students an annotation system they can use
        • double lines underneath main ideas
        • single lines underneath supporting details
        • circle key words/terms
        • jot a brief summary in the side margin

Review of Text or "Lookback" Strategy
Secondary students are often required to read and remember the content of lengthy text. This strategy effectively teaches students to reread a text they have read in order to answer comprehension questions. The advantage to this strategy is that it allows the student time (three days) to consider what has been read (Reis & Leone, 1985).

Lesson 1 - The teacher provides explicit instruction focusing on the question: "Why should I look back?" Answer: "To find information and details I need to remember from the passage." A textbook should be considered a "learning tool" that can be used to help aid reading comprehension. Students must develop a strategy to remember extensive content material and reviewing textbook titles, subtitles, topic sentences, summaries, etc. will aid in reading comprehension.
Lesson 2 - The teacher provides explicit practice instruction focusing on: "When should I look back?" "What should I look for when I look back?"
Lesson 3 - The teacher focuses instruction on: "Where should I look?" Answer:

Students should practice skimming and other strategies for finding answers to specific questions.

Problem-Solution Strategy

The Problem / solution strategy effectively teaches students how to identify specific text structure, and how to summarize this type of passage (Armbruster, Anderson, & Ostertag, 1987). To introduce students to this strategy:

1. Have students draw a line down the center of their page and label the left column "Problem" and the right column "Solution"
2. Have the students practice this analysis on a passage they have previously read. Students should analyze the passage to identify the problem, the action, and the solution (or results) to the problem.
3. Students then summarize the passage by referring to their notes in the problem-solution frame in order to answer the questions below.
   Sentence 1 - Who had the problem and what is the problem?
   Sentence 2 - What action was taken to solve the problem?
   Sentence 3 - What happened as a result of the action?

Semantic Feature Analysis Strategy

The semantic feature analysis strategy is completed before students read the text. This prereading strategy teaches vocabulary by activating prior knowledge, making predictions, and by classifying the new words by their features using a matrix (Anders & Bos, 1986).

1. The teacher creates a list of words that have similarities and places them on the matrix in the left-hand column.
2. The teacher then writes the features associated with these words across the top of the matrix, or asks the students to supply the features associated with these words.
3. The students complete the matrix by placing a check in the column if the word has that feature.
4. Once the matrix is complete and the students have discussed the reasons for their answers, the students should then read the assigned passage.
5. Students review the matrix for any necessary changes.

Objective Analysis Strategy

When participating in objective (form or structural) analysis of a literary work, students are asked to focus on how a work is structured or arranged by the author. Questions may focus on the diction of the work (literary elements such as simile or metaphor), the structure of the plot, the genre (comedy, tragedy, prose, etc.), or the narration / point of view of the work.

Before most authors begin writing, they usually have a definitive **purpose** for writing and usually have chosen a structure or pattern of organization for their writing. They may wish to convey an opinion, explain an idea, describe an event, entertain, provide a sequence of events or steps, provide reasons or rational for an idea, etc. English / Language Arts teachers must be able to demonstrate knowledge of types of text structure and provide students with strategies to facilitate comprehension of these structures.

In order to encourage this type of analysis, the teacher may pose a question such as: Describe the plot structure of the Charles Dickens's novel, *Great Expectations*. In Shakespeare's *King Lear*, how does the plot structure support the audience's emotional reaction of pity and fear?

Reading to Enhance Cultural Awareness and Respect

Secondary English teachers need to provide literary experiences that reflect the multitude of backgrounds of the students in today's schools. Multicultural literature, defined as literature that represents any distinct cultural group through portrayal and rich detail, can play an important role in developing pride in one's heritage and building positive self-concept. Yakota (1993) explains that students benefit from various experiences from cultures other than their own, and these experiences help students understand differing points of view. Students should be encouraged to investigate and research culturally diverse points of view found within important cultural or historical events such as: differing viewpoints about the discovery of America, the Wounded Knee massacre, the Indian wars of the 1890s or immigration laws and patterns.

Yokota (1993) provides well-defined criteria for selecting multicultural literature and explains that a literary work should be culturally accurate and that issues should be represented within the work in ways that reflect the true values and beliefs of the culture. The criterion of **cultural accuracy** serves as an umbrella criterion. Included within this criterion are: richness of cultural details, authentic dialogue and relationships, in-depth treatment of cultural issues, and the inclusion of members of "minority" groups for a purpose (Yakota, 1993).

The details of a story should be written in such a way as to provide insight into the culture described. Details may be a natural part of the story and provide insight into daily life rather than attempting to explain the culture. The literary work should also provide authentic dialogue and relationships among characters. Furthermore, the work should provide an in-depth treatment of cultural issues. It is important to give issues a realistic portrayal and explore them in depth so that readers may be able to formulate informed conclusions about the issues. No matter how minor a character in the story, each of the characters should be regarded as a distinct individual whose life is rooted in his or her culture (Yakota, 1993).

The intent of sharing multicultural literature in the classroom is to provide vicarious experiences from cultures other than the students' own, and these experiences should, in turn, influence the decisions students will make about living in their culturally pluralistic world (Yakota, 1993). Other ideas for promoting literacy include:

- inviting culturally diverse guest speakers into the classroom
- posting information on bulletin boards about famous people of diverse cultures (inventors, mathematicians, etc.)
- sharing works written by diverse authors

Using Technology to Enhance Reading Instruction

Today, the definition of literacy has expanded from traditional notions of reading and writing to include the ability to learn, comprehend, and interact with technology in a meaningful way. Electronic texts introduce new supports as well as new challenges that can have a great impact on an individual's ability to comprehend what he or she reads. The Internet, in particular, provides new text formats, new purposes for reading, and new ways to interact with information (Chau, 2008).

Traditional text forms typically include a combination of two types of media: print and two-dimensional graphics. Electronic texts can integrate a range of symbols and multiple-media formats including icons, animated symbols, photographs, cartoons, advertisements, audio and video clips, virtual reality environments, and new forms of information with nontraditional combinations of font size and color (Brunner & Tally, 1999; Reinking & Chan Lin, 1994; Reading Next Report, 2004).

Images and sounds are combined with written texts to create new ways of conveying meaning, explaining procedures, and communicating interactively (Reading Next Report, 2004). For readers, these multimedia representations demand new ways of thinking about how to access, manipulate, and respond to information.

Thus, technology has evolved into both a facilitator of literacy and a medium of literacy. Effective adolescent literacy programs therefore should use technology as both an instructional tool and an instructional topic (Reading Next Report, 2004, pg. 27).

Supportive Electronic Technologies:

Educational technologies that support the development of students' reading skills may include electronic books / online texts, electronic talking books, programmed reading instruction software and reference / research software.

Electronic Books, also known **as *e-books***, are electronic texts that are presented visually. Accessed in a myriad of different ways including the internet, CD-ROM or a portable e-book reader. This emerging technology has opened the possibility for a large range of new learning experiences for students because of its advantages over traditional printed textbooks. Electronic books are searchable, modifiable (for example, font sizes can be increased to meet the needs of the reader), and come with embedded resources (for example, definitions and details). Electronic books often contain rich multimedia features that cannot be found in textbooks. These frequently include recordings of the text read-aloud, lively animations, music, video and various sound effects. (Korat, 2008).

Electronic Talking Books. The term *electronic talking books* was coined by researchers to refer to electronic texts that also provide embedded speech. The speech component offers a digitized reading of general sections as well as pronunciations of specific words within the text; it supports and coaches students as they read the text of the story (Leu, 2000; McKenna, 1998). For older readers, talking books feature glossary entries, explanatory notes, and simplified rewordings that provide additional background information needed to understand new concepts in texts. Talking books are listed and critiqued by the American Library Association and are readily available for purchase through Amazon.com.

Electronic Reading Systems (E-Readers, Scan & Read Systems) – These software systems: skim headings, turn headings into pre-reading questions, read text aloud, contain dictionaries, synonyms, and thesaurus features, are able to summarize through voice/text notes, answer built-in questions, bookmark sections, highlight main ideas or sections for further research, and review notes and summaries.

- Aspire Reader
- Dolphin Tutor
- GH Player
- Kurzweil 3000
- Read & Write Gold
- Read:OutLoud
- Scan & Read Pro
- Universal Reader
- WYNN:What You Need Now

Programmed Reading Instruction. Various types of software programs, computer-assisted instruction, and integrated learning systems offer programmed reading instruction for students. During the past decade technology has advanced to include programs with voice-activated reading software and software for culturally mediated instruction. **Project LISTEN** (Literacy Innovation that Speech Technology Enables), an award winning program developed at Carnegie Mellon University, has been supported by National Science Foundation and by the U.S. Department of Education. The Project is an initiative to create a novel tool to improve literacy. It works like an automated Reading Tutor which displays stories on computer screen and simultaneously listens to children read loud. This project is described as "an automated reading Tutor."

Internet & other Reference CDs – for exploring inquiry questions and building background development include:

- American Heritage Electronic Dictionary
- Grolier Multimedia Encyclopedia
- The Way Things Work
- The Ultimate Human Body
- Cartopedia
- Street Atlas

The National Reading Panel, which found that: "The rapid development of capabilities of computer technology, particularly in speech recognition and multimedia presentations, promises even more successful applications in literacy for the future".

The International Reading Association Electronic Classroom website, which is part of their Reading Online site, is "dedicated to sharing effective practices and new developments related to the intersection of literacy with technology."

Also, The **What Works Clearinghouse**, established in 2002 by the U.S. Department of Education's Institute of Education Sciences, provides educators, policymakers, researchers, and the public with a central, independent, and trusted source of scientific evidence of what works in education.

Moreover, The **CAST** (Center for Applied Special Technology) web site offers a variety of resources including (1) an online version of the book, *Learning to Read in the Computer Age*; (2) information about CAST products, such as eReader which converts text-to-speech for any electronic text; summaries of research on technology and reading; and (3) descriptions of the principles and applications of Universal Design for Learning.

Journals publishing research on computers and reading instruction include:

- Reading Research Quarterly*
- Reading & Writing Quarterly*
- Reading Research and Instruction*
- Reading and Writing: An Interdisciplinary Journal
- The Computing Teacher*
- Reading Online* (online journal)
- Reading Improvement*
- The Reading Teacher*
- Reading: Literacy and Language
- Journal of Research in Reading
- Journal of Literacy Research
- Reading Psychology
- Journal of Computing in Childhood Education
- Journal of Educational Computing Research
- Computers in Human Behavior
- Journal of Reading Behavior
- Journal of Learning Disabilities
- Journal of Experimental Child Psychology
- Scientific Studies of Reading

Monitoring and Assessing Students' Reading Skills

Teachers need to listen to students read aloud to make judgments about their progress in reading fluency. Systematic observation helps assess student progress and determine instructional needs. Teachers observing students' oral reading fluency should consider each critical aspect of fluent reading: word-reading accuracy, rate, and prosody.

Assessing Accuracy

Measurement of students' word-reading accuracy can take numerous forms. Simply listening to oral reading and counting the number of errors per 100 words can provide invaluable information for the selection of appropriate text for various instructional purposes for an individual or group of students. A running record and miscue analysis (Clay, 1984, 1993) provides more detailed information about the student's accuracy. Through careful examination of error patterns, a teacher can determine which strategies the student is using and which strategies the student is failing to use. For example, observation of a student's attempts to figure out an unknown word might yield evidence of phonemic blending, guessing based on context, or a combination of decoding and contextual analysis. These observations can provide information about areas in need of further instruction to improve word-reading accuracy (Hudson, et al, 2005).

Assessing Rate

Reading rate comprises both word-level automaticity and the speed and fluidity with which a reader moves through connected text. Contextual reading rather than reading words in a list and oral reading rather than silent reading were both found to be the best measures of reading rate. Measuring reading rate should encompass consideration of both word reading automaticity and reading speed in connected text. Assessment of automaticity can include tests of sight-word knowledge or tests of decoding rate. Tests of decoding rate often consist of rapid decoding of non-words. Measurement of reading speed is most typically accomplished through timed readings. Timings of a student's reading of connected text allows a teacher to observe the number of words read correctly and the number of errors made in a given time period (Hudson, et al, 2005).

Assessing Prosody

Prosody is a linguistic term to describe the rhythmic and tonal aspects of speech: the "music" of oral language. Prosodic features are variations in pitch (**intonation**), stress patterns (**syllable prominence**), and duration (length of time) that contribute to expressive reading of a text. When these features are present and appropriate in oral reading, the reader is reading "with expression."

A student's reading **prosody** can be measured only through observation of an oral reading of a connected text. During the reading of a passage, a teacher can listen to the student's inflection, expression, and phrase boundaries. The following is a simple checklist of oral reading prosody observation (Hudson et.al, 2005):

1. Student placed vocal emphasis on appropriate words.
2. Student's voice tone rose and fell at appropriate points in the text.
3. Student's inflection reflected the punctuation in the text (e.g., voice tone rose near the end of a question).

4. In narrative text with dialogue, student used appropriate vocal tone to represent characters' mental states, such as excitement, sadness, fear, or confidence.
5. Student used punctuation to pause appropriately at phrase boundaries.
6. Student used prepositional phrases to pause appropriately at phrase boundaries.
7. Student used subject–verb divisions to pause appropriately at phrase boundaries.
8. Student used conjunctions to pause appropriately at phrase boundaries.

Assessing Reading Comprehension

Instructors often use comprehension questions to test whether students have understood what they have read. In order to test comprehension appropriately, these questions need to be coordinated with the purpose for reading. If the purpose is to find specific information, comprehension questions should focus on that information. If the purpose is to understand an opinion and the arguments that support it, comprehension questions should ask about those points. It is important to note that when the purpose for reading is enjoyment, comprehension questions are beside the point. As a more authentic form of assessment, have students talk or write about why they found the text enjoyable and interesting (or not) (www nclr.org).

Authentic Assessment

In order to provide authentic assessment of students' reading proficiency, a post-listening activity must reflect the real-life uses to which students might put information they have gained through reading.

- It must have a purpose other than assessment
- It must require students to demonstrate their level of reading comprehension by completing some task

To develop authentic assessment activities, consider the type of response that reading a particular selection would elicit in a non-classroom situation. For example, after reading a weather report, one might decide what to wear the next day; after reading a set of instructions, one might repeat them to someone else; after reading a short story, one might discuss the story line with friends.

Use this response type as a base for selecting appropriate post-reading tasks, and then develop a checklist or rubric that will evaluate each student's comprehension of specific parts of the text (www.nclr.org).

In sum, all assessment measures given to students should be used to provide students with a timely, accurate, and constructive picture of their performance. This information can be used by students to correct errors and encourage persistence. Assessment feedback should lead to student **self-assessment** as students correct their reading errors or misunderstanding of concepts and ideas.

References

Anders, P., & Bos, C. (1986). Semantic feature analysis: An interactive strategy for vocabulary development and text comprehension. *Journal of Reading*, 29(7), 610-616.

Alverman, D. and Phelps, S. E. (1994). *Content Reading and Literacy.* Allyn and Bacon: Boston.

Armbruster, B., Anderson, T., & Ostertag, J. (1987). Does text structure/summarization instruction facilitate learning from expository text? *Reading Research Quarterly*, 23, 331-346.

Biancarosa, G., & Snow, C.E. (2004). *Reading Next – A Vision for Action and Research in Middle and High School Literacy: A Report to Carnegie Corporation of New York.* Washington, DC: Alliance for Excellent Education.

Blanchard, J., & Stock, W. (1999). Meta-analysis of research on a multimedia elementary school curriculum using personal and video-game computers. Perceptual and Motor Skills, 88, 329–336.

Bruner, J.S. (1967). *On knowing: Essays for the left hand.* Cambridge, Mass: Harvard University Press.

Chau, M. (2008) The Effects of Electronic Books Designed for Children in Education *FIS2309, Design of Electronic Text, Scroll: University of Toronto. V 1 (2008)*

Colburn, A. (2010). *What Teacher Educators Need to Know about Inquiry-Based Instruction,* http://www.csulb.edu/~acolburn/AETS.htm.
Copyright and Fair Use Guidelines for Teachers: www.mediafestival.org/downloads.html

Cox, C. (1999). *Teaching Language Arts: A Student and Response Centered Classroom.* Allyn and Bacon: Boston.

Hasselbring, T.S., Goin, L., Taylor, R., Bottge, B., and Daley, P. (1997). The Computer Doesn't Embarrass Me. Educational Leadership, 55(3), p.30-33.

Hudson, R., Lane, H., & Pullen, P. (2005). *Reading fluency assessment and instruction: What, why and how?* 2005 International Reading Association (pp.702-714).

Korat, O. (2008). The educational electronic book as a tool for supporting children's emergent literacy in low versus middle SES groups. *Computers & Education, 50*(1), 110-124.

Leu, D. J. (2000). Literacy and technology: Deictic consequences for literacy education in an information age. In M. L. Kamil, P. B. Mosenthal, P. D. Pearson, & R. Barr (Eds.), Handbook of Reading Research: VOL. III (pp. 743-770). Mahwah, N J: Lawrence Erlbaum Associates.

McKenna, M. C. (1998). Electronic texts and the transformation of beginning reading. In D. Reinking, M. C. McKenna, L. D. Labbo, & R. D. Kieffer (Eds.), Handbook of Literacy and Technology Transformations in a Post-Typographic World, (pp. 45-60). Mahwah, N.J., Lawrence Erlbaum Associates.

Pauk, W. (1974). *How to study in college* (3rd ed.). Boston: Houghton Mifflin.
Raphael, T. (1982). Question-answering strategies for children. *The Reading Teacher*, 36(2), 186-191.

Reis, R., & Leone.P. (1985). Teaching text Lookbacks to mildly handicapped students. *Journal of Reading*, 28, 416-420.

Roblyer, M. D. (2003). *Integrating Educational Technology into Teaching.* (3rd Edition), Merrill Prentice Hall , New Jersey.

Rose, D.H., & Mayer, A. (2002). *Teaching Every Student in the Digital Age: Universal Design for Learning.* Association for Supervision and Curriculum Development Alexandria, VA.

Rosenblatt, L. M. (1983). The Literary Transaction: Evocation and Response. *Theory into Practice,* V. 21: 268-277.

Smith, B. D. (1993). *Bridging the Gap.* (4th Edition), Harper Collins, NY.

Staver, J. R., & Bay, M. (1987). Analysis of the project synthesis goal cluster orientation and inquiry emphasis of elementary science textbooks. *Journal of Research in Science Teaching, 24,* 629-643.

Vacca, R.T. & Vacca, J. L. (1999). *Content Area Reading: Literacy and Learning across the Curriculum.* Addison-Wesley: Texas.

Vogel, J. J., Vogel, D. S., Cannon-Bowers, J., Bowers, C. A., Muse, K., & Wright, M. (2006). Computer gaming and interactive simulations for learning: A meta-analysis, Journal of Education Computing Research, 34, 229–243.

Wood, J. (2000). A Marriage Waiting to Happen: Computers and Process Writing, Education Development Center, Inc. (EDC). www.edtechleaders.org

www.benedict.com
www.libraryresources.com
www.mediafestival.org
www.thewritesource.com
www.worldwideschool.org/library/books/hst/biography/TheLifeofChristopherColumbusfromhis own
www.nclr.org

Practice Questions

Use the following excerpt from the *Journal of the First Voyage to America* written by **Christopher Columbus** to answer the following questions:

Sunday morning, October 21,
These are the words of the admiral, says the scribe, La Casas.
He anchored, apparently more to the west, and after having dined, landed. He found but one house, from which the inhabitants were absent; he directed that nothing in it should be touched. He speaks again of the great beauty of the island, even greater than that of the others he had seen. "The singing of the birds," he says, "seems as if a man would never seek to leave this place, and the flocks of parrots which darken the sun, and fowls and birds of so many kinds and so different from ours that it is wonderful. And then there are trees of a thousand sorts, and all with fruit of their kinds. And all have such an odor that it is wonderful, so that I am the most afflicted man in the world not to know them."
They killed a serpent in one of the lakes upon this island, which Las Casas says is the Guana, or what we call the Iguana. In seeking for good water, the Spaniards found a town, from which the inhabitants were going to fly. But some of them rallied, and one of them approached the visitors. Columbus gave him some little bells and glass beads, with which he was much pleased. The Admiral asked him for water, and they brought it gladly to the shore in calabashes.
He still wished to see the king of whom the Indians had spoken, but meant afterward to go to "another very great island, which I believe must be Cipango, which they call Colba (modern day Cuba)." It continues, "and to that other island which they call Bosio" (modern day Haiti or Jamaica) "and the others which are on the way, I will see these in passing. . . . But still, I am determined to go to the mainland and to the city of Quisay and to give your Highnesses' letters to the Grand Khan, and seek a reply and come back with it."
He remained at this island during the twenty-second and twenty-third of October, waiting first for the king, who did not appear, and then for a favorable wind. "To sail round these islands," he says, "one needs many sorts of wind, and it does not blow as men would like." At midnight, between the twenty-third and twenty-fourth, he weighed anchor in order to start for Cuba.
"I have heard these people say that it was very large and of great traffic," he says, "and that there were in it gold and spices, and great ships and merchants.
And they showed me that I should go to it by the west-southwest, and I think so. For I think that if I may trust the signs which all the Indians of these islands have made me, and those whom I am carrying in the ships, for by the tongue I do not understand them, it (Cuba) is the Island of Cipango, of which wonderful things are told, and on the globes which I have seen and in the painted maps, it is in this district." www.worldwideschool.org/library/books/hst/biography/

1. Of the following, which question would aid student reading comprehension on the *literal level?*

   a. What did Columbus give the natives in exchange for water?
   b. Why does Columbus describe the islands in such a positive way?
   c. Why does Columbus need royal letters of introduction to present to the Great Khan?
   d. How will Columbus achieve the main objectives of his voyage?

A is correct. This answer is directly stated in the passage.

2. Of the following, which question would aid student reading comprehension on the *applied level?*

   a. What evidence is presented in the passage that tells how the natives feel about Columbus and his crew?
   b. What did the natives give to Columbus in trade for the hawk's bells and glass beads?
   c. Do you think Columbus will be able to meet with the Great Khan? Why or why not?
   d. Where is Columbus going after he leaves this island?

C is correct. The student will need to use evidence given in the passage in order to draw a conclusion.

3. Which of the following teaching strategies would be most effective in helping students enhance their personal understanding of and respect for diversity and knowledge of cultures found in the reading selection?

   a. Ask students to write a narrative describing the native tribe's use of tools, trade, and communication.
   b. Ask students to rewrite this passage from the natives' point of view and then share their accounts with the class.
   c. Have students visit the library to research the impact the early explorers had on the indigenous peoples of the New World.
   d. Have students draw an illustration of the meeting between the natives and Christopher Columbus and his crew.

B is correct. Asking students to look at events from a different point of view will enhance their personal understanding of and respect for diversity and knowledge of cultures found in the reading selection.

4. Which of the following reading strategies would likely help students apply the highest level of thinking (evaluation) and reading comprehension (critical) levels?

> a. Have students visit the library to research the impact the early explorers had on the indigenous peoples of the new world.
> b. Have students visit the library to research whether or not Christopher Columbus and his voyages were considered a success or failure by modern day historians.
> c. Ask students to work in small groups to compose a *Reader's Theater* script that presents a chronological account of the events of Columbus' life.
> d. Ask students to work in small groups to write a summary of how Columbus solved the problem of lack of water for his crew using a problem-solution organizational pattern.

B is correct. This activity requires higher order thinking at the evaluation level.

5. In addition to comprehension questions concerning main idea, details, inferences, and vocabulary, an 11th grade English / Language Arts teacher often asks students to respond to reading selections in aesthetic ways. Which of the following statements best explains the primary reason this instructional strategy is effective in increasing student understanding and comprehension?

> a. Students of high school age should be allowed to express their opinions and ideas in order to ensure effective psychosocial maturation.
> b. A reader's thoughts and feelings in response to a literary selection are considered very important components of literary interpretation.
> c. Introducing the fine arts in response to good literature may accommodate students with diverse learning styles.
> d. It is important that students learn to interpret literature on varying levels: literal, interpretive, and critical.

B is correct. This answer provides the rational for requiring aesthetic responses to reading.

6. The students in Mr. Downs' 10th grade English class often have difficulty when reading new words. Mr. Downs has taught the students to use structural analysis when trying to determine the meaning of a word. Structural analysis would be most effective with which of the following words?

> a. c'est la vie
> b. void
> c. disgraceful
> d. flounder

C is correct.

7. The students in Mr. Downs' 10th grade English class are having difficulty with reading fluency. Which of the following instructional strategies would be most effective in helping these students read with increased fluency?

> a. Have students use morphemic / structural analysis on unknown words.
> b. Ask students to reread some of their favorite novels and short stories.
> c. Have students participate in several lessons that emphasize metacognitive awareness.
> d. Ask students to write a script for the *Reader's Theater* production.

.

B is correct. Asking students to practice their reading skills by rereading favorite stories is an effective reading strategy for increasing reading fluency.

Directions: Read the following excerpt from ***The Nobel Lecture*** given by **Alexander Solzhenitsyn** as his acceptance speech for the Nobel Prize for Literature; then answer the questions that follow.

> Dostoevsky once enigmatically let drop the phrase: "Beauty will save the world." What does this mean? For a long time I thought it merely a phrase.
> Was such a thing possible? When in our bloodthirsty history did beauty ever save anyone from anything? Ennobled, elevated, yes; but whom has it saved?
> There is, however, something special in the essence of beauty, a special quality in art: the conviction carried by a genuine work of art is absolute and subdues even a resistant heart. A political speech, hasty newspaper comment, a social program, a philosophical system can, as far as appearances are concerned, be built smoothly and consistently on an error or a lie; and what is concealed and distorted will not be immediately clear. But then to counteract it comes a contradictory speech, commentary, program or differently constructed philosophy- and again everything seems smooth and graceful, and again hangs together. That is why they inspire trust-and distrust.
> There is no point asserting and reasserting what the heart cannot believe.

A work of art contains its verification in itself; artificial, strained concepts do not withstand the test of being turned into images; they fall to pieces, turn out to be sickly and pale, convince no one. Works which draw on truth and present it to us in live and concentrated form grip us, compellingly involve us, and no one ever, not even ages hence, will come forth to refute them.

Perhaps then the old trinity of Truth, Goodness, and Beauty is not simply the dressed-up, worn-out formula we thought it in our presumptuous, materialistic youth? If the crowns of these three trees meet, as scholars have asserted, and if the too obvious, too straight sprouts of Truth and Goodness have been knocked down, cut off, not let grow, perhaps the whimsical, unpredictable, unexpected branches of Beauty will work their way through, rise up to that very place, and thus complete the work of all three?

Then what Dostoevsky wrote-"Beauty will save the world"-is not a slip of the tongue but a prophecy. After all, he had a gift of seeing much, a man wondrously filled with light. And in that case could not art and literature, in fact, help the modern world? What little I have managed to learn about this over the years I will try to set forth here today.

8. The organizational pattern found in this passage is:
    a. time order
    b. compare / contrast
    c. definition / explanation
    d. cause / effect

C is correct. In this passage Solzhenitsyn provides an explanation and definition of the phrase, "Beauty will save the world."

9. Solzhenitsyn uses the term, *enigmatically,* in the first sentence of the essay. Of the following, which is the most effective method of unlocking the meaning of this word?
    a. context clues
    b. structural analysis
    c. dictionary
    d. ask a friend

B is correct. Knowledge of the root word, enigma = puzzling, would help determine the word's meaning.

10. Where is the main idea located in this reading selection?
    a. in the first paragraph
    b. in the last paragraph
    c. the main idea is not directly stated, but implied
    d. in the second paragraph

B is correct. Solzhenitsyn's main point is stated in the final paragraph of the essay.

11. The students in Mr. Downs' 10th grade English / language arts class are having difficulty reading and comprehending nonliterary texts. As an instructional strategy, Mr. Downs plans to teach his students to recognize organizational patterns within nonliterary text. Of the following strategies, which would be most effective in helping students identify the organizational pattern of nonliterary text?

    a. Have students use the *Observation / Proof note taking method* to identify main ideas and details important within several passages, then use this information to draw a map of the organizational pattern of each selection.
    b. Have students work in cooperative groups to determine the author's purpose for writing the passages, then apply that knowledge when reading the selections.
    c. Have students work in cooperative groups to write notes of the main points of the passages on *Post-It* notes, then use the notes to create a summary of each passage.
    d. Have students read the passage and create a list of the signal words that are found within the passage which convey the organizational pattern.

D is correct. Signal words (i.e. first, next, second, finally) are often associated with specific organizational patterns (time-order/sequential/chronological) found in nonliterary texts.

Domain II: Chapter 5

Competency 5: Reading literary / nonliterary texts – *The teacher understands reading skills and strategies for various types of nonliterary texts and teaches students to apply these skills and strategies to enhance their lifelong learning.*

The beginning teacher:

- Demonstrates knowledge of types of nonliterary texts (e.g., textbooks, newspapers, manuals, electronic texts, memoranda) and their characteristics.

- Understands purposes for reading nonliterary texts (e.g., for information, for pleasure), reading strategies associated with different purposes and ways to teach students to apply appropriate reading strategies for different purposes.

- Knows strategies for monitoring one's own understanding of nonliterary texts and for addressing comprehension difficulties that arise (e.g., by rereading, using other resources, questioning) and knows how to teach students to use these strategies.

- Demonstrates knowledge of skills for comprehending nonliterary texts (e.g., identifying main ideas and supporting details, summarizing, making inferences, drawing conclusions, analyzing historical and contemporary contexts) and knows how to provide students with opportunities to apply and refine these skills.

- Understands types of text organizers (e.g., overviews, headings, tables of contents, graphic features) and their use in locating and categorizing information.

- Demonstrates knowledge of types of text structure (e.g., chronological order, compare/contrast, cause/effect) and strategies for promoting students' ability to use text structure to facilitate comprehension of nonliterary texts.

- Knows strategies for helping students increase their knowledge of specialized vocabulary in nonliterary texts and for facilitating reading comprehension (e.g., creating graphic organizers, using study strategies such as skimming and scanning, note taking and outlining).

- Knows how to locate, retrieve and retain information from a range of texts, including interpreting information presented in various formats (e.g., maps, graphs) and uses effective instructional strategies to teach students these skills. I. Knows how to evaluate the credibility and accuracy of information in nonliterary texts, including electronic texts, and knows how to teach students to apply these critical-reading skills.

- Demonstrates an understanding of the characteristics and uses of various types of research tools and information sources and promotes students' understanding of and ability to use these resources.

- Understands steps and procedures for engaging in inquiry and research and provides students with learning experiences that promote their knowledge and skills in this area.

Key Terms

Almanac
Annotating
Atlas
Context clues
Cornell Method of Note taking
Dictionary
Educationatlas.com
Encyclopedia
Fishbone Map
Flow chart
Graphic organizer
Graphic organizer
Idea list
Image Description
Internet
Morphemic analysis
National Atlas of the United States of America
Note taking
Outlining
Post-it-notes
Problem-Solution
Road atlas
Scan
Skim
Spider cluster
Structural analysis
T-Chart
Thematic map
Thesaurus
Venn diagram
Web Portals
Weblogs

Skills and Strategies for Reading
Nonliterary Texts

Nonliterary texts may be described as contemporary, traditional and everyday texts that use language in precise and accurate ways to: transact and negotiate relationships or goods and services, report on events and issues, give directions, explain, analyze, argue, persuade, or give opinions. The primary purpose of informational text is to convey information about a topic, typically from someone presumed to know that information to someone presumed not to, with particular linguistic features such as headings and technical vocabulary to help accomplish that purpose. Typical nonliterary text types include: textbooks, newspaper or magazine articles, letters to the editor, brochures, advertisements, reports, and editorials. Typical types and features of nonliterary text include:

Newspaper articles, magazine articles - headlines, photographs, human interest stories; may use colloquial or idiomatic language.

Letters to the editor - praise for a good article; criticism of opinions expressed by the newspaper; suggestions for improving the newspaper; criticism or praise of politicians.

Editorials - the opinion of the newspaper on a particular subject; may use rhetorical devices like metaphors, hyperbole, irony

Advertisements - eye-catching pictures, illustrations or cartoons; humorous or witty remarks with a play on words; exaggerated praise of the product or service offered.

Brochures - information describing a product or service; glossy format; photographs and illustrations.

Reports - factual information; objective style; frequent use of diagrams or photographs to illustrate points.

Comprehending Nonliterary Texts

As stated previously, when authors begin writing, they usually have a definitive **purpose** for writing and usually have chosen a **structure or pattern of organization**. They may wish to convey an opinion, explain an idea, describe an event, entertain, provide a sequence of events or steps, provide reasons or rational for an idea, etc. English / language arts teachers must be able to demonstrate knowledge of types of text structure and provide students with strategies to facilitate comprehension.

Readers can use text structures to aid comprehension by asking the following questions:

- Skim the article for titles, subtitles, headings, and key words. After scanning the text, how do you think the author organized the information?

- Which framework did this author use to organize the information? Chronological? Cause/Effect? Problem/Solution? Compare/Contrast? Description? Directions?

- Does the author use a combination of structures?

- How did the author organize the text to be "reader-friendly"?

- Which text features helped you collect information from the article?

Critical Analysis of a Non-Literary Work

A critical analysis requires the reader to both summarize and evaluate a work *(www.media-awareness.ca)*. In order to critically analyze a nonliterary work, the following steps are recommended:

Read and annotate the work
- Consider the question prompts as you read.
- Take notes – look for author's thesis –
- If the work is a persuasive essay, evaluate the argument for validity
- Is the argument supported by evidence?
- Is information accurate and fairly interpreted?
- Does the author leave out important information?

Develop a thesis.
- Although the reader must identify the author's thesis, the reader must also develop and support an independent response thesis about the author's work.
- In the thesis, the reader must identify the author's main argument, and state whether or not the author achieves this purpose.

Organize the analysis.
- Include essential information in the Introduction. First, introduce the work and the author.
- Then, place the work in context (background information, literary period, interest in the topic, etc.) Next, state the response thesis.

Write the main body of the critique.
- In writing the critique, it is important to give a short overview of the work by briefly summarize only the main points of the book.
- The response evaluation should then address analytical questions.

Developing Reading Comprehension by Increasing Knowledge of Specialized Vocabulary

English / language arts teachers should know strategies for helping students increase their knowledge of specialized vocabulary in nonliterary texts in order to support reading comprehension. Every content area has a large collection of specialized vocabulary that students may or may not be able to understand.

Research on vocabulary instruction suggests that teachers should build student vocabulary by starting with what students already know, providing students with multiple exposures to new terms and concepts, and aiding students' transfer of new vocabulary knowledge to other subjects and reading situations (Alverman & Phelps, 1994).

When a student encounters an unknown word he or she must be aware that several effective methods can be applied to gain meaning of the word. The first method is to use context clues to unlock the word's meaning. **Context clues** are the words and ideas surrounding the unknown word that may give clues to its meaning. This method of vocabulary instruction is very effective because it is useful in building vocabulary by starting with what the student already knows. However, context is not always helpful and students must be taught other means of unlocking the meaning of unknown words.

Students then should try structural or morphemic analysis, to look for familiar word parts (prefixes, roots, and affixes) in order to unlock the meaning of an unknown word. However, **structural** or **morphemic analysis** is sometimes not adequate for meaning. For example, knowledge of the word part, *trans,* does not provide enough information to unlock the meaning of the *transcendentalist movement.* Students must then resort to much slower means of gaining the meaning of an unknown word including asking another student, asking the teacher, or using a dictionary (Alverman & Phelps, 1994).

Strategies to Facilitate Comprehension

When applying the cognitive theory of learning to the English / language arts classroom, a teacher's classroom activities and reading strategies should emphasize the importance of **prior knowledge**, the development of schema (internal networks of knowledge), and understanding the purpose for reading and learning. During the high school years, students are required to comprehend a vast amount of information and then are expected to retain the information for future use. Effective strategies which help students link the information to prior knowledge, develop new schema, and organize nonliterary text information for studying include: **annotating, note taking, outlining**, and creating **graphic organizers**.

Students must understand that the textbook should be considered a learning tool when reading, so they should annotate their text to help develop **metacognitive skills** during reading and retain the information after reading. Since students cannot write in public issued textbooks, an effective study strategy for annotating a text is to require students to write notes on **Post-it notes** and then attach the notes to the pages while reading and studying.

Writing notes on main points, identifying and defining specialized vocabulary, and noting relationships between ideas are all effective study methods to aid students with retention. When reading nonliterary selections, students must also be able to **skim** information to glean the main idea of a selection quickly, and to **scan** information to locate a particular item quickly.

The **Cornell system of note taking** has proven to be a very effective method of teaching students to organize nonliterary text and apply metacognitive skills to monitor their own comprehension. (Smith, 1993) The steps for this method of note taking include: First, draw a vertical line down the paper about two inches from the left side. The paper will then resemble a legal pad. After reading each section, write the main ideas or key terms in the left column with supporting details on the right. Students should then be able to use this information when completing additional assignments such as writing a summary or studying for an exam.

Teachers can also require students to create graphic organizers to guide their note-taking and discussion of nonfiction texts. Completing a **graphic organizer** has proven to be a very effective instructional strategy for students who have difficulty distinguishing between main ideas and supporting details. Additional visual and tactile activities (such as completing outlines, creating charts and diagrams, mapping ideas and relationships) all require active involvement on the part of the student and aid student comprehension and retention. Specific types of graphic organizers can be used for distinct purposes:

- **Spider Cluster** - a graphic aid to help connect supporting ideas to a main idea or point.
- **T-chart** - a graphic aid used to compare and contrast two subjects.
- **Idea List** or **chronological list** - a graphic aid to show ideas which occur in a specific order.
- **Flowchart** - a graphic aid used to visualize the flow of ideas or steps in a procedure or solution.
- **Venn diagram** - a graphic aid used to visualize the relationship or overlap of characteristics of two or more concepts.

Graphic Organizers

Graphic organizers come in many different forms, each one best suited to organizing a particular type of information. The following examples are merely a sampling of the different types and uses of graphic organizers typically used to help high school students comprehend non-literary text. **Graphic organizer**s help students organize and represent knowledge of a subject. Most graphic organizers begin with a main idea (or concept) and then branch out to show how that main idea can be broken down into specific topics. Many more graphic organizers are available from inspiration.com, an educational software company. Examples of graphic organizers available from inspiration.com include:

Descriptive or Thematic Map

Description / Thematic Map:

This graphic organizer consists of a series of shapes in several rows. The top row consists of a diamond in the center with two circles, one on each side, and two vertical rows of rectangles, one on each outer side. The diamond is labeled "Main Idea." The two circles are each labeled "Subordinate Idea" and the top rectangle of each outer row is labeled "Support Detail." Underneath the center diamond is a circle and beneath the circle is a horizontal row of three rectangles. The circle is labeled "Subordinate Idea" and the center rectangle is labeled "Support Detail." Lines connect the shapes of the graphic organizer http://www.inspiration.com.

Image description:
The graphic organizer titled "Network Tree" consists of a series of ovals of two different sizes. At the top are three large ovals, one above a row of two. They are connected by two black lines. At the bottom are two rows of three smaller ovals. One row of three is connected by black lines to a larger oval above them on the right, and one set of three is connected by black lines to a larger oval above them on the left http://www.inspiration.com.

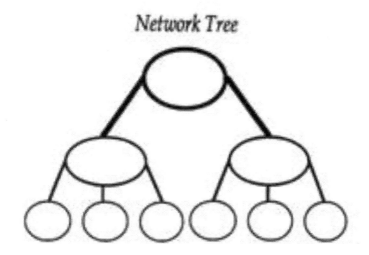

Spider Map:

The graphic organizer titled "Spider Map" consists of a large, central oval with four sets of black lines extending from it. The central oval is labeled "Topic, Concept, or Theme." Four slanted lines extend from the oval, and each one has two horizontal lines attached. Along the side of the slanted line at the top right of the graphic organizer is the label "Main Idea." On one of the horizontal lines at the top left is the label "Detail" http://www.inspiration.com.

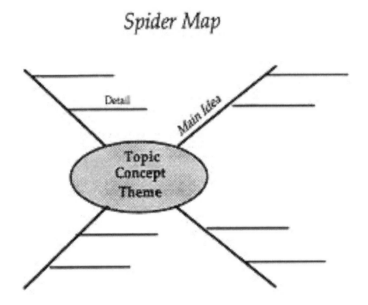

Spider Map

Problem-Solution:

The graphic organizer titled "Problem-Solution Outline" consists of a vertical row of three rectangles. To the left of the top rectangle is the label "Problem." The word "Who" appears at the top right corner, and the words "What" and "Why" appear within the rectangle. An arrow points from the top rectangle to the one in the middle. The middle rectangle is larger than the other two. An arrow cuts through the center of the rectangle, pointing down. To the left of the rectangle is the label "Solution." Within the rectangle, on the left, the words "Attempted Solutions" appear, with the numbers one and two beneath. Within the rectangle, on the right, the word "Results" appears, with the numbers one and two beneath. An arrow points from the center rectangle to the one beneath, which is labeled "End Result" http://www.inspiration.com.

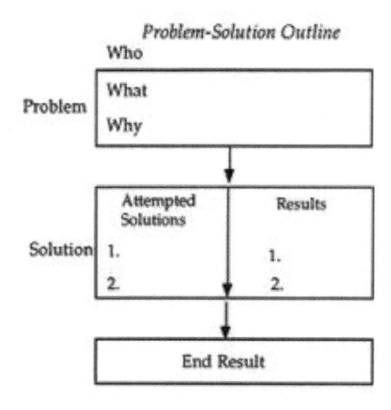

Sequential Episodic Map:

The graphic organizer titled "Sequential Episodic Map" consists of an oval at the top and three vertical rows of boxes beneath. The oval is labeled "Main Idea." The top box on the left is labeled "Cause..." The top box in the middle is labeled "Effect...Cause..." The top box on the right is labeled "Effect..." Lines connect the boxes beneath, and arrows point from the rows to the top boxes. Each box in the second row is labeled "Influence" **http://www.inspiration.com**.

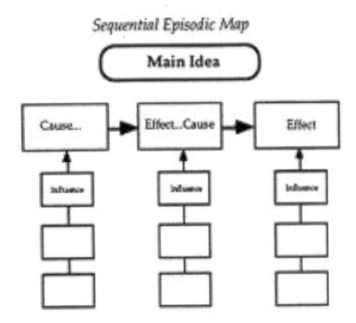

Fishbone Map:

The graphic organizer titled "Fishbone Map" consists of a series of horizontal and slanted lines. In the center of the graphic organizer, is a thick black line with two sets of two slanted lines extending from it in the shape of two arrows pointing to the left. The arrow's lines on the left are labeled "Cause 1" on the top and "Cause 2" on the bottom. The arrow's lines on the right are labeled "Cause 3" on the top and "Cause 4" on the bottom. A horizontal line extends from the top of each arrow. The horizontal line on the left is labeled "Detail." Two horizontal lines extend from the bottom of each arrow. The bottom line on the left is labeled "Detail"
http://www.inspiration.com.

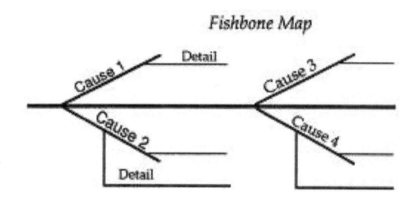

Compare / Contrast Map:

organizer titled "Comparative and
Map" is made up of two ovals at the top, a
rectangles connected by straight and zig-
beneath, and a vertical row of three circles
left. The oval on the top left is labeled
The oval on the top right is labeled
Below this, three rows of three rectangles
to each other and to the top ovals by
lines. Zig-zag lines connect the rectangles
horizontally. The rectangle on the top left
rectangle on the top right are each labeled
Feature." The top rectangle in the center is
"Similar Feature." Brackets to the left of

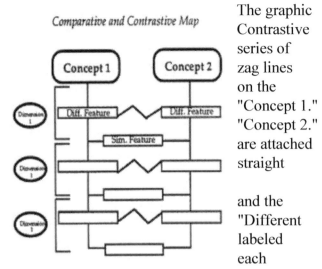

The graphic
Contrastive
series of
zag lines
on the
"Concept 1."
"Concept 2."
are attached
straight

and the
"Different
labeled
each

rectangle in the row on the left indicate each of three circles on the far left of the graphic
organizer. Each of the three circles are labeled "Dimension 1" http://www.inspiration.com.

Continuum Scale:

The graphic organizer titled "Continuum Scale" consists of a straight horizontal line with a short
vertical line at each end. The left end of the line is labeled "Low," and the right end of the line is
labeled "High" http://www.inspiration.com.

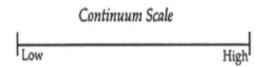

Series of Events Chain:

organizer titled "Series of Events Chain" consists of of three rectangles with arrows pointing down them. Above the top rectangle is the label "Initiating Within the rectangles are the labels "Event 1," and "Event 3," from top to bottom. Above the third the label "Final Event" http://www.inspiration.com.

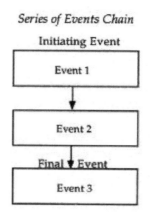

Series of Events Chain

The graphic a vertical row between Event." "Event 2," rectangle is

Benefits of Graphic Organizers

Graphic Organizer aid students' understanding and learning of content, and help students focus their energies on the most important aspect of the material rather than just memorizing the material. Graphic organizers can be used to depict complex concepts, ease information processing demands, and scaffold students' understanding. Graphic organizers can also be used to facilitate writing or give an oral report. In sum, graphic organizers are effective devices for helping students focus on the relationships between main ideas and details, Graphic organizers are typically hierarchical, with the subordinate concepts stemming from the main concept or idea.

Locating and Retrieving Information

In an age when information grows exponentially, it is important for students to learn where to find resource material. A number of useful reference sources are available to help students find information and answer questions including: dictionaries, thesauruses, encyclopedias, almanacs, atlases, and online resources.

The **dictionary** is the most common and basic reference source with which most students are familiar. Today, almost all dictionaries are available on the Internet. Online dictionaries include: Merriam-Webster Dictionary, Cambridge Free Dictionary and Thesaurus, and The Oxford Dictionary. The purpose of the dictionary is to provide the meaning, spelling, origin, and correct pronunciation of words. There are dictionaries for most languages worldwide and a number of language translation dictionaries for student use. There are three types of dictionaries: abridged, unabridged, and specialized. Abridged dictionaries include only those words most commonly used in everyday language. Unabridged dictionaries include all words used in a language. Specialized dictionaries provide information on words that apply to a specific subject such as finance, math, chemistry, or physics (**Dictionary.com** http://dictionary.reference.com/).

A **thesaurus** provides synonyms for words. Most thesaurus are available free on the Internet including: Roget's Thesaurus, Think-Map Visual Thesaurus, and Merriam-Webster Thesaurus. An online thesaurus usually gives a definition, an audio clip for the pronunciation, the origin, and synonyms for the entry word that have the same or similar meanings. For example, "whirlpool" is a synonym for "vortex."

vor·tex

noun \'vȯr-ˌteks\

: a mass of spinning air, liquid, etc., that pulls things into its center

plural **vor·ti·ces** *also* **vor·tex·es**

Full Definition of VORTEX

1: something that resembles a whirlpool <the hellish *vortex* of battle — *Time*>

2 a : a mass of fluid (as a liquid) with a whirling or circular motion that tends to form a cavity or vacuum in the center of the circle and to draw toward this cavity or vacuum bodies subject to its action; *especially* : WHIRLPOOL, EDDY

  b: a region within a body of fluid in which the fluid elements have an angular velocity

See vortex defined for English-language learners »
See vortex defined for kids »

Examples of VORTEX

1.   <a boat sucked down into the *vortex*>

2.   **Origin of VORTEX**

New Latin *vortic-, vortex,* from Latin *vertex, vortex* whirlpool — more at VERTEX

First Known Use: 165

Synonyms

      gulf, maelstrom, whirlpool

Related Words

See **Roget's II: The New Thesaurus, Third Edition**

http://www.bartleby.com/62/

This thesaurus contains 35,000 synonyms in an easy-to-use format. This thesaurus features succinct word definitions and an innovative hyperlinked category index by the Editors of the American Heritage® Dictionary.

An **encyclopedia** is a compilation of articles, descriptions, and explanations written by experts on a variety of subjects. Today, most online encyclopedias also provide audio and video clips, as well as interactive maps, diagrams, graphs, and illustrations. These include: **World Book Online Encyclopedia**, and **Encyclopedia Britannica**. There are typically two types of encyclopedias: general encyclopedias and subject specific encyclopedias. As the name indicates, general encyclopedias contain articles and reference information on an array of topics. Subject encyclopedias contain detailed articles and reference information on specific subjects.

Encyclopedia.com, http://www.encyclopedia.com/, the Internet's premiere free encyclopedia, provides users with more than 57,000 frequently updated articles from the Columbia Encyclopedia, Sixth Edition. Each article is enhanced with links to newspaper and magazine articles as well as pictures and maps - all provided by eLibrary.

Wikipedia
http://en.wikipedia.org/wiki/Main_Page
Wikipedia is a free content wiki encyclopedia written collaboratively by contributors from around the world. Every day thousands of visitors from around the world make tens of thousands of edits and create new articles. It is important to note that Wikipedia, while very popular, is not considered a reliable source by most academics, because of its open format.

An **almanac** contains facts about a variety of topics during a given year. Topics covered in almanacs may include government, history, countries, and weather. Since a new almanac comes out each year, the information is usually very current. *The Old Farmer's Almanac*, is available online. It is one of America's oldest sources of weather, folklore, gardening and other information. Fed States, Fact Monster, CIA: World Fact Book are just a few of the online almanacs available to students. See http://www.refseek.com/directory/almanacs.html for a complete list of online almanacs.

CIA - The World Factbook
https://www.cia.gov/library/publications/the-world-factbook/index.html
The Factbook, first made available on the Internet in June 1997, provides basic information from the US Government.

An **atlas** provides a collection of maps of the countries and geographies throughout the world. A country map will show the borders of a country as well as major political features such as states and cities. Geographical maps include topographical features such as oceans, seas, lakes, mountains, valleys, rivers, and deserts. The **National Atlas of the United States of America** home page contains an online map maker, dynamic maps, and printable maps (http://nationalatlas.gov/).

A **road atlas** contains a collection of road maps. Other specialized atlases provide detailed information on human anatomy, animal anatomy, lakes, rivers of the world, and more. **EducationAtlas.com** contains maps for educators and helps individuals find detailed educational resources and information. Additional specialized atlases are available online as well including: **Census Atlas of the United States, Muscle Atlas, Dermatology Atlas**, etc.

Useful Online Resources for Teachers

Internet Public Library:
   http://www.ipl.org
   Provides all of the basic research tools such as dictionaries and encyclopedias that one would expect to find in a library.

LibrarySpot.com
   http://www.libraryspot.com/
   LibrarySpot.com is a free virtual library resource center for educators and students, librarians and their patrons exploring the Web for valuable research information. Sites featured on **LibrarySpot.com** are hand-selected and reviewed by an editorial team and are usually of exceptional quality, content and utility.

Research Strategies

Students should participate in a variety of research activities that promote active learning and higher order thinking. In today's classrooms the use of technology helps actively involve students in research by helping them acquire, analyze, and evaluate information. Students need to learn to locate and evaluate information for accuracy and validity (Roblyer, 2003).

Students are required to write numerous research papers during high school. Skills in research and organization help students gather information by consulting sources outside the classroom and then sharing the findings with others. A **research paper** is a formal, written presentation of findings based on information gathered from a variety of sources. Effective research writing includes:

- a thesis statement
- supporting facts and details from a variety of sources
- a clear organizational structure
- a bibliography (works cited list) which provides a complete list of sources

Narrowing the Research Topic

One of the first things students must realize is that they need to narrow the scope of their topic. They can narrow their topic by asking themselves the "w" questions so familiar to journalists: Who? What? Where? When? and Why? (and sometimes, How?) These questions can help students locate specific points of interest within a general topic area. For example, to narrow a topic like "foreign languages," a student should begin with the "what" and "when" questions and decide if he or she is interested in "foreign language studies in high school." Asking the "where" question, might help a student arrive at "foreign language studies in high school in Texas." And asking the "who" question might help the student limit the topic again to "Texas state policy regarding foreign language studies in high school." Students must realize that each time they add something specific to a topic, they are placing "restrictors" on it, thereby narrowing it. Consequently, when students conduct a library or Internet search, they will be able to use these "restrictors" as key words (http://writing.colostate.edu/guides/processes/topic/pop15c.cfm).

Considering the Audience and Purpose of Research

Determining the **purpose** of writing a research paper helps the writer narrow a topic. The purpose of research demands particular approaches to a subject in that it will determine the questions that give direction to the research. In the case of a research paper, selecting a purpose for conducting the research will suggest the type of information the student needs to gather in order to address those questions.

Students must also have a clear idea of the **audience** for whom they are writing; this will help determine an appropriate topic and how to present it. Knowing the audience (high school students, teachers, parents, politicians, etc.) requires the student to adapt and limit the topic so that the information presented is appropriate to a specific group of readers.

Moving from Topic to Thesis

It is important to remember that a narrow topic is not the same thing as a **thesis statement.** Unlike a topic, a thesis makes a claim of fact, provides a claim of value, or makes a recommendation about a topic under consideration. For example, a narrowed topic might be "the under emphasis on foreign language in Texas high schools." A focused thesis statement making a claim about this topic might read, "Texas high schools should require elementary students to take at least one course in a foreign language sometime during the 4th through 6th grades." Transforming a workable topic into a possible thesis is really just a continuation of the narrowing process, with an emphasis on what the writer wants to say about a topic. In this way, it is much like the "hypothesis" stage of the scientific method. The writer arrives at a thesis by attempting to make an opinionated statement about the chosen topic.

Using Technology to Aid Research

The Internet vastly increases the number of resources students can utilize when exploring nonfiction topics. Search engines index the content of the web to create an information retrieval system responsive to queries. Descriptions of how that happens change rapidly as programmers and technological developments advance. For example: Wikipedia provides one overview, About.com another.

However, more than 85 percent of online searches start with Google. It is the universal default search engine, a ubiquitous tool for beginning online research, and it's now a transitive verb inscribed in dictionaries. Teachers can narrow the content available from Internet searches by using student-friendly search engines such as **Ask, Yahooligans, Chrome, Foxfire** and **Searchopolis.** This narrow-scope search engine may lead to a more appropriate content on topics from astronomy to quantum physics.

Searchopolis is geared towards children, students and families, and filters out all porn and material that would not be safe for everyone. Searchopolis claims to be the first to do so, and during a test it appeared to function as advertised. Powered by Inktomi, Searchopolis may help students find fast age-appropriate results.

For research assignments that link the English / language arts classroom to content areas, computers can offer a wealth of information. For example: the **National Geographic's Picture Atlas of the World**, *www.nationalgeographic.com/atlas/*, offers rich resources-maps, facts, and video clips about countries all over the world.

Additional Academic search engines for high school students include:

- **Google Scholar** - This Google search engine makes it easy to search for papers, abstracts, citations, and other scholarly literature.
- **iSEEK** - Designed specifically for students and educators, iSEEK is a non-commercial search engine. It delivers results from universities, government sites, and other noncommercial providers.
- **OJOSE** - The Online Journal Search Engine (OJOSE) searches online journals and books. This search engine is best for students who are looking for scientific materials.
- **Scirus** - This search engine claims to have the most comprehensive scientific search engine on the Web. More than 450 million scientific items are included in Scirus' index.
- **DMOZ** - Though technically not a search engine (it's more of a directory), DMOZ contains content that is hand-picked by editors who are experts in their field. You can find over five million links on DMOZ.

Critiquing Sources

Once students have gathered sources for their research paper, they must then evaluate the material found. This is especially true of resources found on the Internet. The articles in scientific publications are previously scrutinized by scientific evaluation before being published. Scientific journals have a system called peer review, which means that all articles are reviewed by researchers within the field before publication to guarantee scientific quality. In contrast, anyone can publish anything on the Internet, so there is no safeguard for evaluation. Students must therefore develop the skills to judge the quality of information found on the Internet.

Considering this, evaluation is mostly about judging the quality of the information found. By asking a number of questions, students can ascertain if the information can be used for their research paper (www.libraryresources.com):

Author - Who is the author? Can you find any information about him/her? Can this information be verified?

Subject and perspective - How does the material cover the subject? Sometimes all that is needed is an overview of the subject; sometimes specific aspects of a subject are needed. The material chosen should suit the student's information needs.

Facts & details - Is the material correct? Are the facts right? It is naturally easier to be certain as to what is correct when dealing with a known subject. However, encyclopedias can be used to compare facts with the material found.

Is the text objective or does the author put forward his or her own views? Is the material unique or are you finding similar or better information from other sources?

Purpose and target groups -What is the purpose of the text? What does the author want to achieve by it? Does he want to inform, provoke, or persuade?

Audience - Who is the intended audience: researchers, school students, or the public? Is the material relevant and up to date?

Publisher - Which organization is responsible for the information?

References - Which other articles or sources has the author used or quoted? Does the author reference the sources in a bibliography?

Citing Sources

It is essential that students understand and apply the fair use / copyright rules that protect copyrighted information. The first place to begin this endeavor is by teaching students about fair use / copyright law.

Students may be surprised to learn that the myriad media materials and electronic information found online must not only be subject to critical evaluation, but also must be cited as reference sources when integrated into class work. Students must be taught to assume that everything they find online is copyrighted and protected.

Copyright: Fair Use Practices for Students

Federal copyright laws protect the creative work of artists, musicians, writers, and photographers. "Fair Use" is a provision of U.S. copyright law that permits students and teachers to use portions of copyrighted materials for educational purposes. Students should consider the fair use guidelines below when creating projects or writing research papers. Answering the four questions posed below can help students determine how to use copyrighted material properly. http://www.copyright.gov/title17/

1. What is the purpose and character of use?
Nonprofit, educational, and personal uses are most likely to fall under the fair use category. Also at issue here is whether the copied material is being used to help create something new or simply being copied verbatim.
2. What is the nature of the copyrighted work?
Generally speaking, students and teachers have more leeway to copy factual works and published works than imaginative and unpublished works.
3. How much of the work will be used?
Fair use includes portion limitations. Less is always better. Students may use music, video, and texts, but guidelines for these materials vary. A general guideline for a student multimedia project is to use 10 percent (or less) of a work, but not more than: 3 minutes of a video, 30 seconds of a song, and 5 photos from an artist's collection.

The videos and music being copied must be legally acquired.

4. What effect does the use have on the potential market for the work?
Students may never distribute or sell their projects to mass audiences, and may keep only two copies of the project. Be aware that federal law also maintains time limitations. Students may keep a project for two years and must not harm the author or copyright holder's profits. Always students must cite all your sources; the copyright holder of any material used for a class project must be given proper credit. And be aware that these guidelines apply to material on the Web (text, images, multimedia objects) which is protected under copyright law.

Penalties
Students are subject to litigation if they do not follow these guidelines.
- Be careful. Copyright infringement is considered intellectual theft!
- Be sure to follow the 10% rule and document your sources carefully.
- Students may be fined up to $100,000 for not following the Fair Use guidelines, even if unaware of these laws.

Seek Permission to Use
Students can ask for, and in many cases, receive permission to use a whole song or extensive images if a request is made to the copyright holder and proof of permission is kept.

Works Cited: Documentation Formats
Students should understand the importance of using acceptable formats for communicating the various forms of discourse; the three most common formats for documentation include: The Modern Language Association (MLA), The American Psychological Association (APA), and the Chicago Manual of Style. A brief review of the MLA style is presented.

The Modern Language Association Style
The Modern Language Association (MLA) is involved with the study and teaching of language and literature. This MLA documentation style, used in many research papers, especially in high schools, is as follows (www.thewritesource.com):

Book
Okuda, Michael, and Denise Okuda. Star Trek Chronology: The History of the Future. New York: Pocket, 2013.

Journal Article
Wilcox, Rhonda V. "Shifting Roles and Synthetic Women in Star Trek: The Next Generation." Studies in Popular Culture 13.2 (2013): 53-65.

Newspaper or Journal Article
Di Rado, Alicia. "Trekking through College: Classes Explore Modern Society Using the World of Star Trek." Los Angeles Times 15 Mar. 2013: A3.

Book Article or Chapter
James, Nancy E. "Two Sides of Paradise: The Eden Myth According to Kirk and Spock." Spectrum of the Fantastic. Ed. Donald Palumbo. Westport, CT: Greenwood, 1988: 219 223.

Encyclopedia Article (and other well-known reference books)
Sturgeon, Theodore. "Science Fiction." The Encyclopedia Americana. International ed., 2013.

Encyclopedia Article (and less familiar reference books)
Horn, Maurice. "Flash Gordon." The World Encyclopedia of Comics. Ed. Maurice Horn. 2 vols. New York: Chelsea, 2013.

Reference Book (and other books featuring reprinted articles)
Shayon, Robert Lewis. "The Interplanetary Spock." Saturday Review 17 June 2013: 46. Rpt. in Contemporary Literary Criticism. Ed. Sharon R. Gunton. Vol. 17. Detroit: Gale Research, 2013.

MLA Format of On-Line Electronic Entry
Author or editor. "Title." Book title. Printed version information. Site title. Volume or issue number. Date posted. Name of subscription service, library name and location. Listserv name. 00 pp. Sponsoring organization. Date accessed <Electronic address>.

Sample Website Citation
Lynch, Tim. "DSN Trials and Tribble-ations Review." Psi Phi: Bradley's Science Fiction Club. 1996. Bradley University. 8 Oct. 2013. http://www.bradley.edu/campusorg/psiphi/DS9/ep/503r.html.

Sample Newspaper or Magazine Article on the Internet
Andreadis, Athena. "The Enterprise Finds Twin Earths Everywhere It Goes, But Future Colonizers of Distant Planets Won't Be So Lucky." Astronomy Jan. 1999: 64-68. Academic Universe. Lexis-Nexis. B. Davis Schwartz Memorial Lib., Brookville, NY. 7 Feb. 2013. http://web.lexis-nexis.com/universe.

Methods of Inquiry and Investigation

Students should be prompted to research topics which hold their interest. When helping students, teachers should ensure that a variety of sources are available for student use. Teachers may choose to apply specific lesson designs to promote higher order thinking and active student involvement when conducting research:

- **Inquiry lessons** require that the student pose questions and then research the answers. The teacher's role during inquiry is to serve as a facilitator by structuring the learning environment to support learning. The teacher also supports and scaffolds the students when they are working to answer their inquiries.

- **Discovery lessons** require that the teacher pose students challenging questions and then ask students to work together to research the answer to the question through trial and error experimentation.

Inquiry

Inquiry-based instruction requires that a teacher create a classroom where students are engaged in open-ended, student-centered, and hands-on activities. During an inquiry lesson students are required to: pose questions, solve problems, and create answers or tentative generalizations.

Staver and Bay (1987) described a method of teaching inquiry (structured inquiry) during which students were given a problem to solve, a method for solving the problem, and necessary materials, but not the expected outcomes. Students were to discover a relationship and generalize from the data collected. Similarly, in guided inquiry lessons, students must also figure out a method for solving the problem given. And, in open inquiry lessons, students must also formulate the problem they will investigate. Open inquiry most closely mimics the actions of "real" scientists.

Students more easily learn observable ideas via inquiry-based instruction (especially the learning cycle) than ideas considered theoretical. For example in a science class, inquiry-based instruction is likely to be effective for showing many students that chemical reaction rates depend on the concentrations of reactants. Students can even investigate how reaction rates depend on concentration. On the other hand, inquiry-based methods are poor as a means toward helping most students understand how scientists *explain* the phenomena, via the kinetic-molecular theory.

To help students benefit from inquiry-based instruction teachers should:
1. Orient activities toward concrete (or observable) concepts (What characteristics in this story make it a folk tale?)
2. Emphasize activities centered on operational questions - questions that students can answer directly via investigation (Are their similar folk tales from other regions of the world?)
3. Emphasize activities using materials and situations familiar to students (How is this folk tale like other folk tales that you know?).
4. Choose activities which build on students' prior knowledge (For example: Work in small groups to write a folk tale. Be sure your folk tale includes all the characteristics of a typical folk tale previously researched).

Discovery Learning

Discovery learning is inquiry-based. It is based on constructivist learning theory in that it takes place in problem solving situations where the student draws on his or her own past experience and existing knowledge to discover new facts and relationships. During an "inquiry" lesson, students interact with the world by exploring and manipulating objects, wrestling with questions and controversies, or performing experiments (Bruner, 1967). As a result, students may be more likely to remember concepts and knowledge discovered on their own. Lessons that are based upon discovery learning include: guided discovery, problem-based learning, simulation-based learning, case-based learning, and incidental learning.

Proponents of **discovery learning** believe that these types of lessons have advantages, including:

- encouraging active engagement
- promoting motivation
- promoting autonomy, responsibility, and independence
- promoting the development of creativity and problem solving skills in a unique learning experience

Critics of **discovery learning** have sometimes cited disadvantages including:

- at times this type of lesson will create cognitive overload
- the potential exists for the student to produce misconceptions
- teachers may fail to detect problems and misconceptions students encounter

References

Abrams, M. H. (1971). Introduction: Orientation of Critical Theories in *The Mirror and the Lamp: Romantic Theory and the Critical Tradition*. Galaxy: Oxford University Press.

Bruner, J.S. (1967). On knowing: Essays for the left hand. Cambridge, Mass: Harvard University Press.

Colburn, A. (2010). *What Teacher Educators Need to Know about Inquiry-Based Instruction*, **http://www.csulb.edu/~acolburn/AETS.htm**.

Guerin, W. et. al. *Critical Approaches to Literature* (4th edition). (1999). Galaxy: Oxford University Press.

Roblyer, M. D. (2003). *Integrating Educational Technology into Teaching.* (3rd Edition), Merrill Prentice Hall, New Jersey.

Rosenblatt, L. M. (1983). The Literary Transaction: Evocation and Response. *Theory into Practice,* V. 21: 268-277.

Smith, B. D. (1993). *Bridging the Gap.* (4th Edition), Harper Collins, New York.

Staver, J. R., & Bay, M. (1987). Analysis of the project synthesis goal cluster orientation and inquiry emphasis of elementary science textbooks. *Journal of Research in Science Teaching, 24,* 629-643.

Tchudi, S. and Mitchell, D. (1999). *Exploring and Teaching the English Language Arts* (4th edition). Addison Wesley Longman, Inc.: NY.

Wood, J. (2000). A Marriage Waiting to Happen: Computers and Process Writing, Education Development Center, Inc. (EDC).

www.benedict.com
http://www.copyright.gov/title17/
http://www.edtechleaders.org
http://www.inspiration.com
http://www.k12reader.com/reading-fluency-and-instruction/
www.libraryresources.com
www.media-awareness.ca
www.mediafestival.org
www.rlwclarke.net
www.thewritesource.com
www.walterforeman.com/files/papers/compare.htm
http://writing.colostate.edu/guides/processes/topic/pop15c.cfm.
www.thewritesource.com

Practice Questions

1. The graphic organizer which would best support student understanding when asked to compare and contrast two newspaper articles is the _____.

      a. Flow chart
      b. Spider chart
      c. T-chart
      d. Précis

C is correct. A "T-chart" is a graphic aid used to compare and contrast two subjects.

2. Read the following paragraph to determine the author's organizational structure.

Take the following steps to make an ecologically friendly window cleaner for your home. First, purchase a spray bottle or recycle one from your home. Make certain it is cleaned out and rinsed really well. Then, combine one cup of each of the vinegar, water and alcohol and mix well. Next, pour the solution into the spray bottle and start cleaning. This solution may be used on almost any surface. I find that it works better than Windex and is friendly on the wallet. It cleans sinks and doorknobs terrific. You can also add a few drops of tea tree oil or orange oil for scent, but these are also natural disinfectants.

      a. Cause / effect
      b. Chronological
      c. Problem / solution
      d. Definition

B is correct. The reader must follow certain steps in order to make Windex. Therefore, this paragraph is written using "chronological" structure.

3. Which type of graphic organizer which would best support student understanding of the (How to Make Windex) paragraph above?

      a. Flow chart
      b. Spider chart
      c. T-chart
      d. Précis

A is correct. A Flow Chart graphic organizer is often used to outline ideas or steps of a procedure.

4. An electronic source is more advantageous to a researcher than a printed document for all of the following reasons EXCEPT:

      a. the researcher can easily locate specific words or phrases within the source using the "find" feature.
      b. once downloaded, the electronic version can easily be retrieved.
      c. the researcher can easily focus on the main ideas and details within the document.
      d. once downloaded, the electronic document can be easily stored.

C is correct. This is not an advantage to using an electronic resource. A,B & D are advantages to using electronic sources.

5. Of the following, which question would be the most important to ask when analyzing a reference source for a research paper?
      a. What search engine was used to locate the source?
      b. When was the source located?
      c. Are the facts and details within the source correct?
      d. How many sources are needed for the research assignment?

C is correct.

6. Of the following documentation formats, which one follows the MLA style of formatting an article citation?

a. Wilcox, Rhonda V. "Shifting Roles and Synthetic Women in Star Trek: The Next Generation." *Studies in Popular Culture.* 13.2 (1991): 53-65.

b. J. Brian. Steel Wills, A Battle from the Start: The Life of Nathan Bedford Forrest (New York: HarperCollins, 1992), 187.

c. Smith, T. (2005). Mid-life crisis: how to find happiness and fulfillment in a loving relationship. *The Psychology of Love.* Harper Collins: NY

d. Williams, Joanna, "What to expect from your 6-month-old." *American Baby* (New York: HarperCollins, 2005), 304.

A is correct. This is MLA formatting for an article citation.

7. Which of the following strategies would be <u>most</u> effective in helping students **improve their reading rates and reading fluency?**

a. Allowing frequent opportunities for students to read (and reread) texts with subject matter that they have selected and that has great interest to them.

b. Expanding students' vocabulary knowledge by assigning challenging texts at and beyond their instructional reading level.

c. Encouraging students to use various comprehension strategies such as self-monitoring, predicting, and questioning.

d. Administering timed reading tests to students each week to motivate them to read more quickly and accurately.

A is correct.

8. To promote students' reading fluency, a teacher plans activities in which students and their assigned small group will engage in a Reader's Theater assignment. When the teacher assembles reading materials for this purpose, it would be most important to assign each small group a passages that:

a. the students have previewed and selected themselves.

b. everyone in the group is capable of reading aloud - with no more than 5 word recognition errors per 100 words of text.

c. at least one student in the group is capable of reading aloud, allowing that student to scaffold others.

d. the students have been reading in connection with content-area study.

B is correct.

Domain II: Chapter 6

Competency 6: Literature – *The teacher understands literary elements, genres and movements and demonstrates knowledge of a substantial body of literature.*

The beginning teacher:

- Demonstrates knowledge of genres and their characteristics through analysis of literary texts.
- Demonstrates knowledge of literary elements and devices, including ways in which they contribute to meaning and style, through analysis of literary texts.
- Demonstrates knowledge of major literary movements in American, British and world literature, including their characteristics, the historical contexts from which they emerged, major authors and their impact on literature and representative works and their themes.
- Demonstrates knowledge of a substantial body of classic and contemporary American literature.
- Demonstrates knowledge of a substantial body of classic and contemporary British literature.
- Demonstrates knowledge of a substantial body of classic and contemporary world literature.
- Demonstrates knowledge of a substantial body of young adult literature.
- Demonstrates knowledge of various critical approaches to literature.

Key Terms

Aesthetic
Allegory
Alliteration
Allusion
Anachronism
Analogy
Antagonist
Antithesis
Apostrophe
Assonance
Ballad
Canon
Catharsis
Cause / effect
Character
Climax
Compare / contrast
Connotation
Consonance
Couplet
Definition
Denotation
Denouement
Drama
Dynamic character
Efferent
Epic
Essay
Eulogy
Euphemism
Existentialism
Exposition
Fable
Fairy tales
Falling action
Farce
Figurative language
First person narrative
Flashback
Flat character

Foreshadowing
Genre
Gothic fiction
Green Critic
Haiku
Hyperbole
Imagery
Irony
Legend
Malapropism
Meiosis
Metaphor
Metaphysical Poetry
Metonymy
Mimetic Approach
Motif
Muse
Myth
Narration
Neoclassicism
Novel
Octave
Ode
Omniscient
Onomatopoeia
Palindrome
Pantoum
Paradox
Parody
Pastoral ode
Pathos
Personification
Point of view
Pragmatic analysis
Quatrain
Quintet
Refrain
Resonance
Rising action
Round character

Satire
Septet
Sestet
Short story
Simile
Soliloquy
Stanza
Static character
Stress
Surrealism
Symbolism

Synecdoche
Tercet
Theme
Time order or sequence
Tone / mood
Tragedy
Understatement
Verbal representation
Victorian Era
Villanelle
Young Adult literature

Literary Elements, Genres and Movements

Teachers of English should be able to demonstrate knowledge of the literary elements and devices that contribute to meaning and style. The basic elements of literature are plot, theme, setting, character, point-of-view, conflict, symbolism, tone, and irony. An in-depth study of literature requires that students move beyond these basic elements of literature into higher order thinking; therefore, it is important that secondary English teachers become knowledgeable of the many **literary elements** used by authors to convey human emotion and understanding.

Alliteration - the repetition of initial consonant sounds in two or more words in a line of writing; often used for poetic effect. Alliteration is based on sound not spelling. Example: luscious lemons; trespasser's reproach. "Tell all the truth, but tell it slant," **Emily Dickinson**.

Allusion - reference to a well-known person, place, object, event, literary work, or work of art. The use of allusion implies shared literary and cultural experiences between author and reader. Example: When Susan lost her job, she became a Scrooge, refusing to buy anything but the basic necessities. (Referencing a character from **Charles Dickens,'** *A Christmas Carol*.)

Allusions from a Variety of Sources Contribute to Literature - An allusion is an indirect and brief reference to a well-known person, character, events, or a place in a story. Allusion in a story allows the reader to visualize a concept or a situation and relate the story to its time. A story, a paragraph, or a poem can allude to a person, a character in a novel or movie, myth, historical event, the Bible, a particular setting or an era. The reader has to be familiar with the allusion in order to understand the prose or poem that contains it.

A modern example is found in the Harry Potter's series where **J.K. Rowling** frequently alluded to folklores and mythological names. For instance, Remus Lupin's code name as Rumulus in *Harry Potter and the* **DEATHLY HOLLOWS** was alluded from Romulus found in early Greek Mythology.

HAMLET, notably one of **Shakespeare**'s greatest plays depended heavily on allusions to support Shakespeare's ideas and viewpoints. The character Hercules was alluded from Greek and Roman mythology where he was known for his strength. In Act 1, Scene 2, line 140, Hamlet compares his deceased father to Hyperion, Titan God of Light, who represents virtue and honor and in contrast compares his Uncle Claudius to a satyr, a Greek mythic fusion of man and goat. Satyrs are known for their rudeness and over indulgence, which accurately describes the character, Claudius: *"So excellent a king, that was to this Hyperion to a satyr"* (i.ii.143-144).

Biblical references are found quite often in literature. The following allusion is to the biblical story of Jonah who is swallowed alive by a whale. *"As the cave's roof collapsed, he was swallowed up in the dust like Jonah, and only his frantic scrabbling behind a wall of rock indicated that there was anyone still alive."*

Some allusions are in reference to other works that are popular within the Western canon. For example, the following allusion is to Ebenezer Scrooge, the main character in **Charles Dickens'** famous novel, *A Christmas Carol*: "Christy didn't like to spend money. She was no Scrooge, but she seldom purchased anything except the bare necessities."

Anachronism - placing an event, person, or object out of its proper chronological place. Anachronisms can be used purposefully, for humorous effect, or accidentally, the result of poor research. Example: In the film, *Apollo 13*, there were several accidental anachronisms: the use of the modern NASA logo, and the use of a Beatles' song that was not released until after the time of the Apollo 13 incident (www.americanpoems.com).

Analogy - an inference that two dissimilar things share common traits. In **Robert Frost's** poem, *The Onset,* the poet reveals depth of thought through analogy: winter compared to death and spring compared to life (www.americanpocms.com/poets/robertfrost):

The Onset
Always the same, when on a fated night
At last the gathered snow lets down as white
As may be in dark woods, and with a song
It shall not make again all winter long
Of hissing on the yet uncovered ground,
I almost stumble looking up and round,
As one who overtaken by the end
Gives up his errand, and lets death descend
Upon him where he is, with nothing done
To evil, no important triumph won,
More than if life had never been begun.
Yet all the precedent is on my side:
I know that winter death has never tried
The earth but it has failed: the snow may heap
In long storms an undrifted four feet deep
As measured again maple, birch, and oak,
It cannot check the peeper's silver croak;
And I shall see the snow all go down hill
In water of a slender April rill
That flashes tail through last year's withered brake
And dead weeds, like a disappearing snake.
Nothing will be left white but here a birch,
And there a clump of houses with a church.

Antagonist-a character or force in conflict with the main (protagonist) character. In **Edgar Allan Poe's** short story, ***The Tell-Tale Heart,*** the central opponent (antagonist) is a madman and murderer.

Antithesis-A figure of speech in which a thought is balanced with a contrasting thought in parallel arrangements of words and phrases. Example: from, ***A Tale of Two Cities,*** "it was the best of times, it was the worst of times."

Anthropomorphism – when inanimate objects or animals are given human characteristics. Example: **George Orwell's *Animal Farm***.

Apostrophe-when a character turns away from the audience and directly addresses an absent person or a personified quality. Apostrophe allows the character the opportunity to think aloud. The use of apostrophe is often considered too theatrical for modern poets. In the sonnet, ***Great is My Envy of You***, the Renaissance scholar, **Francesco Petrarch (1304-1374),** uses apostrophe to reveal his envy of the earth which envelopes the body of his dead lover, Laura (www.americanpoems.com):

Great is My Envy of You
Great is my envy of you, earth, in your greed
Holding her in invisible embrace
Denying me the look of the sweet face
Where I found peace from all my strife at need!
Great is my envy of heaven which can lead
And lock within itself in avarice
That spirit from its lovely biding-place
And leave so many others here to bleed!
Great is my envy of those souls whose reward
Is the gentle heaven of her company.
Which I so fiercely sought beneath these skies!
Great is my envy of death whose curt heard sword
Carried her whom I called my life away;
Me he disdains, and mocks me from her eyes!

Archetype Hero – a character on a dangerous adventure or quest. Example: **Homer's *Iliad*, *The Odyssey*; Luke Skywalker** from the ***Star Wars* series.** The following characteristics are associated with an archetype hero:

- Unusual circumstances of birth; sometimes in danger or born into royalty
- Leaves family or land and lives with others
- An event, sometimes traumatic, leads to adventure or quest
- Has a special weapon only he can wield
- Always has supernatural help
- Must prove himself many times while on adventure
- When the he dies, he is rewarded spiritually

Archaic - old-fashioned: words no longer in common use. Example: using the term "spooning" for the word "kissing."

Assonance - is the repetition of vowel sounds to create internal rhyming within phrases or sentences and together with alliteration and consonance serves as one of the building blocks of verse. For example, in the phrase "**Do you** like bl**ue**?," the /uː/ ("o"/"ou"/"ue" sound) is repeated within the sentence and is assonant.

Catharsis - the reader or audience feels compassion with the protagonist and experiences a sense of relief when watching a protagonist overcome great odds to survive.

Character - a person in a story, poem or play. Even if the character is an animal or a god, the character will have human characteristics. A writer can reveal a character in numerous ways: through the characters actions, speech, or thoughts.

> **Static character** - a character who does not change during the course of the story
> **Dynamic character** - a character who changes in some way during the story
> **Flat character** - exhibits few personality traits
> **Round character** - complex characters in a story

Climax - the moment of the greatest emotional tension or suspense in a story or novel.

Colloquialisms (colloquial expressions) – expressions used in informal situations. The use of colloquial expressions in a piece of literature gives the reader insight into the life of a character. Colloquial expressions help a writer form strong connections with readers. Example: "Over and over, I would read her account of the turning point in her career--the night she got her first standing ovation, hours after *being dumped* by her fiancé because she wouldn't quit acting." (from K.D. Miller's, "Standing Up Naked and Turning Around Very Slowly." *Writers Talking*, ed. by John Metcalf and Claire Wilkshire. Porcupine's Quill, 2003.)

Connotation - a hidden meaning of a word usually determined by the context in which the word is used. Words may have negative or positive connotations. Example: thin = positive; skinny = negative.

Consonance - an example of near rhyme - the repetition of terminal consonant sounds, often used by poets to create rhyme. Example: *drunk* and *milk,* from the last line of **Samuel Taylor Coleridge's (1772-1834)** *Kubla Khan* or *A Vision in a Dream:*

> Weave a circle round him thrice,
> And close your eyes with holy dread,
> For he on honey-dew hath fed,
> And drunk the milk of Paradise.

Couplet - A **heroic couplet** is a traditional form of English poetry, commonly used for epic and narrative poetry; it refers to poems constructed from a sequence of rhyming pairs of iambic pentameter lines. The rhyme is always masculine. Use of the heroic couplet was first pioneered by **Geoffrey Chaucer** in the *Legend of Good Women* and *The Canterbury Tales*. Chaucer is also widely credited with the first extensive use of iambic pentameter.

Denouement - a French term that literally means "untying the knot," used to describe the moment of climax resolution in a story.

Denotation - the literal dictionary meaning(s) of a word.

Dialect – a variety of language used by people in a particular group or geographic region. Example: *How ya'll doin?*

Diction – an author's choice of words, based on effectiveness.

Eulogy - A speech or writing to praise or honor someone, most commonly spoken at a funeral. Example: The eulogy for **Julius Caesar** given by Mark Antony in **Shakespeare's** play.

Euphemism [YOO-fuhm-izm] - A device where a direct, unpleasant expression is replaced by an indirect, pleasant phrase. Example, he has "passed away" is a euphemistic expression for he is "dead." She is "in a family way," is a euphemistic expression for she is "pregnant." In George Orwell's novel, 1984, the author describes a person's condition as being an "unperson" instead of dead.

Existentialism - was popularized by the writer, **Sartre**. Existentialists believe that man determines his own destiny by the choices he makes. Existentialism is anchored in reality, not idealized life. The most important aspect of life is living free, establishing one's individual "existence" and personality. Existentialism became fashionable in the post-World War years as a way to reassert the importance of human individuality and freedom. Two of the first literary authors important to existentialism were the Czech writer, **Franz Kafka,** and the Russian writer, **Fyodor Dostoyevsky**. Dostoyevsky's ***Notes from Underground*** portrays a man who is unable to fit into society, ultimately becoming unhappy with the identities he creates for himself.

First-person Narrative - occurs in a literary work when one character in the story tells the story from his point of view.

Flashback - a section of a literary work that interrupts the sequence of events to relate to an event from an earlier time. A critical reader needs to be aware of the order of events within the plot arrangement; a flashback informs the reader about events that take place before the current scene being read.

Figure of speech (figurative language)-writing or language not meant for literal interpretation; instead, these words are out of their literal meaning or out of their ordinary use in order to add beauty or emotional intensity or to transfer meaning by comparing or identifying one thing with another. Figures of speech may include **simile, metaphor, personification, hyperbole,** or **symbolism.**

Foreshadowing - a hint that prepares readers for what occurs later in the work. In the film, *Jaws,* the audience always knows the shark is coming when the distinct music plays.

Hyperbole- an exaggerated expression or overstatement. Examples: I am so hungry, *I could eat a horse*. We waited *an eternity* for the play to end.

Image, Imagery - descriptive language that addresses the senses of the real or imagined world. The descriptive or figurative language used in literature evokes mental images, not only in the visual sense, but also to the other senses or the emotions. In the poem, ***The Negro Speaks of Rivers,*** poet **Langston Hughes** uses the visual imagery of the great rivers of the Earth to paint a picture of the struggles experienced by the African race throughout time (www.americanpoems.com/poets):

The Negro Speaks of Rivers

I've known rivers;
I've known rivers ancient as the world and older than the
flow of human blood in human veins.
My soul has grown deep like the rivers.
I bathed in the Euphrates when dawns were young.
I built my hut near the Congo and it lulled me to sleep.
I looked upon the Nile and raised the pyramids above it.
I heard the singing of the Mississippi when Abe Lincoln
Went down to New Orleans, and I've seen its muddy
bosom turn all golden in the sunset.
I've known rivers:
Ancient, dusky rivers,

My soul has grown deep like the rivers.

Irony- an unexpected disparity between what is spoken or written and the reality or expectation of the situation. Verbal irony is when the author says one thing and means something else. Dramatic irony takes place when the audience perceives something that the character does not know. Example: Dramatic irony is revealed in the following poem by **e. e. cummings** in which the author describes the character's emptiness of real patriotism and reverence even though the words expound love for his country as he slaughters the patriotic phrases and drones on and on in mindless verbiage (www.americanpoems.com):

Next to of course god america i
next to of course god america i
love you land of the pilgrims' and so forth oh
say can you see by the dawn's early my
country 'tis of centuries come and go
and are no more what of it we should worry
in every language even deafanddumb
they sons acclaim your glorious name by garry
by jingo by gee by gosh by gum
why talk of beauty what could be more
beautiful than these heroic happy dead
who rushed like lions to the roaring slaughter
they did not stop to think they died instead
then shall the voice of liberty be mute?"
He spoke. And drank rapidly a glass of water.

Jargon – specialized language used in a particular profession or subject (content) area. In literature, **jargon** can be found in the works of renowned writers like Shakespeare or Charles Dickens; their jargon related to the expressions used during their time. Modern writers use jargon to make it easier for readers to relate to the work http://literarydevices.net.
Modern-day examples include:
- On cloud nine: extremely happy
- Sweet tooth: someone who loves sweets
- Shrink: psychiatrist
- Poker face: a blank or unreadable expression
- Ball park figure: an estimated number or value
- Back Burner: to give low priority, delay something until a later date

Malapropism (MAL-a-prop-izm) (from French "mal a propos" meaning "ill to purpose") - the mistaken substitution of one word for another that sounds similar, generally for comic effect, as in *"He laid prostate on the ground"* for *"prostrate."* The term is named for the character, Mrs. Malaprop, in **Richard Brinsley Seridan's** play, ***The Rivals*** (1775), who made frequent misapplications of words. Archie Bunker, the main character of the popular 1970's television show, *All in the Family,* often used malapropisms in his comical lines.

Meiosis (my-OH-sis) - an understatement; the presentation of a word or phrase with underemphasis in order to achieve a greater effect, such as, "World War II was a bit of a mess for England." The poet, **Randall Jarrell** (1914-1965), uses meiosis or understatement in the last line of his World War II poem about an aircraft machine gunner sitting in the ball turret, a plastic compartment housed on the underside of an aircraft bomber. When the gunner tracked the enemy planes with his machine gun, he revolved with the turret; hunched upside down in his plexiglas sphere, he looked like a fetus in the womb (www.americanpoems.com):

The Death of the Ball Turret Gunner
From my mother's sleep, I fell into the State
And I hunched in its belly till my wet fur froze,
Six miles from earth, loosed from its dream of life,
I woke to black flack and the nightmare fighters.
When I died they washed me out of the turret with a hose.

Metaphor - a figure of speech in which a word or phrase is implicitly compared to something else creating an analogy, without the use of words such as like or as. Shakespeare uses metaphor throughout his work: the character Macbeth laments, "life is a brief candle," "life is a walking shadow," "life is a poor player," "life is a tale told by an idiot." Some authors use extended metaphor where the entire work is organized into a comparison. An example can be found in the following excerpt from, **e. e. cummings**' poem, "she being Brand" in which he compares a woman to an automobile (www.americanpoems.com/poets):

she being Brand
she being Brand
-new; and you
know consequently a
little stiff i was
careful of her and(having
thoroughly oiled the universal
joint tested my gas felt of
her radiator made sure her springs were O.
K.) i went right to it flooded-the-carburetor cranked her
up, slipped the
clutch(and then somehow got into reverse she
kicked what
the hell)next

minute i was back in neutral tried and
again slo-wly; bare-ly nudg-ing my
lev-er Rightoh

Metonymy [meh-TAHN-ih-mee] - A figure of speech in which the name of one object is substituted for that of another object closely associated with it. Example: Newscasters often use the phrase, *the White House,* to describe the actions of the president of the United States.

Motif [moh-TEEF] - A thematic element recurring frequently in a work of literature. The motif or theme of darkness is found in the gothic novels of the Bronte sisters. The stories are set within the dark dreary moors and the harsh weather of England. Examples: **Charlotte Bronte (1816-1855),** *Jane Eyre;* **Emily Bronte (1818/1848), Wuthering Heights; Anne Bronte (1820-1849),** *The Tenant of Wildfell Hall.*

Muse -The term *muse* (from Latin *mens* and English *mind)* denotes *memory* or *a reminder.* In ancient times the earliest poets and storytellers had no books, so they relied on their memories in order to share their works with others. In mythology, a muse is a source of inspiration, or a guiding genius. In Greek mythology, the nine daughters of **Zeus** and **Mnemosyne** were known as the **Muses**, each paired with an individual art or science (www.litertureonline.com):

> **Calliope** (kuh-LY-uh-pee) - Muse of epic poetry
> **Clio** (KLY-oh or KLEE-oh) - Muse of history
> **Erato** (EHR-uh-toh) - Muse of lyric and love poetry
> **Euterpe** (yoo-TUR-pee) - Muse of music, especially wind instruments
> **Melpomene** (mel-PAH-muh-nee) - Muse of tragedy
> **Polymnia** (pah-LIM-nee-uh) - Muse of sacred poetry
> **Terpsichore** (turp-SIK-uh-ree) - Muse of dance and choral song
> **Thalia** (thuh-LY-uh) - Muse of comedy
> **Urania** (yooh-RAY-nee-uh) - Muse of astronomy

Narration - a story told in fiction, nonfiction, poetry, or drama. Narration may be limited, and told from the point of view of one character in either first or third person; or it may be omniscient, in which the narrator reveals to the audience or reader what the characters think and feel.

Neoclassicism - adherence to virtues thought to be characteristic of classical literature: elegance, correctness, simplicity, dignity, restraint, order, and proportion; neoclassicism sometimes modifies a classic in order to comment on contemporary conditions.

Onomatopoeia (ahn-uh-mah-tuh-PEE-uh) - the use of words that imitate sounds. Examples: *clang, sizzle, chirp, bong, bang, clatter, rattle.*

Oxymoron (ahk-see-MOR-ahn) -The conjunction of words which, at first view, seem to be contradictory or incongruous, but whose surprising juxtaposition expresses a truth or dramatic effect, such as *military intelligence, jumbo shrimp, deafening silence.*

Palindrome - A word, verse, or sentence in which the sequence of letters is the same forward and backward, as the words, *madam, radar, Bob, peep,* or the sentence (a word-order palindrome), *A man, a plan, a canal: Panama.*

Paradox - A statement which appears contradictory or absurd to common sense yet can be seen as true when viewed from the writer's point of view. **John Donne's** sonnet, ***Death Be Not Proud***, argues that death shall die and humans will triumph over death, a thought which seems untrue, but explained to be true in Donne's sonnet (*www.poets.org)*:

> **Death, Be Not Proud**
> Death, be not proud, though some have called thee
> Mighty and dreadful, for thou are not so;
> For those whom thou think'st thou dost overthrow
> Die not, poor Death, nor yet canst thou kill me.
> From rest and sleep, which but thy pictures be,
> Much pleasure; then from thee much more must flow,
> And soonest our best men with thee do go,
> Rest of their bones, and soul's delivery.
> Thou'art slave to fate, chance, kings, and desperate men,
> And dost with poison, war, and sickness dwell,
> And poppy'or charms can make us sleep as well
> And better than thy stroke; why swell'st thou then?
> One short sleep past, we wake eternally,
> And death shall be no more; Death, thou shalt die.

Pastoral ode - Odes were first developed by poets writing in ancient Greek (Pindar) and Latin (Horace.) Forms of odes appear in many of the cultures that were influenced by the Greeks. Odes have a formal poetic diction, and generally deal with a serious subject. Keats's ***Ode on a Grecian Urn*** is a romantic ode, a dignified but highly lyrical (emotional) poem in which the author addresses an urn and the images on it. The romantic ode was at the pinnacle of its popularity in the 19th Century. It is the result of an author's deep meditation on the person or object.

Pathos - A scene or passage in a work evoking great emotion in the audience or reader. For example, in **Jane Austen's** novel, ***Pride and Prejudice***, Mr. Darcy persuades Elizabeth to reconsider her disposition of him through pathos in his letter when he informs her of Mr. Wickham's offenses. Elizabeth feels pity when she reads that he had deceived Mr. Darcy out of 2,000 pounds, and tried to elope with the younger Miss Darcy for her money. This emotion causes Elizabeth to absolve her own obstinacy, and supports the readers' hope that Mr. Darcy and Elizabeth will end up together (www.janeausten.org*)*.

Personification - A type of figurative language in which distinctive human characteristics, e.g., honesty, joy, etc., are attributed to an animal, inanimate object, or idea. Nature is personified in the following line from **Rachel Carson's** literary work, *Silent Sprint*: "It is not possible to add pesticides to water anywhere without threatening the purity of water everywhere. Seldom if ever does Nature operate in closed and separate compartments, and she has not done so in distributing the earth's water supply."

Plot - the sequence of events in a short story, novel, or drama. High school students are often asked to construct a **plot graph** of events when analyzing a novel or short story.

Point of view - from whose perspective the story is being told, such as a character within the story or an omniscient (all knowing) narrator, and what their vantage point is:

    First Person - the story is told from the point of view of one character at a time.
    Third Person - the story is told by someone who stands outside the story.
    Omniscient - the narrator knows everything about the characters and events and reveals details that even the characters themselves could not reveal.
    Limited omniscient - the narrator knows the thoughts and feelings of one character.

Pyramid-a graphic design that illustrates the structure of a typical five-act play:

    Exposition-introduction, background information
    Rising action-the events leading up to the climax
    Climax-the point of highest dramatic tension or a major turning point in
    the action of a play, story or other work of literature. It is the point at
    which the rising action is reversed to the falling action
    Falling action-action after the climax leading to the denouement
    Catastrophe-the final action that completes the unraveling of the plot

Romanticism - An 18th century movement placing artistic emphasis on imagination and emotion. These works emphasized rebellion against social conventions. Writers from the Romantic period include: **William Wordsworth, Samuel Taylor Coleridge, Lord Byron Shelley, John Keats, Jane Austen,** and **Sir Walter Scott.**

Satire - A style of writing that uses humor to criticize people, governments, or ideas. The writer's intent is usually to correct an injustice or social wrong. Example: **Jonathan Swift** (1667-1745), author and satirist, famous for *Gulliver's Travels* (1726) wrote the satirical essay, *A Modest Proposal* (1729), in order to heighten awareness of the inhumane treatment of the Irish by the English government. In the proposal, he suggests that the Irish eat their own children since they are all dirty, uneducated people who cannot feed themselves. He devoted much of his writing to the struggle for Ireland against English hegemony.

Setting - the time and place in which the events of a literary work occur.

Simile - a figure of speech that makes an explicit comparison using words such as like, as, than or seems. Example: In the following excerpt from the poem, ***By the Sea***, by **William Wordsworth (1770-1850)** a comparison is made of the evening by the sea to a nun's quiet manner.

> ### *By the Sea*
> It is a beauteous evening, calm and free;
> The holy time is quiet as a nun
> Breathless with adoration; the broad sun
> Is sinking down in its tranquility;

Soliloquy - A speech delivered by a character as he talks aloud to himself and reveals his state of mind. A soliloquy gives the illusion of being unspoken reflections. A famous soliloquy in **William Shakespeare's Hamlet**, when Hamlet contemplates suicide and laments aloud, "to be or not to be, that is the question." A soliloquy is similar in nature to an **aside** - lines spoken directly to the audience by an actor.

Surrealism - expresses thought uncontrolled by logical reasoning or moral codes. For example, **Lewis Carroll's** novel, ***Alice's Adventures in Wonderland***, tells the story of Alice's experiences in a surreal (dream-like) world at the bottom of a rabbit hole.

Symbolism / Symbol - when a writer uses visible objects or action to suggest some further meaning. The writer reveals the symbolism in the work by repetition, using dramatic scenes, description, or dialogue. Interpretation of symbolism can move the reader from literal interpretation of the words or object to an abstract idea or concept. Example: In the following excerpt from the poem, ***The Road Not Taken,*** by **Robert Frost**, the author's symbolic use of the crossroads symbolize the choices one must make in life (www.americanpoems.com/poets/robertfrost):

The Road Not Taken
Two roads diverged in a yellow wood,
And sorry I could not travel both
And be one traveler, long I stood
And looked down one as far as I could
To where it bent in the undergrowth;
then took the other, as just as fair,
And having perhaps the better claim,
Because it was grassy and wanted wear;
Though as for that the passing there
Had worn them really about the same

Synecdoche [suh-NEK-duh-kee] – A figure of speech in which a part of something stands for the whole or the whole for a part. Example: A prisoner is placed *behind bars* (prison), the term *wheels* are used for *automobile,* and the neighborhood gossip is described as a *wagging tongue.* Synecdoche is closely associated with **metonymy**.

Theme - The central idea, topic, message, or insight into life revealed through a literary work. Example: **Robert Frost's** famous poem, ***Stopping by Woods on a Snowy Evening,*** allows the reader to contemplate the theme of life's many responsibilities, "miles to go before I sleep," and the attraction that death offers "woods lovely, dark and deep" for a chance to rest.

Tone - A writer's style, attitude, or expression toward the subject. A poem or literary work can evoke feelings of love, bitterness, sadness, playfulness, etc. Tone can also refer to the overall mood of a poem or literary work, in the sense of the pervading atmosphere and emotions intended by the writer. Example: **Kate Chopin's, *The Story of an Hour***, depicts a widow's emotions ranging from the grief of losing her husband to the joyful freedom of liberation from an oppressive male-dominated life. This short story, with a twist of an ending, allows the reader to understand the reasons the widow suddenly dies after hearing that her husband was alive.

Literary Genres

Reading literature not only stirs the imagination but also offers insight into the hearts and minds of humankind, thus leading the reader to a greater understanding of people and their behaviors. As a story unfolds, life's struggles are revealed through the descriptions, actions, and words of characters. However, reading literature in order to discover insights into the human condition is not enough; students must learn to read carefully and critically in order to develop analytical skills. It is through reading, thinking, talking, and writing about literature that students develop these skills and broaden their perspectives of the world. In order to help students with this understanding, secondary English teachers need to demonstrate an understanding of the major literary genres and become familiar with examples of works from each genre.

Allegory - A symbolic fictional narrative that conveys a second meaning not explicit in the narrative. Characters and events represent virtues and vices and often bear descriptive names, such as "Christian" or "Faith." Example: **John Bunyan, *Pilgrims Progress;* George Orwell, *Animal Farm.***

Ballad - A story told or sung to music. A ballad usually includes a refrain (a repeated section) for effect. *The Rime of the Ancient Mariner*, a narrative poem by **Samuel Taylor Coleridge, published in 1798** in the first edition of *Lyrical Ballads,* depicts the travels of a seaman who must live a life of penance wandering the seas after committing the sin of killing an albatross, one of God's creatures. Another example can be found in the Scottish ballad, ***Bonny Barbara Allan,*** which describes the death of a young lover:

Bonny Barbara Allan
It was in and about the Martinmas time,
When the green leaves were a fallin',
That Sir John Graeme, in the West Country,
Fell in love with Barbara Allan.

He sent his man down through the town
To the place where she was dwellin'
O haste and come to my master dear,
Gin ye be Barbara Allan.

Comedy - A play intended to entertain and amuse the audience or reader. Example: **William Shakespeare's *A Midsummer Night's Dream.***

Drama - A play, usually consisting of five acts. Plays are categorized based on author's intent: satire, comedy, tragedy, etc.

Epic - A long poem reflecting the values of a society. An epic poem usually contains a protagonist, the lead character, and an antagonist, a character who opposes or competes with the protagonist (who may possess supernatural powers). Example: *The Iliad* and *The Odyssey* by **Homer.**

Essay - A work usually written by an opinionated expert with an authoritative tone. Example: **Ralph Waldo Emerson**, wrote essays on love, nature, intellect, and art.

Fable - A tale in which animals take on human characteristics; a fable is usually written to provide a moral lesson (didactic) or to illustrate man's shortcomings. Examples: **Aesop's Fables** believed to have been written by a slave in ancient 6th century: *The Fox and the Grapes, The Tortoise and the Hare.*

Fairy Tale - A type of folktale, based on oral tradition that features some sort of magical element, begins with the phrase "Once upon a time" and usually ends happily with the main character overcoming a dilemma. Examples: **Cinderella, Little Red Riding Hood, Rapunzel.** (See Hans Christian Anderson in this chapter).

Farce - A light, dramatic composition that uses highly improbable situations, stereotyped characters, exaggerations, and violence. It is generally regarded as inferior to comedy because of its crude characterizations and implausible plots. The term FARCE was first used in 15th-century France to describe the elements of clowning, acrobatics, caricature, and indecency found together within a single form of entertainment.

Legend - A story of traditional, enduring quality from earlier times. Examples include: Arthurian legends from medieval lore about King Arthur of Britain and the knights of the round table, with legendary characters such as Sir Lancelot, Guinevere, Merlin; and, Native American legends concerning the formation of the earth, or explanation for the seasons, such as: *The Legend of the Bluebonnet.*

Myth(s) - A myth relates to the deeds of extraordinary beings and speaks a common truth about life; myth analysis usually focuses on stages of a hero's life: miraculous birth, initiation, fight for community, death, and resurrection. Myths are concerned with cycles: fertility and seasons.

Novel -The term novel is derived from *novella*, Italian for compact, realistic fiction, often ribald; a prose tale that became popular during the Renaissance. A novel is the longest example of fictional prose. Examples: **Leo Tolstoy, *War and Peace;* John Steinbeck, *The Grapes of Wrath;* Charles Dickens, *Hard Times;* Herman Melville, *Moby-Dick*.** Gothic novels were set in medieval times of castles, kings and knights (the time of the Goths); the definition was broadened to include romantic fiction set in a dark, mysterious setting, with ghosts, madness, supernatural, or revengeful elements. Examples include **Emily Bronte, *Wuthering Heights*** and **Charlotte Bronte, *Jane Eyre.***

Parody is an imitation or exaggeration of a particular writer, artist or a genre written deliberately to produce a comic effect. The writer achieves the humorous effect in parody by imitating and overstressing noticeable features of a famous piece of literature just as in caricatures, certain peculiarities of a person are highlighted to achieve a humorous effect. **Parody** is often confused with satire. Often used by writers to develop satire, parody differs from satire in that it mimics a subject directly to produce a comical effect. Satire, on the other hand, makes fun of a subject without a direct imitation. Moreover, satire aims at correcting shortcomings in society by criticizing them http://literarydevices.net/parody/. **Examples: Miguel de Cervantes'** parody, **Don Quixote**, describes how Quixote and his overweight sidekick, Sancho, delude themselves into thinking that they are knights entrusted with the obligation of saving the world. **Shakespeare's** Sonnet **13** provides an example of parody of traditional love poems commonly found in Shakespeare's day. He presents an anti-love poem **theme** in a manner of a love poem mocking the exaggerated comparisons they made:

My mistress' eyes are nothing like the sun;
Coral is far more red than her lips' red;
If snow be white, why then her breasts are dun;
If hairs be wires, black wires grow on her head.
I have seen roses damasked, red and white,
But no such roses see I in her cheeks. . .

Poem - A literary work containing rhythm including: **sonnet, ode, pastoral,** and **villanelle.** Other examples are **blank verse** and dramatic **monologue.** (See Poetry section in this chapter.)

Romance - An imaginative story concerning conflicts between heroes and villains written in popular language. Example: **Chaucer's** *Canterbury Tales*.

Satire - a work written to ridicule human vices, folly, abuses, or shortcomings, sometimes with the intent to bring about improvement. Example: *A Modest Proposal*, a satire written by **Jonathan Swift** in 1729, proposed a solution to the poverty and overpopulation found in Ireland. In the essay, Swift recommended, in a very logical voice, that the two major problems found in Ireland, overpopulation and famine, could be corrected if everyone would simply eat the Irish babies born to the many breeders, the women of poverty.

Science Fiction - A story which describes the impact of current or future scientific and technological developments on society. Examples: **Ray Bradbury,** *The Martian Chronicles*; **Ursula K. le Guin,** *The Left Hand of Darkness*; **Lois Lowery,** *The Giver*; **Suzanne Collins:** *The Hunger Games, Mocking Jay, and Catching Fire*; **Madeleine L'Engle,** *A Wrinkle in Time*; **Cormac McCarthy,** *The Road*.

Short story - A short narrative story written to create an impact upon the reader. Examples of renowned short story writers include: **Ernest Hemingway, William Faulkner, James Joyce, Shirley Jackson, Flannery O'Connor, Guy De Maupassant, Edgar Allan Poe,** and **Pushkin.**

Tragedy - a drama with a serious and dignified character in which the protagonist has a tragic flaw that brings about his downfall. Example: **William Shakespeare**, ***Romeo and Juliet.*** After a tragic occurrence in the play, a catharsis or purging of emotion takes place.

Poetry Analysis and Terms

Two important aspects of poetry must be considered during analysis: theme / meaning (the author's message) and genre / structure (by what means). Interpretation of the theme or meaning of a poem involves analysis based on imagery, symbolism, or figurative language and is usually considered the most important aspect of poetry. The meaning of a poem can be interpreted by the reader on two levels: figurative or literal. Very rarely are poems meant for literal interpretation. More often, the author has a contemplative meaning for the poem which describes some aspect of life's experiences or understanding.

Poets use imagery, symbolism, and figurative language to represent objects, actions, feelings, thoughts, and ideas from life. An image may involve sight, smell, hearing, taste, body movement, or intellectual thought. The form or structure of a poem is conveyed through analysis of rhyme, rhythm, meter, and poetic genre (www.poetrymajic.com).

Close attention should be given to the examples and excerpts contained within this section of this chapter, as they are representative of poetry found within the secondary English curriculum for high school students. When studying this chapter, it may be helpful to examine a 10th or 11th grade literature book adopted for high school students in order to find additional examples of poetic works.

Ballad - a story told or sung to music. Traditional folk ballads have been passed down through generations. Most ballads have four-line stanzas and follow an ABAB or ABCD rhyme scheme. (See **Ballad** under the previous **Literary Genres** section of this chapter.) A ballad usually includes a refrain, a repeated section, for effect. Examples: *The Rime of the Ancient Mariner*, a narrative poem by **Samuel Taylor Coleridge,** describes the travels of a seaman who must live a life of penance wandering the seas after committing the sin of killing an albatross, one of God's creatures.

Blank Verse - is written in iambic pentameter; consisting of unrhymed, five-stress lines. Examples of blank verse are found in the work of **William Wordsworth, Samuel Taylor Coleridge, John Milton**, and other Romantic period writers.

Epic - a lengthy, **narrative poem** of a serious subject containing details of heroic deeds and events significant to a culture or nation. An epic poem usually contains a protagonist, the lead character, and an antagonist, a character who opposes or competes with the protagonist who may possess supernatural powers. Examples: **Homer's** Greek epic, *The Odyssey*; the Old English epic poem**, *Beowulf.***

Foot - (see **meter**) the basic unit in the measurement of a line of metrical poetry. Except for a spondee, a foot usually has one stressed syllable and one or more unstressed syllables. The five basic descriptions of metrical feet are as follows:

- **Iambic** - an unstressed syllable followed by a stressed syllable (this beat or pattern closely resembles the natural rhythm of speech).

Example: She walked with angels standing round.
- **Trochaic** - a stressed followed by an unstressed syllable.
  Example: Singing soft with harpers sound.
- **Anapestic** - two unstressed syllables followed by a stressed syllable.
  Example: The Gregorian spoke like the mist on the glen.
- **Dactylic** - a stressed syllable followed by two unstressed syllables.
  Example: Unwilling / death how you / cry for me / cry for me.

Names for the line lengths include:
- One foot – monometer
- Two feet – dimeter
- Three feet – trimeter
- Four feet – tetrameter
- Five feet – pentameter
- Six feet – hexameter
- Seven feet – septameter
- Eight feet- octameter

Free Verse - a poem with no regular meter, line length or rhyme; usually written as a narrative.

Haiku (HIGH-koo) - a Japanese form of poetry usually consisting of 17 syllables, three unrhymed lines of five, seven, and five syllables. Haikus are strongly influenced by Zen Buddhism, and provide brief descriptions of nature that capture a thought or an understanding. Traditionally, haikus contain either a direct or indirect reference to a season. The dominant characteristic of the poem lies with its ability to stir the senses. It is contemplative poetry that encompasses nature, color, season, contrasts, and surprise (www.poetryconnection.net). Example by **Matsuo Basho**:

Old pond ...
A frog leaps in
water's sound.

Image, imagery - descriptive language that addresses the senses of the real or imagined world. The descriptive or figurative language used in literature evokes mental images, not only in the visual sense, but also to the other senses or the emotions. Imagery can be found in the poem below by **William Carlos William**:

Poem
As the cat
climbed over
the top of
the jamcloset
first the right
forefoot
carefully
then the hind
stepped down
into the pit of
the empty
flowerpot

Limerick - a light, humorous five line verse: lines one, two, and five are of three feet and lines three and four are of two feet, with a rhyme scheme of aabba. The limerick was named for the Irish town, Limerick. Limericks were popularized by **Edward Lear** in his ***Book of Nonsense*** published in 1846:

There was a young lady named Bright
Who traveled much faster than light
She started one day
In a relative way,
And returned on the previous night.

Lyric-usually a short poem told or sung by a single speaker involving love, sadness, or the natural world.

Meter - (see **foot**) The word meter originates from the Greek, *metron,* meaning "to measure," and refers to the "beat" of the poem; thus, meter pertains to the structure of the poem. The word meter also refers to the number of **feet** in a line. (monometer-one; dimeter-two; trimeter-three; tetrameter-four; pentameter-five; hexameter-six). Poetry is measured in feet. A foot is a combination of two or three stressed and / or unstressed syllables.

Metaphysical poetry - A popular form of poetry during the 17th century. Brief and concentrated in meaning and sometimes cynical. Metaphysical poetry often employs a blend of formal and colloquial language written in extended metaphors to describe the subjects of love, law, medicine, philosophy, and religion. Example: ***The Flea,*** a poem by **John Donne (1572-1631)** (www.online-literature.com):

The Flea

Mark but this flea, and mark in this
How little that which thou deny'st me is;
It sucked me first, and now sucks thee,
And in this flea our two bloods mingled be;
A sin, nor shame, nor loss of maidenhead,
Yet this enjoys before it woo,
And pampered swells with one blood make of two,
And this, alas, is more than, married are.
This flea is you and I, and this
Our marriage bed, and marriage temple is;
Though parents grudge, and you, we're met
And cloistered in these living walls of jet.
Though use make you apt to kill me,
Let not to that, self-murder added be,
And sacrilege, three sins in killing three.
Cruel and sudden, hast thou since
Purpled my nail in blood of innocence.
Wherein could this flea guilty be,
Except in that drop which it sucked from thee?
Yet thou triumph'st, and say'st that thou
Find'st not thyself, nor me, the weaker now;
'Tis true; then learn how false, fears be;
Just so much honor, when thou yield'st to me,
Will waste, as this flea's death took life from thee.

Pantoum - a poem consisting of four-line stanzas with lines rhyming alternately; the second and fourth lines of each stanza are repeated to form the first and third lines of the succeeding stanza; the first and third lines of the first stanza form the second and fourth of the last stanza, but in reverse order, so that the opening and closing lines of the poem are identical. The theme is conveyed in the second two lines of each quatrain, while the first two lines present an image or allusion.

Refrain - a stanza, line, part of a line, or phrase, generally pertinent to the central topic, which is repeated at regular intervals throughout a poem, most often at the end of a stanza. Example: The word, *"Quoth the raven, nevermore,"* in **Edgar Allan Poe's, *The Raven***.

Rhythm -The rhythm of a poem is determined by the way a line is spoken or voiced; rhythm is usually determined by the end words of each line. When analyzing the rhyme scheme of a poem, label the end of a line with a letter, using a new letter every time a new rhyming sound occurs. The following stanza is written in ABAB pattern:

> Sweet baby boy in cradle safe, (A)
> Tucked and warm in blanket's fold (B)
> There he lays, a tiny waif. (A)
> How soon, how soon a man of bold (B)

Rhyme - provides pleasure to the reader in the sound and cadence of a poem; rhyme is often associated with music and beat. It is difficult to analyze the rhyme in poems written in previous time periods. Rhyme usually occurs at the end of a line of poetry; however, some poets may use internal rhyme. Example: Oh happy maiden all of *fair*, may I take your hand I *dare*.

Sonnet - a poem of fourteen lines written in iambic pentameter. Sonnets are categorized into two types:

Petrarchan (Italian) Sonnet - consists of eight rhyming lines (octave) and six rhyming lines (sestet). The octave develops a thought and the sestet is the completion or comment upon the thought. Many of the **Petrarchan** sonnets, penned by the great Italian poet, **Fransesco Petrarch (1304-1375),** use an Italian rhyme scheme to describe the torturous love he felt for his beloved Laura. Even after her death, Petrarch described the feelings he had for Laura and he believed her spirit watched over him in life and would guide him to paradise after his death www.todayinliterature.com:

> ***All Silent Now Lie Earth and Wind and Sky***
> All silent now lie earth and wind and sky,
> And sleep enfolds all animals and birds.
> Night turns the wheel of stars. No wave disturbs
> The wide unrippled sameness of the sea.
>
> But I, I wake and brood, rage, weep, my eyes
> Always behold my love, my foe, my pain.
> I am a war. Here wrath and sorrow reign,
> Yet solely in her image I find peace.
>
> It was her healing hand gave me my wound,
> And where the pure and living spring wells forth
> I drink at once sweet water, bitter gall;
>
> Storm-driven and extreme, remote from land,
> A thousand times I suffer birth and death,

Swept far from any salvage of my soul.

Shakespearean or Elizabethan (English) Sonnet - consists of three rhyming quatrains (four lines each) which introduce the subject, and a couplet (two rhyming lines) that provide a conclusion. Example: **Shakespeare's Sonnett 116:**

Sonnet 116
Let me not to the marriage of true minds
Admit impediments. Love is not love
Which alters when it alteration finds,
Or bends with the remover to remove:

O no! it is an ever-fixéd mark
That looks on tempests and is never shaken;
It is the star to every wandering bark,
Whose Worth's unknown, although his height be taken.

Love's not Time's fool, though rosy lips and cheeks
Within his bending sickle's compass come;
Love alters not with his brief hours and weeks,
But bears it out even to the edge of doom:

If this be error and upon me proved,
I never writ, nor no man ever loved

Stanza -The number of lines in a stanza unit: *couplet* (2), *tercet* (3), *quatrain* (4), *quintet (5), sestet* (6), *septet* (7), and *octave (8).*

Periods of American literature, Major Authors, and Representative Works

American literature can be categorized into seven literary time-periods: (1) **The Colonial Era** (1620-1776); (2) **The Early American Revolutionary Era** (1776-1830); (3) **The American Renaissance** (1830-1865); (4) **American Realism** (1865-1920); (5) **American Modernism** (1913-45); (6) **Post Modern** (1945-1970); and, **Contemporary** (1970 – present).

The Colonial Era (1620-1776)

The first category of American literature, **The Colonial Era**, occurred during the years 1620 to 1776. American literature began with the establishment of the first European colonies in North America by the religious group known as separatists. One small group set sail for North America upon the ship *Mayflower* in 1620. These colonists, known as Puritans, were religious reformers who were critical of the political and religious doctrines established by the Church of England and chose to leave England rather than conform. These groups soon joined other religious colonies in the New England area to establish a government and live by the Puritan strict moral code and strong work ethic. Much of the literature originating from the Puritans involves the struggle of mankind with sin and salvation. (Painting by Henry Gibbs)

The southern colonies of colonial America, established during this time period, differed from the small farming endeavors common in the northern colonies. Plantations, large estates of farmland, were established and worked with slave labor throughout the southern colonies. Many of the plantation owners regarded themselves as the ruling aristocracy of the region and life evolved into a socially stratified society dependent upon slave labor for success (Davis, et al., 1995). Representative works from this time period include:

- Anne Bradstreet (1612-*1679), To My Dear and Loving Husband*
- Edward Taylor (1642-1729), *Huswifery*
- Mary Rowlandson (1635 -1711), *A Narrative on the Captivity and Restoration of Mrs. Mary Rowlandson*
- Essays by Jonathan Edwards (1703-1758)

The works of colonial poets **Anne Bradstreet** and **Edward Taylor** reflect the plain style of the Puritan writer. Both Bradstreet and Taylor experienced the harshness of early colonial life that brought death of loved ones, harsh living conditions, and strict religious customs. An excerpt from **Edward Taylor's** poem, *Huswifery* (housekeeping) reflects the puritan belief system. In this poem Taylor uses the spinning wheel and weaver as an analogy of man's relationship to God, the creator (Bradbury & Ruland, 1992; Davis, et al, 1995):

Huswifery
. . . Make me, 0 Lord, Thy spinning wheel complete.
Thy holy word my distaff make for me
Make mine affections Thy swift flyers neat
And make my soul Thy holy spoole to be
My conversation make to be The reel
And reel the yarn thereon spun of Thy wheel

Another example of the Puritan way of life is demonstrated in this excerpt from **Jonathan Edwards'** "fire and brimstone" sermon:

Sinners in the Hands of an Angry God
... once the day of mercy is past, your most lamentable and dolorous cries and shrieks will be in vain; you will be wholly lost and thrown away of God, as to any regard to your welfare. God will have no other use to put you to but to suffer misery (www.jonathanedwards.com).

The Early American Era (1776-1830)
The second category of American literature, **The Early American Era**, occurred during the years 1776 to 1830. Literature from this time period reflects pride in the growing young nation (Davis, et al., 1995). Representative authors from this era include:

- Benjamin Franklin (1706-1790), *Poor Richard's Almanac, The Autobiography of Benjamin Franklin*
- Thomas Jefferson (1743-1826), *The Declaration of Independence*
- Olaudah Equiano (1745-1797), *Autobiography*
- Phyllis Wheatley (1753-1784), *To His Excellency, General Washington, Poems on Various Subjects: Religious and Moral, Hymn to the Evening*
- Philip Freneau (1752-1832), *The Indian Burying Ground, The Rising Glory of America*
- James Fenimore Cooper (1789-1851), *The Last of the Mohicans*
- Washington Irving (1783-1859), *The Legend of Sleepy Hollow, Rip Van Winkle*

The Work of Benjamin Franklin

Early American statesman, **Benjamin Franklin** wrote his autobiography at the age of 65; this work provides an insight into Franklin's character as well as a description of life during the 18th century. The following excerpt from his autobiography provides insight into Franklin's moral concerns:

The Autobiography of Benjamin Franklin

. . . It was about this time I conceived the bold and arduous project of arriving at moral perfection. I wished to live without committing any fault at any time. I would conquer all that either natural inclination, custom or company might lead me into. As I knew, or thought I knew, what was right and wrong, I did not see why I might not always do the one and avoid the other. But I soon found I had undertaken a task of more difficulty than I had imagined (www.ushistory.org).

The Work of Phyllis Wheatley

Phyllis Wheatley became famous at a young age for her poetry and eventually gained freedom from slavery as an adult. Phyllis was taught to read and write as a young girl in Boston, Massachusetts even though she was a slave. However, her freedom did not grant her happiness as her children died young and she died in poverty at age 30. During the Revolutionary War, Phyllis penned a letter in the form of a poem entitled, *To His Excellency, General Washington*, which supported the patriots' cause. The poem praised the brave deeds of General George Washington in his fight for American freedom. The following excerpt depicts Wheatley's use of personification of the new nation as the goddess, Columbia (www.earlyamerica.com):

To His Excellency, General Washington
.. . Anon Britannia droops the pensive head,
While round increase the rising hills of dead.
Ah! Cruel blindness to Columbia's state!
Lament thy thirst of boundless power too late.
Proceed great Chief, with virtue on thy side,
Thy ev'ry action let the goddess guide.
A crown, a mansion, and a throne that shine,
With gold unfading, Washington, be thine.

The Work of Olaudah Equiano

Slave **Olaudah Equiano** (1745-1797) wrote a narrative which described his capture and journey from Africa to the New World. Almost everything we know about the first ten years of Equiano's life we find from Equiano's own account in *The Interesting Narrative of the Life of Olaudah Equiano, or Gustavus Vassa, the African,* published in 1789.

In this, Equiano tells us that he was born around the year 1745 in an area called 'Eboe' in Guinea. Ibo (or Igbo) is one of the main languages of present day Nigeria. Equiano tells us that he was the son of a chief, and that at about the age of eleven he and his sister were kidnapped while out playing, and were marched to the coast and put onboard a slave ship. Equiano then endured the passage on a slave ship bound for the New World. This narrative stirred the fires for the abolitionists who were against slavery.

The American Renaissance (1830-1865)

The third major period of **American literature**, known as **The American Renaissance**, occurred during the years 1830 through 1865, a time of heightened awareness of the American culture and spirit that had been freed from European bondage. **Ralph Waldo Emerson** and his circle of writers, reformers, and artists would lead a rebirth of thought known as **Transcendentalism**.

Transcendentalism, derived from the philosophy of Kant who believed that "all knowledge transcendental is concerned not with objects but with our mode of knowing objects." Emerson explained the basis of transcendentalism belief as the spark of divinity that lies within man. Emerson further purports that everything in the world is a microcosm of existence and that the individual soul is identical to the world soul, or "Over-Soul." Transcendentalists also believed that through meditation, by communing with nature, through work and art, man could transcend his senses and attain an understanding of beauty, goodness and truth. (Bradbury & Ruland, 1992; Davis, et al., 1995; www.pbs.org). Representative authors from this era include:

- Nathaniel Hawthorne (1804-1864), *The Scarlet Letter, The House of the Seven Gables*
- Edgar Allan Poe (1809-1849), *The Raven, The Murders in the Rue Morgue*
- Ralph Waldo Emerson (1803-1882**), *Essays, Woodnotes***
- Henry David Thoreau (1817-1862**), *Walden, Civil Disobedience***
- Walt Whitman (1813-1892)*, **Leaves of Grass, I Hear America Singing***
- Emily Dickinson (1830-1886)*, **Complete Poems and Letters***

The Work of Ralph Waldo Emerson

As a leader in the Transcendentalist movement, **Ralph Waldo Emerson** expressed his belief that the meaning of life could be found as one explores the natural world, finding a connection to God, the universe, and every living thing (www.transcendentalists.com).

An awe of nature is exhibited in **Ralph Waldo Emerson's** poem, *The Snowstorm*. In the poem, Emerson uses extended metaphor to compare nature's force during a snowstorm to an architect creating a building. Emerson's poem conveys the message that man cannot surpass the beauty built by nature (www.transcendentalists.com):

The Snowstorm
> ... Come see the north wind's masonry.
> Out of an unseen quarry evermore
> Furnished with tile, the fierce artificer
> Curves his white bastions with projected roof
> Round every windward stake, or tree, or door.

...Standing on the bare ground-my head bathed by the blithe air and uplifted into infinite space-all man egotism vanishes. I become a transparent eyeball; I am nothing; I see all; the currents of the Universal Being circulate through me; I am part or parcel of God.

The Work of Henry David Thoreau

Another naturalist and writer of this era, **Henry David Thoreau** expressed his views and philosophy of life in his essay, *Walden*. In the essay, Thoreau laments that life has become too complicated and that men should try to simplify their lives in order to discover their own spiritual journey (www.transcendentalists.com).

In his essay, *Walden*, Thoreau wrote:
Why should we be in such desperate haste to succeed, and in such desperate enterprises? If a man does not keep pace with his companions, perhaps it is because he hears a different drummer. Let him step to the music which he hears, however measured or far away.

Emily Dickinson

A highly recognized poet of the American Renaissance, **Emily Dickinson**, died before

achieving any type of recognition for her literary talent. Dickinson wrote over 1,700 poems in a unique style containing strong imagery and forceful language. Many of Dickinson's poems reflected her life lived in solitude.

In the poem, *There is a Solitude of Space*, Dickinson expresses the contrast between the solitude found in life and that found within one's soul. Dickinson believed that the profound privacy found within the soul will end with death. The excerpt below demonstrates this point (www.onlineliterature.com/dickinson):

There is a Solitude of Space
There is a solitude of space
A solitude of sea
A solitude of death, but these
Society shall be
Compared with that profounder site
The polar privacy
A soul admitted to itself Finite
Infinity

The Work of Walt Whitman

Walt Whitman's poem, *I Hear America Singing*, proved very popular during the American Renaissance as it celebrated the spirit of Americans who worked hard with pride and purpose. The excerpt below demonstrates Whitman's expression of pride in the working man (www.onlineliterature.com):

I Hear America Singing
I hear America singing, the varied carols I hear,
Those mechanics, each one singing his as it should be blithe and strong,
The carpenter singing his as he measures his plank or beam,
The mason singing his as he makes ready for work, or leaves off work.

American Realism (1865-1920)

The fourth major division of **American literature**, known as the era of **American Realism**, occurred during the years 1865 through 1920, a time of great transformation. America was changing from an agricultural nation into a modern industrial nation. This era began with the Civil War, a time of conflict over economics and slavery. After the war's devastating effect, the changes during the following years were extraordinary. Millions of settlers moved out West: miners, ranchers, farmers and the railroad all changed the face of America. Electricity, barbed wire, and mass-produced consumer goods became commonplace in America. The numerous waves of immigrants brought cheap labor for industry. Soon, a small group of industrialists became America's new royalty; at the same time, child labor became common place. The harsh reality of these challenges soon became the subject for the writers of this time (Bradbury & Ruland, 1992; Davis, et al., 1995). Representative authors from this era include:

- Mark Twain (Samuel Langhorne Clemens) **(1835-1910),** *The Innocents Abroad, Huckleberry Finn, Tom Sawyer*
- Stephen Crane (1871-1900), *The Red Badge of Courage*
- Frederick Douglass (1818-1895), *The Life and Times of Frederick Douglass, My Bondage and My Freedom*
- Abraham Lincoln (1809-1865), *the Gettysburg Address*
- Robert E. Lee (1807-1870), **collection of essays and letters**
- Willa Cather (1873-1947), *O Pioneers!, My Antonia, One of Ours*

The Work of Frederick Douglass

One well-known author of the American Realism Era, **Frederick Douglass** experienced both slavery and freedom during his lifetime. Although born into slavery, he escaped from slavery while on a train trip. Douglass wrote extensively about his enslavement during his childhood. The following excerpt is taken from ***My Bondage and My Freedom*** (www.frederickdouglass.org):

. . . Although slavery was a delicate subject, and very cautiously talked about among grownup people in Maryland, I frequently talked about it-and that very freely-with the white boys. I would, sometimes, say to them, while seated on a curbstone or a cellar door, "1 wish 1 could be free, as you will be when you get to be men. You will be free, you know, as soon as you are twenty-one, and can go where you like, but I am a slave for life. Have I not as good a right to be free as you have?

The Work of Robert E. Lee

Military leader and politician, **Robert E. Lee**, the leading general of the Confederacy, was truly grieved to see the United States torn apart by the Civil War. The following excerpt, taken from a letter written to his son, expresses his frustration about the nation's imminent war (www.civilwarhome.com):

... As an American citizen, I take great pride in my country, her prosperity and institutions, and would defend any state if her rights were invaded. But I can anticipate no greater calamity for the country than a dissolution of the Union. It would be an accumulation of all the evils we complain of, and I am willing to sacrifice everything but honor for its preservation. I hope, therefore, that all constitutional means will be exhausted before there is a resort to force.

The Work of Willa Cather

During the American Realism Era, **Willa Cather** penned the novel, ***O Pioneers!*** This novel is somewhat autobiographical as it is based on Cather's childhood experiences on the Nebraska prairie. The novel contains vivid descriptions of the harsh conditions the immigrants withstood in order to survive. The main character, Alexandra, exhibits the strong, moral character needed for survival after her father dies. She and her brothers endure many years of hard work in order to succeed. The following excerpt, from Willa Cather's novel, ***O Pioneers***, describes the bitter conditions of the Nebraska prairie (www.americanliterature.com):

… The homesteads were few and far apart; here and there a windmill gaunt against the sky, a sod house crouching in a hollow. But the great fact was the land itself, which seemed to overwhelm the little beginnings of human society that struggled in its somber wastes. It was from facing this vast hardness that the boy's mouth had become so bitter; because he felt that men were too weak to make any mark here, that the land wanted to be let alone, to preserve its own fierce strength, its peculiar, savage kind of beauty, its uninterrupted mournfulness. The wagon jolted along over the frozen road. The two friends had less to say to each other than usual, as if the cold had somehow penetrated to their hearts.

American Modernism (1913-1945)

The fifth major division of American literature, known as the era of **American Modernism**, occurred during the years 1913 through 1945. As America moved into the twentieth century, a sense of optimism was established as industrial strength promised a place of importance among the nations of the world. However, a great economic depression and two World Wars would dominate this era between the years 1914 and 1945. World War I, thought to be the war to end all wars, did not bring the prosperity and peace that was promised. The war left many people with a distrust of established religious and political doctrines and people looked for new ideas to explain the complex experiences of modern life (Bradbury & Ruland, 1992; Davis, et al., 1995).

The Work of F. Scott Fitzgerald

One of the most important literary works originating from this era was **F. Scott Fitzgerald's** (1896-1940) novel, ***The Great Gatsby***, a story about wealthy, self-centered characters during the roaring 1920s.

 Nick Carraway, the narrator of the novel, is a young bachelor from a patrician Midwestern family, who graduates from Yale in 1915. After fighting in World War I, he returns to the Midwest before settling in Texas City to "learn the bond business." Despite his wealthy upbringing, Nick lives very modestly in a rented bungalow between two mansions in West Egg on Long Island Sound. Across the bay lies East Egg, inhabited by the "old aristocracy," including Tom and Daisy Buchanan. Tom's glory days are behind him, and although engaging and attractive, Daisy is pampered and superficial, ignoring her three-year-old daughter. Nick learns that Tom has a mistress.

Nick receives an invitation one weekend and attends a party hosted by a man named Gatsby; the guests do not know much about Gatsby. A close, friendship between Nick and Gatsby begins. Nick explains how Gatsby had fallen in love with Daisy in 1917 while serving as an Army Lieutenant stationed near Daisy's hometown, Louisville. After the war, Gatsby came east to live near Daisy, where he hopes she will visit. Daisy invites Gatsby and Nick to her mansion, where her husband (Tom) discovers that Gatsby loves Daisy. As they depart, Tom insists he and Gatsby switch cars; and as he stops by Wilson's garage for gas he flaunts Gatsby's roadster. At the hotel Tom confronts Gatsby about their affair. Gatsby reveals that the reason Daisy married Tom was because he (Gatsby) was too poor to marry Daisy. Daisy runs out of the hotel, with Gatsby following her to his car where she insists on driving home as it will calm her nerves. Tom, believing he has bested Gatsby, leaves with Nick and Jordan.

Meanwhile, George Wilson is suspicious that his wife, Myrtle, is having an affair with Tom and argues with her. Myrtle runs outside as Gatsby's roadster approaches (believing it to be Tom), only to be struck and killed by the car. Daisy and Gatsby speed away. Later, Wilson appears at Gatsby's mansion with a gun. Wilson finds Gatsby floating in his pool and kills him before committing suicide (*www.online-literature.com*).

The Imagist Movement

During the Modern era of American literature, poets rebelled against the romanticized sentimentality found in works of previous decades. These poets expressed life in concrete terms using everyday language of the common man. Poets during this time presented new forms of writing using strong imagery. These poets were known as imagists. The leader of the imagist movement was **Ezra Pound** (1885-1972), *In a Station of the Metro, The River Merchant's Wife* (Davis, et al., 1995; www.poets.org).

During the American Modernism era, writers began to explore new techniques of writing such as the **stream-of-consciousness technique**. This technique attempted to present a character's associated thoughts similar to the associations found within the brain while thinking. Nobel Prize winning author **William Faulkner** (1897-1962) used stream-of-consciousness narration along with dialect to depict conflict among the tormented characters in his novels and short stories (Davis, et al., 1995; www.poets.org).

Representative works from this era include:

- Ezra Pound (1885-1972), *The River Merchant's Wife, In Station of the Metro, Ione, Dead the Long Year*
- T. S. Eliot, (1888-1965), *Prelude, The Wasteland, The Hollow Man, The Love Song of J. Alfred Prufrock*
- William Carlos Williams (1883-1963), *Spring and All, In the American Grain, Pictures from Breughel and Other*
- Robert Frost (1874-1963), *A Boy's Will, North of Boston, New Hampshire, Steeple Bush*
- Ernest Hemingway (1899-1961) *For Whom The Bell Tolls, The Old Man and The Sea*
- William Faulkner (1897-1962), *The Sound and The Fury, As I Lay Dying, The Optimist'Daughter*
- Eudora Welty (1909-2001), *A Worn Path*
- John Steinbeck (1902-1968), *The Grapes of Wrath, Of Mice and Men, Tortilla Flat, East of Eden, The Winter of Our Discontent*
- F.Scott Fitzgerald (1896-1940), *The Great Gatsby*

The Work of T.S. Eliot As the modern age descends upon America, many writers express frustration with the spiritual coldness of modern society. Writers from the Modern era of American Literature often let the reader infer and interpret the true meaning of their work. This

point is exampled in **T. S. Elliot's** poem, ***The Wasteland***, wherein the author describes a sick, modern urban society filled with materialistic desires. In the poem, Eliot questions the traditions and values established by American society. Another work by Eliot, ***The Love Song of J. Alfred Prufrock***, explores the internal struggles of a man who is hesitant to declare his love for a woman. The work describes the character of the man who vacillates over the decision to tell the woman of his love and ponders his life in either circumstance (Bradbury & Ruland, 1992; Davis, et al., 1995; www.americanliterature.com). The following excerpt describes the character's inner conflict:

The Love Song of J. Alfred Prufrock
. . . And the afternoon, the evening, sleeps so peacefully!
Smoothed by long fingers,
Asleep . . . tired ... or it malingers,
Stretched on the floor, here beside you and me.
Should I, after tea and cakes and ices,
Have the strength to force the moment to its crisis?
But though I have wept and fasted, wept and prayed,
Though I have seen my head (grown slightly bald) brought in upon a platter,
I am no prophet-and here's no great matter;
I have seen the moment of my greatness flicker,
And I have seen the eternal Footman hold my coat, and snicker,
And in short, I was afraid

The Work of John Steinbeck

During the 1930s, America experienced an economic depression and a severe drought. These events caused major suffering across America, especially among the working poor. **John Steinbeck's** novel, ***The Grapes of Wrath***, is considered by many to be the greatest American novel ever written. In it, Steinbeck portrays the life of the Joad family, a displaced Oklahoma farm family, as they travel across America to Texas in search of work as migrant workers. Steinbeck received the 1962 **Nobel Prize in Literature** for this work.

Steinbeck begins the novel with an analogy describing a turtle's journey across a highway to foreshadow the Joad family's harsh journey. The inference the reader must make about the turtle's tenacity and strength are analogous to the strength and endurance found within the Joad family (www.ac.wwu.edu).The following excerpt describes the struggle:

. . .At last he started to climb the embankment. Front clawed feet reached forward but did not touch. The hind feet kicked his shell along, and it scraped on the grass, and on the gravel. As the embankment grew steeper and steeper, the more frantic were the efforts of the land turtle. Pushing hind legs strained and slipped, boosting the shell along, and the horny head protruded as far as the neck could stretch. Little by little the shell slid up the embankment until at last a parapet cut straight across its line of march, the shoulder of the road, a concrete wall four inches high. As though they worked independently, the hind legs pushed the shell against the wall. The head upraised and peered over the wall to the broad smooth plain of cement. Now the hands, braced on top of the wall, strained and lifted, and the shell rested its front end on the wall.

The Work of Robert Frost
Another well-known poet during the era of American Modernism, **Robert Frost**, was very popular with the American public during his lifetime. Frost's work often exhibited common language and universal themes. His work leaves a profound impact upon the reader with its insights into the complexities of man's behavior. Among his most popular poems are *Stopping by the Woods on a Snowy Evening, Birches,* and *Mending Wall.* The following excerpt, from the poem, *Mending Wall,* reflects the common language and psychological insight typical of Frost's work (www.poets.org):

Mending Wall
... There is where we will never need the wall;
He is all pine and I am apple orchard.
My apple trees will never get across
And eat the cones under his pines, I tell him.
He only says, "Good fences make good neighbors."

The Post Modern Era (1945-1970)
Postmodernism is difficult to define and there is little agreement on the exact characteristics, scope, and importance of postmodern literature. However, instead of the modernist quest for meaning in a chaotic world, the postmodern author presents the possibility of meaning, and the postmodern novel is often a parody of this quest (Bradbury & Ruland, 1992). Representative works from this era include:

- Arthur Miller (1915-2005)**, *Death of a Salesman***
- Kurt Vonnegut (1922–2007)**, Slaughterhouse-Five,** and **Breakfast of Champions**

The Contemporary Era (1970 - present)
Contemporary writing in modern-day America includes the work of male writers as well as the work of women, Mexican-Americans, Asians, Hispanics, and Native-Americans. This multicultural collection of writers reflects the changing canon and its concerns and complexities in America culture. For centuries, works written by writers outside of the classic Greek and Latin tradition were often disregarded. The work of women and people of color had to wait centuries before their status was recognized. It is quite common now for high school students across the country to read literary works representative of myriad races and cultures (Bradbury & Ruland, 1992; Davis, et al., 1995). Representative works from the Contemporary era in American literature include:

- Amy Tan *(1952-), **The Joy Luck Club, The Bonesetter's Daughter***
- Maya Angelou (1928- 2014), ***I Know Why the Caged Bird Sings***
- Toni Morrison (1931-), ***The Bluest Eye***
- N. Scott Momaday (1934-), ***The Ancient Child, The Names: A Memoir***
- Sandra Cisneros (1954-), ***The House on Mango Street, Straw into Gold***
- William Safire (1929- 2009), ***The Metamorphosis of Everyday, Words of wisdom: More Good Advice***
- Ana Quidlen (1953-), ***Cats***
- Alice Walker (1944-), ***The Color Purple***
- Larry McMurtry (1936-), ***The Last Picture Show, Terms of Endearment, Lonesome Dove***

Periods of British literature, Major Authors, and Representative Works

British literature can be categorized into seven major literary periods: (1) Middle Ages (440-1485), (2) English Renaissance (1485-1660), (3) Restoration and Enlightenment (1660-1798), (4) Flowering of Romanticism (1798-1832), (5) Victorian (1832-1901), (6) Emerging Modernism (1901-1950), and (7) Contemporary Era (1950-present).

The Middle Ages
The Middle Ages represent the 1,000-year time period when civilization evolved and Europe was established. The literature developed during this time period falls between the classical age of the Greeks and Romans and the time of the rebirth of civilization known as the Renaissance (Coyle & Peck, 2002; Davis, et al., 1995). This era can be further subdivided into **Old English (450 – 1066)** and **Middle English (1066 – 1550)**.

Old English literature (or **Anglo-Saxon literature**) encompasses literature written in Old English (also called Anglo-Saxon), during the 600-year Anglo-Saxon period of England, from the mid-5th century to the Norman Conquest of 1066. Representative work from Old English time period includes:

Beowulf (author unknown, 8th century, **Old English**)

Beowulf, the oldest surviving English **epic**, tells the story of Beowulf, the hero-king, who believes the world is controlled by one's fate and destiny. The story describes the life of kings and soldiers as they battle evil. In the story Beowulf's father, Ecgbeow, is banished from his kingdom because he kills a man from a noble family and cannot pay the restitution payment demanded by the family. Ecgbeow moves to the kingdom of the Danes and pledges loyalty to the king in return for payment of his debt. Ecgbeow then marries the king's daughter and has a son, Beowulf. Many years later, when the kingdom is terrorized by trolls, Beowulf volunteers to slay the enemy in exchange for the debt owed by his father.

In the poem, Beowulf, a hero of the Geats, battles three antagonists: Grendel, who attacks the resident warriors of the mead hall of Hroðgar (the king of the Danes), Grendel's mother, and a fierce dragon. Beowulf slays Grendel, the enemy-troll, and is rewarded for his bravery and becomes king. Beowulf rules his people for many years until his kingdom is terrorized by a dragon. He goes to battle with the dragon and kills the dragon, but is mortally wounded in the effort. Scholars believe that the story of *Beowulf* is a retelling of an older, pagan tale changed to include Christian elements, thus providing principles for how to live life as a good Christian. (http://lnstar.com/literature/beowulf).

Middle English literature is written in the form of the English language known as Middle English, from the 12th century until the 1470s, when the Chancery Standard, a form of London-based English, became widespread and the printing press came into use. Middle English Literature usually involves themes of religion, courtly love, and Arthurian tales. Representative works from The Middle Age time period include:

- Dante Alighieri, *The Divine Comedy* (1231-1265)
- Geoffrey Chaucer, *The Canterbury Tales* (1340-1400)

Geoffrey Chaucer's work, *The Canterbury Tales* is a long narrative poem describing of a group of thirty people from all levels of society who travel as pilgrims to Canterbury, England. As a member of the king's household, Chaucer is sent on diplomatic errands throughout Europe. From all these travels, he gains knowledge of society at many levels in order to write *The Canterbury Tales*. The pilgrims tell stories in order to make time pass pleasantly as they travel from London to Canterbury. The dramatic interaction between the tales and the framing story allows Chaucer to develop the individual personalities of the pilgrims. A brief synopsis of several of the tales are provided below (www.librarius.com).

The Wife of Bath's Prologue and Tale

One of the most well-known of ***The Canterbury Tales*** is the tale from ***The Wife of Bath***. The wife's tale tells the story of romance and conflict between the sexes. As punishment for raping a disagreeable woman a knight must find out what women most desire. The unpleasant woman says she will help him, if he marries her. After the two spend time together, the knight falls in love with the woman and she is transformed into a beautiful younger woman. The wife of Bath is an independent woman and claims she has acquired her knowledge of love and marriage from experience. She rejects the strict interpretation of scriptural authority that inhibits the lives of women (www.librarius.com).

The Knight's Tale

The Knight's Tale describes two young knights that want the same beautiful woman, Emily. The story describes the characteristics of knighthood and chivalry and discusses love, courtly manners, brotherhood, and loyalty. Several fights and battles are described until the knights meet their death on the battlefield (www.librarius.com).

The Merchant's Tale

The Merchant's Tale describes an older knight who decides he should marry a young woman. In the tale, the older knight describes the meaning of love, marriage, truth, and faithfulness (www.librarius.com).

The English Renaissance (1550-1660)

The second major period of development in British literary history, the English Renaissance, occurred during the years 1550 to 1660. This period can be further subdivided into the **Elizabethan period (1550 – 1625)** and the **Puritan Period (1625 – 1660).** The Renaissance describes an era during which man desired to recover the classical past of the Greeks and Romans, relished and explored the physical and temporal world, developed passion for discovery and invention, and developed an interest in gaining personal knowledge and power which often conflicted with existing religious doctrine. Renaissance literature reflected humanistic values. Humanists believed that human beings were the vital and intriguing base of creation. These values are reflected in many European literary works of this era (Coyle & Peck, 2002; Davis, et al., 1995). Representative works from this time period include:

- Cervantes, ***Don Quixote***
- Petrarch, ***Love Sonnets***
- Machiavelli, ***The Prince***
- Sir Philip Sidney, ***Arcadia, Astrophil, Stella***
- Edmund Spenser, ***The Faerie Queene***
- John Milton, ***Paradise Lost***
- John Bunyan, ***Pilgrim's Progress***
- William Shakespeare, ***King Lear, Richard II, Twelfth Night***

John Bunyan's work, *Pilgrim's Progress,* is an **allegory** of Christian travels from the City of Destruction to the Celestial City. Along the way, man discovers the challenges and benefits encountered by believers on a spiritual journey toward Christianity.

William Shakespeare, the world renown playwright, is considered by many scholars to be unequalled by any other writer due to his ability to depict the range and depth of human emotion through his comedies and tragedies. Shakespeare's work has been translated into almost every language worldwide, and his works are still performed across the globe. Shakespeare plays include *Romeo and Juliet, King Lear, Julius Caesar, A Midsummer Night's Dream, Richard II, Richard III, The Tempest,* and *Hamlet.*

Shakespeare's play, *Richard II,* earned a reputation among Elizabethan audiences as politically subversive. In the play, Richard, the legal, rightful ruler of England who was ordained by God, is shown to be a weak and ineffective king who focuses more upon shallow appearances than responsibilities. The play, written entirely in verse, uses the literary device of extended metaphor to compare England to a garden and later to compare the reigning king to a lion and the sun. In the play, the comparison of Queen Elizabeth to Richard is obvious to the audience due to her lack of an heir and inclination toward heavy taxation. Sixteenth-century critics often viewed the play as a politically dangerous commentary on the monarchy. It was not until the 18th century that the play began to generate literary, rather than political, interest. The main issues in the play focus on the nature of kingship and examine the conflict between the legal and divine right to rule, and the effectiveness of the ruler. In the play the controversy lies with whether or not Bolingbroke deposed Richard or if Richard caused his own usurpation (www.allshakespeare.com).

Shakespeare's *Hamlet*, a tragedy written between 1599 and 1601, is set in the Kingdom of Denmark and describes Prince Hamlet's revenge on his uncle Claudius for murdering the elder King Hamlet, Claudius's own brother and Prince Hamlet's father, and then succeeding to the throne. Claudius also married Gertrude, King Hamlet's widow and mother of Prince Hamlet. The play portrays Hamlet's real and feigned madness—from overwhelming grief to seething rage, and explores themes of treachery, revenge, incest, and moral corruption (www.librarius.com).

Shakespeare's *Julius Caesar*, a tragedy written in 1599, describes the 44 BC conspiracy against the Roman dictator Julius Caesar, his assassination and the defeat of the conspirators at the Battle of Philippi. Caesar is not the central character of the play; he appears in only three scenes, and is killed at the beginning of the third act. The protagonist of the play is Marcus Brutus, and the central psychological drama is his struggle between the conflicting demands of honor, patriotism, and friendship. It is believed that the play reflects the general anxiety of England over succession of leadership. At the time of its creation and first performance, Queen Elizabeth, a strong ruler, was elderly and had refused to name a successor, leading to worries that a civil war similar to that of Rome might prevail after her death (www.librarius.com).

Shakespeare's, *A Midsummer Night's Dream*, was written around 1594 to 1596. The play portrays the events surrounding the marriage of the Duke of Athens (Theseus) and the Queen of the Amazons (Hippolyta). During a four-day festival, Theseus commissions his Master of the Revels, Philostrate, to find suitable amusements for the occasion. Egeus, an Athenian nobleman, marches into Theseus's court with his daughter, Hermia, and two young men, Demetrius and Lysander. Egeus wishes Hermia to marry Demetrius, but Hermia is in love with Lysander and refuses to comply. Theseus gives Hermia until his wedding to consider her options, warning her that disobeying her father's wishes could result in her being sent to a convent or even executed. Nonetheless, Hermia and Lysander plan to escape Athens the following night and marry in the house of Lysander's aunt. They make their intentions known to Hermia's friend Helena, who was once engaged to Demetrius and still loves him even though he jilted her. Hoping to regain his love, Helena tells Demetrius of the elopement that Hermia and Lysander have planned. At the appointed time, Demetrius stalks into the woods after his intended bride and her lover; Helena follows behind him. In these woods are two groups of characters. The first is a band of fairies, including Oberon, the fairy king, and Titania, his queen. The second is a band of Athenian craftsmen rehearsing a play that they hope to perform for the Duke and his bride.

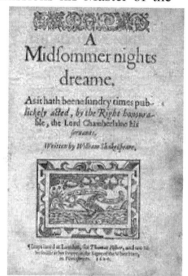

After correcting a mistaken attempt of giving a love potion to the wrong man, Puck spreads the love potion on Lysander's eyelids, and by morning all is well. Theseus and Hippolyta discover the sleeping lovers in the forest and take them back to Athens to be married—Demetrius now loves Helena, and Lysander now loves Hermia. After the group wedding, the lovers watch Bottom and his fellow craftsmen perform their play, a fumbling, hilarious version of the story of Pyramus and Thisbe. When the play is completed, the lovers sleep together; the fairies briefly emerge to bless the sleeping couples with a protective charm and then disappear. Only Puck remains, to ask the audience for its forgiveness and approval and to urge it to remember the play as though it had all been a dream (http:// www.librarius.com).

The Merchant of Venice Antonio, a Venetian merchant, complains to his friends that he suffers from a melancholy that he cannot explain. His friend Bassanio is desperately in need of money to court Portia, a wealthy heiress who lives in the city of Belmont. Bassanio asks Antonio for a loan in order to travel to Portia's estate. Antonio agrees, but is unable to make the loan himself because his own money is all invested. Antonio suggests that Bassanio secure the loan from one of the city's moneylenders. In Belmont, Portia expresses sadness over the terms of her father's will, which stipulates that she must marry the man who correctly chooses one of three caskets. None of Portia's current suitors are to her liking, and she and her lady-in-waiting, Nerissa, fondly remember a visit paid some time before by Bassanio. In Venice, Antonio and Bassanio approach Shylock, a Jewish moneylender, for a loan.

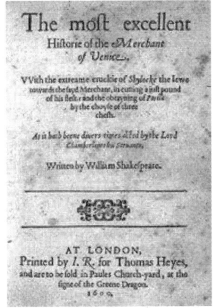

Shylock has a long-standing grudge against Antonio but offers to lend Bassanio three thousand ducats with no interest. Shylock adds, however, that should the loan go unpaid, Shylock will be entitled to a pound of Antonio's own flesh.

In Belmont, Portia welcomes the prince of Morocco, who has come in an attempt to choose the right casket in order to marry her. The prince studies the inscriptions on the three caskets and chooses the gold one, which proves to be an incorrect choice. The second suitor, Shylock, picks the silver casket, which is also incorrect. Despite Portia's request that he wait before choosing, Bassanio immediately picks the correct casket, which is made of lead.

The wedding celebration is cut short by the news that Antonio has lost his ships, and has forfeited
his bond to Shylock. Bassanio and Gratiano immediately travel to Venice to try and save Antonio's life. After they leave, Portia tells Nerissa that they will go to Venice disguised as men. Disguised as a law clerk, Portia informs Shylock that he is guilty of conspiring against the life of a Venetian citizen, which means he must turn over half of his property to the state and the other half to Antonio. The Duke spares Shylock's life and takes a fine instead of Shylock's property. Lorenzo and Jessica are pleased to learn of their inheritance from Shylock, and the joyful news arrives that Antonio's ships have in fact made it back safely. The group celebrates its good fortune (http:// www.librarius.com).

Paradise Lost

John Milton's epic poem, *Paradise Lost,* takes the reader on a journey through Christian theology in an attempt to answer Christianity's most difficult questions. Milton attempts to explain the rise and fall of evil in heaven and man's struggle with knowledge and sin. Milton's work tries to explain why God has given man a chance to live in a fallen world by sacrificing his only son to help save man from himself (www. paradise-lost.com).

Metaphysical Poetry
During the English Renaissance, **John Donne** (1572-1631) composed a popular form of poetry that was brief and concentrated in meaning and sometimes cynical; this **metaphysical** poetry often employed a blend of formal and colloquial language written in extended metaphors to describe the subjects of love, law, medicine, philosophy, and religion. The poems often shocked and aroused the reader. (example: The Flea)

The Restoration and Enlightenment (1660-1798)
The third major division of British Literature, The Restoration and the Enlightenment, occurred during the years **1660 to 1798.** This **"age of enlightenment,"** also known as the **Neoclassical Period,** brought forth writers and thinkers that redefined God's relationship to the world and to mankind. Writers such as Voltaire, and Rousseau believed God made man, but man could function independently of God through rational thinking and action. These thinkers believed that man could discover the hidden laws of nature and make the world a better place. During the Enlightenment, emphasis was placed on the separation of church and state and there grew an increasing demand for political justice and civil liberty. The 18th century was a relatively peaceful time that supported the growth of the merchant (middle) class and promoted economic growth and trade. Artists and writers began to write for this growing merchant class audience instead of to nobility and the aristocracy (Coyle & Peck, 2002; Davis, et al., 1995). Representative authors from The Restoration and Enlightenment era include:

- John Dryden, (1631-1700), *The Indian Queen, An Essay on Dramatic Poesy*
- Daniel Defoe, (1660-1731), *Robinson Crusoe*
- Jonathan Swift (1667-1745), *Gulliver's Travels, A Modest Proposal*
- Alexander Pope (1688-1744), *The Rape of the Lock, An Essay on Man*
- Samuel Johnson, *A Dictionary of the English Language*

Daniel Defoe based his famous novel, ***Robinson Crusoe,*** on the true story of William Selkirk, who went to sea in 1704; and, as a form of punishment, was put ashore on an uninhabited island in the South Pacific, where he survived until his rescue in 1709. Dafoe's character, Robinson

Crusoe, took to the sea despite parental warnings and suffered a number of misfortunes at the hands of Barbary pirates and the elements. Finally Crusoe is shipwrecked off South America. With the aid of salvaged materials from the ship, Crusoe manages to survive on the island. He stays on the island 28 years, and adapts to his alien environment. After many lonely years, he sees a strange footprint in the sand. This discovery leads to an encounter with savages and their prisoners, one of whom he helps to escape. Crusoe names the frightened native, Man Friday, and befriends him. Finally after many years, Crusoe and Friday are rescued by an English ship and returned home to England (www.online literature.com).

Gulliver's Travels

Jonathan Swift wrote the satire, *Gulliver's Travels*, in 1726. In the story, Gulliver, a ship's surgeon, tells of his shipwreck on the island of Lilliput, where the people were only six inches tall. Their actions, controversies, and concerns are depicted as ridiculous. Their political arguments about nonsensical subjects such as on what end should an egg be broken mock the English political and religious debates of Swift's time. On his travels Gulliver meets various other strange tribes of people with silly concerns: extremely tall people, weird scientists, and philosophers who spend their time trying to extract sunshine from cucumbers. In the final section of the book, Gulliver meets two groups of people: a tribe of horsemen who live with reason, simplicity, and dignity and a group called the "Yahoos" who look like humans, but live with sin and violence. Despite its dark themes, the book was an immediate success and has remained a favorite with adults who enjoy the satire and children who like the adventurous travel story (www.bibliomania.com).

The Age of Romanticism (1798-1832)

The fourth major division of **British Literature**, the era of **Romanticism**, occurred during the years 1798 to 1832. The Romantic age of literature was born during a time of revolution throughout the world in areas such as France, China, and the United States. Like the revolutionists, writers during the Romantic age of literature formulated a challenge in their own way against the rationalism and materialism of the dominant culture. From the romantic perspectives, each individual held within himself an eternal conflict between rational thought and emotional self-interest. Many of the works of literature authored during this period revealed a romantic protagonist in turmoil that ended with the tragic triumph of emotion over reason.

The Romantic era celebrated the natural world and gave importance to developing the spontaneous, unaffected, emotional person, who held God's natural world and all its beauty in high regard. Romantic writers believed that seeking one's inner truth and beauty could lead to a deeper connection to others. However, the journey into self-understanding carried with it a melancholy side in that the world often proved to be a place of great suffering and death. Thus, the romantic period of literature involved works of social reality depicting the harsh cruelties of the world (Coyle & Peck, 2002; Davis, et al., 1995). Representative works during the age of Romanticism include:

- William Wordsworth (1770-1850), *Lyrical Ballads, The Prelude*
- William Blake (1757-1827), *Songs of Innocence, Songs of Experience*
- Samuel Taylor Coleridge (1772-1834), *The Rime of the Ancient Mariner, Kubla Khan*
- Charlotte Bronte (1816-1855), *Jane Eyre*
- Emily Bronte (1818-1848), *Wuthering Heights*
- Anne Bronte (1820-1849), *The Tenant of Wildfell Hall*
- Percy B. Shelley (1792-1822), *The Assassins, The Revolt of Islam, Mont Blanc*
- John Keats (1795-1821), *To Autumn, Ode on a Grecian Urn*
- Jane Austen (1775-1817), *Pride and Prejudice, Sense and Sensibility*
- Sir Walter Scott (1771 -1832), *Ivanhoe, Rob Roy*

Songs of Innocence

In his lyrical poems, ***Songs of Innocence***, **William Blake** (1757-1827) presents the naive and hopeful view of a child living in the squalid conditions of London's lower classes. Contrasted with that theme is the message from ***Songs of Experience***, a set of poems that tempers the naive outlook found in the child with the more cynical perspectives of adults who have experienced life's blows. Blake describes his poems as presenting the two contrasting states of the human soul. For example, in the poem, *The Chimney Sweep*er from " *Songs of Experience,"* Blake attacks the moral authoritarianism and religious fallacy during this time period by describing the hypocrisy of a child's parents who sell their child into the slavery of indentured servitude and then congratulate themselves on having done their duty to God, Church, and King. In another poem from *Songs of Experience* entitled *The Tyger* (1794), Blake ponders the purpose of a universe in which God has created both the tiger and the lamb (www.online-literature.com):

The Tyger

Tyger! Tyger! burning bright
In the forests of the night,
What immortal hand or eye
Could frame thy fearful symmetry?
In what distant deeps or skies
Burnt the fire of thine eyes?
On what wings dare he aspire?
What the hand dare seize the fire?
And what shoulder, and what art.
Could twist the sinews of thy heart?
And when thy heart began to beat,
What dread hand? and what dread feet?
What the hammer? what the chain?
In what furnace was thy brain?
What the anvil? what dread grasp
Dare its deadly terrors clasp?
When the stars threw down their spears,
And watered heaven with their tears,
Did he smile his work to see?
Did he who made the Lamb make thee?
Tyger! Tyger! burning bright
In the forests of the night,
What immortal hand or eye
Dare frame thy fearful symmetry?

Rime of the Ancient Mariner

Samuel Taylor Coleridge's poem, *The Rime of the Ancient Mariner*, is another work penned during the age of Romanticism. Coleridge's poem presents a poetic imitation of a folk ballad meant to guide the reader on an exotic journey to the mysterious, supernatural world. Coleridge's intent was to give the reader a taste of exotic travel while directing the mind to the beauty and the wonderment of the natural world. *The Rime of the Ancient Mariner* describes the travels of a seaman who must live a life of penance wandering the seas after committing the sin of killing an albatross, one of God's creatures (www.online-literature.com).

William Wordsworth's poetry

The work of **William Wordsworth** (177-1850) is said to embody the spirit of reform found during this romantic period. Heavily influenced by the French revolution, Wordsworth's poetry incorporated the language of the common man and conveyed the spirit of revolution. His work describes the relationship of man to the natural world and stressed the importance of a strong, inner, spiritual strength that could be called upon during life's trials and tribulations. In his poems *The Prelude* and *Tinturn Abbey*, Wordsworth captures the spirit of the age in that he describes the celebration of life found in a child, the frustration of the adult once that naivety was lost, and the frustration found in life as one attempts to understand loss (www.online literature.com).

The Victorian Period (1832-1901)

The fifth major division of **British Literature**, the **Victorian Period**, occurred during the years 1832 to 1901. The Victorian Era of Great Britain occurred during the height of the British industrial revolution. This time period is named for Queen Victoria whose reign witnessed great changes in society. Economically, the most important change came as the economy shifted away from rural farm life into a more urban economy based on trade and manufacturing. The Industrial Revolution created profound economic and social changes for the people, including a mass migration of workers to industrial towns. These changes also brought about the expansion of newspapers and the periodical press; debate about political and social issues played an important role in everyday life. The "Victorian novel" was born during this era, with its emphasis on the **realistic** portrayal of social life. During the Victorian era, science grew into the discipline it is today and many people devoted their time to the study of natural history. **Charles Darwin's** work, ***On the Origin of Species****,* published in 1859, had a tremendous effect on the popular mindset during of this time (Coyle & Peck, 2002; Davis, et al., 1995; www.wwnorton.com/nael/victorian). Representative works by British authors during the Victorian Era include:

- Alfred Lord Tennyson (1809-1892), ***Ulysses, The Charge of the Light Brigade***
- Charles Dickens (1812-1870), ***David Copperfield, Great Expectations***
- Lewis Carroll, (Charles Lutwidge Dodgson, 1832-1898), ***Alice's Adventures in Wonderland***
- Thomas Hardy (1840-1928), ***The Man He Killed, Hap***
- Oscar Wilde (1854-1900), ***The Importance of Being Earnest, The Picture of Dorian Gray***

The Work of Alfred Lord Tennyson

 **Alfred Lord Tennyson** (1809-1892) is often regarded as the chief representative of the Victorian age in poetry. Tennyson succeeded Wordsworth as Poet Laureate in 1850. In 1842 the two-volume book entitled, *Poems*, established his reputation as a writer and included the poems *The Lady of Shalott, The Lotus-eaters, Marte d'Arthur,* and *Ulysses*.

Among Tennyson's major poetic achievements is the eulogy mourning the death of his friend Arthur Hallam, *In Memoriam*, published in 1850. The patriotic poem, *Charge of the Light Brigade*, published in 1855, is one of Tennyson's best known works. This poem was written to memorialize a suicidal cavalry charge over open terrain by British forces during the Crimean War (1854-1856). In the charge, 247 of 637 men were killed or wounded. The following excerpt reveals the rhythmic cadence found within his work (www.onlineliterature.com/tennyson):

The Charge of the Light Brigade
>Half a league, half a league,
>Half a league onward,
>All in the valley of Death
>Rode the six hundred.
>"Forward, the Light Brigade!
>"Charge for the guns!" he said:
>Into the valley of Death
>Rode the six hundred.
>"Forward, the Light Brigade!"
>Was there a man dismay'd?
>Not tho' the soldier knew
>Someone had blunder'd:
>Their's not to make reply,
>Their's not to reason why,
>Their's but to do and die:

The Work of Charles Dickens

Charles Dickens was the son of poor parents who were placed in debtors' prison when Charles was a child. During the time of his father's imprisonment, Charles worked at Warren's Blacking Factory. When his father was released, 12 year-old Dickens attended school in London, even though his mother wanted him to continue working in the factory to help the family. At the age of 15, he found employment as an office boy for an attorney, while he studied shorthand at night. His brief stint at the Blacking Factory haunted him all of his life and the harsh life of child labor would emerge in his work, most notably, in his novels, ***David Copperfield*** and ***Great Expectations*** (www.victorianweb.org/authors/dickens/dickensbio).

Emerging Modernism (1901-1959)

The sixth major division of **British Literature, Emerging Modernism**, occurred during the years 1901 to 1959. The modernist era of literature took place during a time of great upheaval and change. Before World War I, most people considered warfare a rite of passage for young men. However, the horror and brutality of World War I from poison gas, trench warfare, and machine guns caused a high death rate that was unsurpassed in previous wars. This generation became known as the *lost generation* because of the great numbers of deaths. The additional horrors experienced during World War II from 1940 to 1945 from nuclear weapons, genocide, and massive loss of life added to the people's unrest with existing religious and political doctrines. The backlash of these experiences caused people to question the established beliefs set forth by religion, science, and politics. German philosopher, **Nietzsche**, claimed that God was dead.

In a search for meaning of man's existence, **Carl Jung** suggested that all human beings share a common spiritual and psychic heritage. Moreover, scientific breakthroughs (i.e., Albert Einstein's Theory of Relativity; Heisenberg's work with electrons) made people feel that science, not God, could explain life's meaning. The common theme found within the literature of this time concerned death and mortality. Also, changes in society were reflected in the literature of the era through changes in form and structure. Innovative writing techniques such as stream of consciousness can be seen in **James Joyce's** (1882-1941) novel, ***Ulysses,*** and in **Virginia Woolf's** (1882-1941) novel, ***To the Lighthouse*** (Coyle & Peck, 2002; Davis, et al., 1995). Representative works by British authors during the Emerging Modernism era include:

- T. S. Elliot (1888-1965), ***The Wasteland, The Hollow Men, Preludes, Journey of the Magi***
- George Bernard Shaw (1856-1950), ***Pygmalion***
- William Butler Yeats (1865-1939), ***The Wild Swans at Coole, Sailing to Byzantium***
- D. H. Lawrence (1885-1930), ***Goose Fair, The Rocking-Horse Winner***
- James Joyce (1882-1941), ***Ulysses, Araby***

- Dylan Thomas (1914-1953), *Do Not Go Gentle into That Good Night*
- Virginia Woolf (1882-1941)*, Mrs. Dalloway, A Room of One's Own*
- George Orwell *(1903-1950,) Animal Farm*

The Wasteland

T. S. Eliot (1888-1965), wrote his famous poem, *The Wasteland,* to describe a sick, modern urban society filled with materialistic desires during the Emerging Modernism era. In the poem, Eliot questioned the traditions and values established by society.

Dylan Thomas
Irish poet **Dylan Thomas's** father was close to death in 1952 when Thomas expressed his rage against death through the poem, *Do Not Go Gentle into That Good Night* (www.online-literature.com):

Do Not Go Gentle into That Good Night
Do not go gentle into that good night,
Old age should burn and rave at close of day;
Rage, rage against the dying of the light.
Though wise men at their end know dark is right,
Because their words had forked no lightning they
Do not go gentle into that good night.
Good men, the last wave by, crying how bright
Their frail deeds might have danced in a green bay,
Rage, rage against the dying of the light.
Wild men who caught and sang the sun in flight,
And learn, too late, they grieved it on its way,
Do not go gentle into that good night.
Grave men, near death, who see with blinding sight
Blind eyes could blazed like meteors and be gay,
Rage, rage against the dying of the light.
And you, my father, there on the sad height,
Curse, bless me now with your fierce tears, I pray,
Do not go gentle into that good night.
Rage, rage against the dying of the light.

The Work of William Butler Yeats

Another poet from the Emerging Modernism era, Irish poet and playwright **William Butler Yeats** spent his boyhood summers in Ireland and grew to love the beauty found in the Irish countryside and Irish culture. His early works often reflected the beauty of art and the natural world and its existence beyond mans' mortality. Yeats' works take the reader to a world beyond death by imagining an existence of immortality found within art or nature. Many of Yeats' poems, ***The Wild Swans at Coole, When You Are Old,*** *and* ***The Lake Isle of Innisfree****,* concern overcoming life's disappointments of lost love and man's mortality. The excerpt below from the poem, ***Sailing to Byzantium****,* exemplifies the symbolism used by Yeats to describe a time and place from the past which reflected an ideal life found in art that extended beyond man's mortality (www.online-literature.com):

Sailing to Byzantium
... An aged man is but a paltry thing,
A tattered coat upon a stick, unless
Should clap its hands and sing, and louder sing
For every tatter in its mortal dress,
Nor is there singing school but studying
Monuments of its own magnificence;
And therefore I have sailed the seas and come
To the holy city of Byzantium...
. . . Once out of nature I shall never take
My bodily form from any natural thing.
But such a form as Grecian goldsmiths make
Of hammered gold and gold enameling
To keep a drowsy Emperor awake;
Or set upon a golden bough to sing
To lords and ladies of Byzantium
Of what is past, or passing, or to come.

Contemporary Era (1950-present)

The **Contemporary Era** of **British literature** occurred from post-World War II, 1950 to present. Literature of this period, also known as the **Post Modernism Era**, continues to scrutinize the moral and political dilemmas that contemporary society offers. During the 1960s many British writers attacked the injustices of Britain's class system. During the latter half of the 20th century the voices of women and minority writers were heard as well in response to the social injustices found within the world (Coyle & Peck, 2002; Davis, et al., 1995). Representative works by British authors during the Contemporary era include:

- Doris Lessing (1919-), *No Witchcraft for Sale, African Stories, A Sunrise on the Veld, Under my Skin*
- Ted Hughes (1930-1998), *The Rain Horse, Hawk in the Rain, Crow, Moortown* and *The Horses*
- Harold Pinter (1930-2008), *The Homecoming, The Dumb Waiter, The Caretaker*
- George Orwell (1903-1950), *Animal Farm, 1984*

The Work of George Orwell

George Orwell's (1903-1950) futuristic novel, **1984**, painted a bleak picture of the future as the government maintained tighter and tighter control over people's everyday lives. For example, Orwell's criticism of British colonial government is depicted in his short story, *Shooting an Elephant.* As a police officer in colonial India, Orwell was forced to shoot an elephant that had gone wild in a marketplace. He shot the elephant not so much that it was causing havoc, but to save face as a British police officer in front of the natives. Thus, Orwell reveals the irony of British colonial rule (Coyle & Peck, 2002; Davis, et al., 1995).

During the Emerging Modernism era, **George Orwell**, a democratic socialist, wrote the novel *Animal Farm* as a satire against Joseph Stalin and hostile-direct Stalinism. The novel describes how animals overtake a farm to escape the farmers' tyranny. However, the pigs in the story treat the other animals more harshly than the farmers did. The most famous quotation from the work is, "All animals are equal, but some animals are more equal than others" (www.online-literature.com).

The Work of Doris Lessing

Doris Lessing's work criticizes the British class system. Her childhood experiences in Rhodesia are reflected in her works which describe the people of Africa. Her short story, *No Witchcraft for Sale,* explores the cultural and racial gaps found in the relationship between a deeply religious family and their black servant, Gideon (www.onlineliterature).

The Work of Ted Hughes

Poet **Ted Hughes** spent much of his childhood in rural West Yorkshire and learned to appreciate and respect the natural world. Many of his contemporary works both for children and adults reflect this love of nature; he became Poet Laureate of England in 1984. This sense of awe for the beauty of nature is evidenced in this excerpt from his poem ***The Horses***:

The Horses
. . . And the big planets hanging
I turned
Stumbling in the fever of a dream, down towards
The dark woods, from the kindling tops.
And came to the horses.
There, still they stood.
But now steaming and glistening under the flow of light.

The Work of Harold Pinter

Contemporary British author, **Harold Pinter** (1930-2008), explained that many of his plays describe commonplace situations during which a gradual introduction of menace and mystery takes place. Pinter uses this style in the one-act play, *The Dumb Waiter,* about two hired killers employed by a mysterious organization to murder an unknown victim. In this play, Pinter adds an element of comedy, provided through the characters' brilliant small-talk behind which the two men hide their growing anxiety. Their discussion over whether it is more proper to say "light the kettle" or "light the gas" is wildly comic and terrifying in its absurdity (www.online-literature.com).

World literature, Major Authors, and Works

The Ancient World

Classical Era
Greek Classical and Hellenistic Periods (8ᵗʰ to 2ⁿᵈ centuries B.C.) and Roman Classical Period (1ˢᵗ century to 5ᵗʰ century)

Literature that falls within the ancient time period is representative of the early civilizations of man. Ancient literature originates from the rural, oral storytelling traditions of early civilizations. The ubiquitous theme found within many of these works involves the conflicting relationship between man and the celestial world of the gods (Coyle & Peck, 2002). Representative works from this time period from the civilizations that developed in the Mediterranean region of the world include:

- *The Epic of Gilgamesh* (7th century B.C.)
- Homer, *The Iliad* and *The Odyssey* (700 B.C.)
- *Aesop's Fables* (500 B.C.)
- Plato, *The Republic* (400 B.C.)
- Aristotle, *Metaphysics* (400 B.C.)

The Epic of Gilgamesh (7th century B.C.), a Babylonian epic, is most likely the oldest written story on Earth. Filled with symbolism, the epic describes the life of the Sumerian King Gilgamesh. Gilgamesh, half-human half-god, is a young, arrogant king who begins his reign by alienating himself from his people, claiming first sexual rights to new brides and other women in the Sumerian kingdom of Uruk. The God, Anu, creates a friend named Enkidu for the young king who guides and mentors the king. Enkidu is an uncivilized man who lives among the beasts. Together the civilized Gilgamesh and wild-man Enkidu form a lasting friendship and have adventures while traveling to the edge of the world in search of immortality and the meaning of life. While on this journey, Gilgamesh learns that the essence of life is change and death is the end result. The moral of the story was that mankind had to accept this fate and live life wisely. *The Epic of Gilgamesh* predates Hebrew and Greek literature by almost a thousand years (Coyle & Peck, 2002; Davis, et al., 1995).

Homer's *The Iliad* and ***The Odyssey*** (700 B.C.) is a two-part Greek legend that blends mythical knowledge and ancient Greek history to describe the exploits of Achilles during the Trojan War. The story of *The Iliad* is a salute to heroes. The story begins after the wars have been raging for ten years. Homer describes the cause of the war (known as the Judgment of Paris). At a wedding, Eris, the goddess of discord, rolls a golden apple on the floor which is inscribed, "for the fairest." The favored Prince of Troy, Paris, has to decide which of three goddesses will receive the apple. The goddess Aphrodite bribes Paris into picking her; in return, Paris will receive Helen, the wife of Menelaus who is the most beautiful woman in the world. Paris then steals Helen and takes her and the Spartan treasure back to the city of Troy. Seeking revenge, the Greek Kings sail to Troy to rescue Helen and the treasure. The main characters in the story include: Agamemnon, the Sparta King, Achilles, the great savage warrior, Patroklos, the close friend of Achilles, Hector, the beloved family man who dies in battle and considered Trojan's greatest warrior, and Paris, the spoiled prince. The war ends when the people of Troy are tricked into hauling a great wooden horse into their city. The horse is filled with soldiers who emerge from the horse after dark and destroy the city of Troy (Coyle & Peck, 2002; Davis, et al., 1995).

A Brief Summary of Greek Mythology

The Greeks believed in many gods (and many generations of gods) and believed these gods had both supernatural powers and human weaknesses. The greatest beings in Greek Mythology are the twelve Olympian gods who take their name from the place of their dwelling, Mount Olympus.

Zeus – is the ruler of the Olympian gods and god of the sky, thunder and justice, Zeus overthrows his father Cronus, and then draws lots with his brothers, Poseidon and Hades, for share of the world. Zeus wins the draw and became the supreme ruler of the gods. Although married to Hera, Zeus is famous for his many affairs. He is also known to punish those that lie or break oaths. He was the rain god, and the cloud gatherer, who wielded the terrible thunderbolt. He is represented as the god of justice and mercy, the protector of the weak, and the punisher of the wicked (Graves, 1965; www.greekmythology.com).

Poseidon – is the god of the sea, earthquakes and horses. His prize (from the drawing with his brothers, Zeus and Hades) was to become lord of the sea, so he was widely worshiped by seamen. He married Amphitrite, a granddaughter of the Titan Oceanus. At one point he desires Demeter. Demeter asks him to make the most beautiful animal that the world had ever seen. So to impress her, Poseidon creates the first horse. Poseidon's weapon is a trident, which can shake the earth, and shatter any object. He is second only to Zeus in power amongst the gods. He is greedy and quarrelsome, and always in dispute with other gods as he tries to concur their cities (Graves, 1965; www.greekmythology.com).

Hades - is the brother of Zeus and Posiden. He received the worst draw and became the lord of the underworld, ruling over the dead. He is greedy and concerned with increasing the number of subjects. Hades is also the god of wealth, due to the precious metals mined from the earth. His helmet makes him invisible. Hades abducted his wife, Persephone. Hades is the King of the dead, but death itself is another god, Thanatos (Graves, 1965; www.greekmythology.com).

Hestia - is the sister of Zeus, and goddess of hearth and home. She is the virgin goddess, and is considered to be very kind. She is the Goddess of the hearth, and the symbol of the house around which a newborn child is carried before it is received into the family. Each city had a public hearth dedicated to Hestia, which contained a perpetual fire (Graves, 1965; www.greekmythology.com).

Hera – is the goddess of women, marriage and childbirth and is married to Zeus. She was raised by the Titans, Ocean and Tethys. Zeus courted Hera unsuccessfully, and then turned to trickery, changing himself into cuckoo bird, in order to win her. When Hera saw the cuckoo bird, she felt sorry for the bird, and held it to her breast to comfort it. Zeus then resumed his normal form and raped her. She then was forced to marry Zeus in order to hide her shame. In retaliation, Hera convinced the other gods to revolt against Zeus. She drugged Zeus, and the gods bound Zeus to a couch tying the rope into many knots. When the gods began to quarrel, Briareus overheard the argument and slipped in to free Zeus who sprung from the couch and siezed his thunderbolt. In fear, the gods fell to their knees begging and pleading for mercy. Zeus seizes Hera and hangs her from the sky with gold chains. She weeps in pain all night, but none of the others dare to free her. Her weeping prevents Zeus from sleeping and the next morning he agrees to release her if she swears to never rebel again. She agrees, but lives out her life in rebellion, often trying to outwit him. Most stories concerning Hera involve her jealous revenge for Zeus's infidelities (Graves, 1965; www.greekmythology.com).

Aris – is the god of war, son of Zeus and Hera, and is disliked by both parents. As the god of war, he is considered murderous, but also cowardly. When caught in an act of adultery with Aphrodite (by her husband, Hephaestus) he is publically ridiculed (Graves, 1965; www.greekmythology.com).

Athena – is the goddess of wisdom, reason, intelligent activity, arts, and literature. The daughter of Zeus, she sprang full grown in armor from his forehead, so she has no mother. She is fierce and brave in battle and is the goddess of the city, handicrafts, and agriculture. She invented the bridle (which permitted man to tame horses) the trumpet, the flute, the pot, the rake, the plow, the yoke, the ship, and the chariot. She is the embodiment of wisdom, reason, and purity. She is Zeus's favorite child and is allowed to use his weapons and his thunderbolt (Graves, 1965; www.greekmythology.com).

Apollo - is the god of the sun, light, healing, medicine, music, poetry, prophecy, archery and truth. He is the son of Zeus and Leto, and the twin brother of Artemis. He is known as "The

Archer" for shooting with a silver bow. He is also the god of healing, because he taught mankind to use medicine. He is considered the god of truth and light and is unable to tell a lie. Each day Apollo's task is to harness his chariot with four horses and drive the Sun across the sky. He is famous for his oracle at Delphi and for playing a golden lyre. People visit the oracle from all over the Greek world in order to learn their future (Graves, 1965; www.greekmythology.com).

Aphrodite - is the Goddess of love, desire, beauty, and fertility. In addition to her natural gifts, she has a magical girdle that compels anyone she wishes to desire her. There are two accounts of her birth. One is that she is the daughter of Zeus and Dione; the other refers to when Cronus castrates Uranus and tossed his severed genitals into the sea. Aphrodite then arises from the sea foam on a giant scallop and walks to shore in Cyprus (Graves, 1965; www.greekmythology.com).

Hermes - The fastest of the gods and messenger to all the other gods. Hermes is the son of Zeus and Maia. He is Zeus' messenger. He is the fastest of the gods and wears winged sandals, a winged hat, and carries a magic wand. He is the god of thieves, the god of commerce, and the guide for the dead to the underworld. He invented the lyre, the pipes, the musical scale, astronomy, weights and measures, boxing, gymnastics, and the care of olive trees (Graves, 1965; www.greekmythology.com).

Artemis - The daughter of Zeus and Leto and the twin sister of Apollo. She is goddess of chastity, virginity, the hunt, the moon, and the natural environment. She is the goddess of all wild things and is the huntsman of the gods. She is also the protector of the young. Like Apollo, she hunts with silver arrows. She is associated with the moon, and is a virgin goddess. She also presides over childbirth, which originated with Leto's painless childbirth when Artemis was born.

Hephaestus - Hephaestus is the son of Zeus and Hera. He is the god of fire and the forge. Some claim that Hera alone produced him and that he had no father. He is the only god to be physically ugly and lame. Accounts as to how he became lame vary. Some say that Hera, upset by having an ugly child, flung him from Mount Olympus into the sea, breaking his legs. Others say that he took Hera's side in an argument with Zeus, so Zeus flung him off Mount Olympus. He is the blacksmith and weapons maker for the gods. He is the patron god of both smiths and weavers and is kind and peace-loving. His wife is Aphrodite.

Stories from Greek mythology are always included in high school curriculum. Following are several story synopses from Greek mythology.

Daedalus and Icarus

Daedalus was a famous sculptor and builder who built a great maze called "The Labyrinth" under the Palace of Knossos in Crete in which King Minos kept a monster, Minotaur - the half-man half-bull. The structure consisted of such a complicated maze of tunnels that it was impossible to escape. After the maze was complete, King Minos did not want Daedalus to reveal it's secret to anyone else, so he imprisoned him and his only son Icarus in a tall tower. Daedalus and Icarus wanted to escape. After observing the birds from the windows of the tower, Daedalus decided to construct wings of bird feathers and wax for him and his son so they could escape. After tying the wings onto his son, Daedalus warned his son not to fly too high in the sky as the sun would melt the wax. However, once Icarus begins to fly, he is so fascinated with the flight that he forgets about his father's  warnings and soared high into the air. As Icarus climbed into the sky his wings began to melt and fall apart, causing him to plunge into the sea.

Theseus and Ariadne

King Minos (the King of Crete) had a powerful navy of which all of Greece was afraid. He agreed with King Aegeus (of Athens) that he will not attack Athens if the people of Athens agree to send seven boys and seven girls as food for the Minotaur every year. When it comes time to  send the boys and girls to Crete, Prince Theseus (the son of King Aegeus) wants to save the children and all those who may be sent in the future. So, he decided to go with the children in order to kill the Minotaur. King Aegeus begged his son not to go as he was afraid he would be devoured by the Minotaur. But Theseus insisted and he set sail for Crete in a boat with a black sail, promising his father that he will change the boat's sail to a white one to signal that he has won and is returning home. When Theseus and the children arrive in Crete they are met by King Minos and his daughter Ariadne. Princess Ariadne immediately falls in love with Prince Theseus and decides to help him with his mission. That night she gives a sword to Theseus along with a ball of thread and instructs him to tie the ball of string to the door of the labyrinth where the Minotaur lives. He could then unroll it as he moved through the maze in order to find his way back after he kills the Minotaur with the sword. Prince Theseus did exactly as instructed, and he found the Minotaur. He killed the monster and was able to leave the labyrinth using the thread to guide him.

Pandora's Box

Pandora was created by Hephaestus, the god of craftsmanship using water and earth. After Prometheus stole fire from Mount Olympus, Zeus sought reprisal by handing Pandora to Epimetheus, the brother of Prometheus. At the same time, Pandora was given a box that she was ordered not to open under any circumstances. Despite this warning, Pandora opened the box and the evils contained within escaped into the world. Pandora immediately closed the box, trapping Hope inside. In other versions, Hope does come out, though the main purpose of the myth of Pandora was to address why evil exists in the world.

Troilus and Cressida, the tragedy by **William Shakespeare**, is believed to have been written in 1602. The play is not a conventional tragedy, since its protagonist (Troilus) does not die. Instead, the play ends on a very bleak note with the death of the noble Trojan, Hector, and the destruction of love between Troilus and Cressida. Throughout the play, the tone lurches wildly between bawdy comedy and tragic gloom, and readers and theatre-goers have frequently found it difficult to understand how one is meant to respond to the characters. However, several characteristic elements of the play (the most notable being its constant questioning of intrinsic values such as hierarchy, honor, and love) have often been viewed as distinctly "modern.

Ancient works from India

The **Upanishads** are a collection of philosophical texts which form the theoretical basis for the Hindu religion. They are also known as Vedanta, the end of the veda. The Upanishads are considered by orthodox Hindus to contain revealed truths (Sruti) concerning the nature of ultimate reality (Brahman) and describing the character and form of human salvation (Moksha). The Upanishads have been passed down in oral tradition.

More than 200 Upanishads are known, of which the first dozen or so are the oldest and most important and are referred to as the principal or main Upanishads. Historians believe the chief Upanishads were composed over a wide period ranging from the Pre-Buddhist period to the early centuries. The Upanishads were collectively considered amongst the *most influential books ever written*. Their significance has been recognized by writers and scholars such as Schopenhauer, Emerson and Thoreau, among others.

International Voices

Literature is a primary medium for insight into the rich cultural dynamics of our world. As students read authors from a multitude of backgrounds, they begin to build bridges of understanding over which they can cross into other cultures (Davis, et al., 1995).

The Work of Chinua Achebe

One of the most influential West African writers in the twentieth century, **Chinua Achebe** (1930- 2013) of **West Africa**, is best known for his novel, **Things Fall Apart**.

As a young man attending university, he was disturbed by the false image of Africa presented by European writers such as Joseph Conrad. Achebe began writing his first novel, **Things Fall Apart (1958),** as a direct refutation of the image of Nigeria presented by western writers.

Achebe hoped to foster respect for all and to reverse the distorted representation of Africa that European writers had delivered to European audiences and show the adverse impact that colonialism had upon indigenous cultures. In the novel, **Things Fall Apart**, Achebe creates a complex and sympathetic portrait of a traditional village culture in Africa.

Achebe fiercely resents the stereotype of Africa as a primitive land, the "heart of darkness," as Joseph Conrad called it. Throughout the novel Achebe reveals how African cultures vary among themselves and how they change over time. When the characters speak, they use an elevated diction which is meant to convey the sense of the Ibo language. Achebe develops the main character, Chief Okonkwo, as a strong, courageous leader who had achieved material success in life, but still carried a resentment of his weak father and the effect it had on his life. Okonkwo's killing of Ikemefuna and his rejection of his son invoke little sympathy; his rigidity and heavy-handedness lead to his downfall (www.wsu.edu/achebe).

The Work of Pablo Neruda

Chilean poet and diplomat, **Pablo Neruda** (1904-1973), was awarded the Nobel Prize in Literature in 1971. Neruda is the most widely read of the South American poets.

From the 1940s on, his works reflected the political struggle of the left and the socio-historical developments in South America. He also wrote love poems. **Neruda's Twenty Love Poems** and **A Song of Despair** (1924) sold over a million copies since it first appeared. In much of his work, Neruda examines Latin American history from a Marxist point of view, and shows his deep knowledge about the history, geography, and politics of the continent. The central theme of his work is the struggle for social justice. His poetry uses earthy imagery to create a strong and vigorous experience for the reader. Neruda's poem, **Discoverers of Chile**, is a historical account of the attempts by early explorers to conquer the native Incan area in South America now known as Chile. The following excerpt reveals Neruda's use of strong imagery (www.lnstar.com/literature/Pablo):

Discoverers of Chile

. . . Almagro brought his wrinkled lighting down from the north.
And day and night he bent over this country
Between gunshots and twilight, as if over a letter.

Shadow of thorn, shadow of thistle and of wax.
The Spaniard, alone with his dried-up body made up
Watching the shadowy tactics of the soil.
My slim nation has a body made up
Of night, snow, and sand.

The Work of Alexander Solzhenitsyn

Author, **Alexander Solzhenitsyn,** (1918-2008) was born in the (former) **Soviet Union**. He attended Rostov University and during World War II joined the Red Army, and rose to the rank of captain. While serving on the German front in 1945, he was arrested for criticizing Joseph Stalin in a letter to a friend and was found guilty and sent to prison in Kazakhstan. His first novel, **One Day in the Life of Ivan Denisovich**, set in a labor camp, was initially banned. In 1970 he was awarded the Nobel Prize in Literature for his autobiographical novel, *The Gulag Archipelago*, but was not allowed to collect it in Stockholm.

Solzhenitsyn continued to write and his novel, **August 1914**, was banned in the Soviet Union but was published abroad. This was followed by his prison memoirs, *The Gulag Archipelago*. Soon afterwards, he was arrested and charged with treason, stripped of his citizenship, and deported from the Soviet Union. Solzhenitsyn collected the Nobel Prize in Literature in 1974, and lived in Vermont (in the United States) where he continued to write. In 1994, Mikhail Gorbachev restored Solzhenitsyn's citizenship and the charge of treason was dropped; he then returned to his home country. In the following excerpt from the novel, *The Gulag Archipelago*, Solzhenitsyn explores his own emotional reactions to the harsh events of his life (www.nobelprize.org/literature/ laureates/1970/solzhenitsyn-autobio.html):

The Gulag Archipelago
... It was granted to me to carry away from my prison years on my bent back, which nearly broke beneath its load, this essential experience: how a human being becomes evil and now good. In the intoxication of youthful successes I had felt myself to be infallible, and I was therefore cruel. In the surfeit of power I was a murderer and an oppressor. In my most evil moments I was convinced that I was doing good, and I was well supplied with systematic arguments. It was only when I lay there on rotting prison straw that I sensed within myself the first stirrings of good. Gradually it was disclosed to me that the line separating good and evil passes not through states, nor between classes, nor between political parties either, but right through every human heart, and through all human hearts. This line shifts. Inside us, it oscillates with the years. Even within hearts overwhelmed by evil, one small bridgehead of good is retained; and even in the best of all hearts, there remains a small corner of evil.

The Work of Christina Stead

Regarded as one of **Australia**'s greatest writers, **Christina Stead** was the recipient of the Patrick White Award in 1974. Her earliest major work was the novel, **THE MAN WHO LOVED CHILDREN**, which initially was not well- received. When it was re-released in 1965, the novel gained critical acclaim for its sensitive fictional account of her own adolescent love-hate relationship with her father. Her second autobiographical novel, **FOR LOVE ALONE**, is the story of a young woman who wants to write but is worried her desire for love and marriage will get in the way of her ambitions. Stead died in Sydney on March 31, 1983, at the age of 80.

The Work of Nadine Gordimer

South African (1923-2014) writer and political activist, **Nadine Gordimer,** was awarded the 1991 Nobel Prize in Literature. Her writing dealt with moral and racial issues, particularly apartheid in South Africa. She was active in the anti-apartheid movement, joining the African National Congress during the days when the organization was banned. She has recently been active in HIV/AIDS causes. Her first novel, *The Lying Days* (1953), was based largely on her own life and set in her home town (http://nobelprize.org).

The Work of Wole Soyink

Nigerian writer **Wole Soyink** was born on 13 July 1934 at Abeokuta, near Ibadan. During the civil war in Nigeria, Soyinka appealed in an article for cease-fire. For this he was arrested, accused of conspiring with the Biafra rebels, and was held as a political prisoner for 22 months until 1969. Soyinka has published 20 literary works (drama, novels, and poetry). He writes in English and his literary language is marked by great scope and richness of words. Soyinka has been influenced by, among others, the Irish writer, J.M. Synge, but links with the traditional popular African theatre with its combination of dance, music, and action. Among Soyinka's plays are ***The Swamp Dwellers*** (1958), ***The Strong Breed*** (1966), ***The Road*** (1965) and ***Death and the King's Horseman*** (1975).

He received the Nobel Prize for Literature in 1986 (http://nobelprize.org/nobel_prizes/literature/laureates/1986/soyinka-bio.html).

The Work of Derek Walcott

Caribbean writer **Derek Walcott** (1930) was born in Castries, Saint Lucia, in the **West Indies**. As a young man he trained as a painter and then as a writer, influenced by modernist poets T. S. Eliot and Ezra Pound. Exploring the Caribbean and its history in a colonialist and post-colonialist context, his collection ***In a Green Night: Poems 1948-1960*** *(1962)* gained an international public profile. Walcott was awarded the Nobel Prize in Literature in 1992, the first Caribbean writer to receive the honor.

The Work of Bertold Brecht

German playwright **Bertold Brecht's** (1898 - 1956) epic theatre departed from the conventions of theatrical illusion. His drama developed as a social and ideological forum for leftist causes. His most acclaimed work is ***Mother Courage and Her Children***. Although set in the 1600s, the play is relevant to contemporary society, and often regarded as one of the finest anti-war plays ever written (http://plays.about.com/od/playwrights/a/brecht.htm).

The Work of Sidonie Gabrielle Colette

French author **Sidonie Gabrielle Colette** (1873-1954) was concerned with feminine independence in experiencing the joys and sorrows of love. Her first success**,** ***The Vagabond***, (1955), was followed by its sequel, ***The Shackle***, (1964), and in time by ***Chéri*** (1929), ***La Maison de Claudine*** (1922), and ***My Mother's House*** (1953), a novelized autobiography of her early years.

The Work of Gabriel García Márquez

Columbian writer **Gabriel Garcia Marquez**, (1927 -), known affectionately as **Gabo** throughout Latin America, is considered one of the most significant authors of the 20th century. He was awarded the Nobel Prize in Literature in 1982. In his large body of fictional works, the concepts of time and history are incredibly important. In novels such as ***One Hundred Years of Solitude***, time is mutable and the epic history of one family line is told with frequent allusions to both the past and present. In the story, Marquez tells the multi-generational story of the Buendía family, whose patriarch, José Arcadio Buendía, founds the town of Macondo, the metaphoric Colombia. In other tales, such as ***Love in the Time of Cholera***, ***Death Constant Beyond Love,*** and ***Chronicle of a Death Foretold***, the past is fictionalized but based on true historical or social events.

The Work of Chinese poets: Tang Poetry

Tang poetry refers to **Chinese** poetry written in or around the time of and in the characteristic style of China's Tang dynasty, (618-907). Tang poetry was written during the **Golden Age of Chinese poetry**. There were almost 50,000 Tang poems written by over 2,200 authors during the Tang Dynasty. During this time period, poetry was considered an important part of social life at all levels of society. Scholars were required to master poetry for the civil service examinations, but the art was theoretically available to everyone. This led to a large record of poetry and poets, a partial record of which survives today. Two of the most famous poets of the period were **Du Fu** and **Li Bai**. **Li Bai** (701-762), a Chinese poet also known in the West as **Li Po**, is a major Chinese poet of the Tang dynasty period:

A Song of an Autumn Midnight

A slip of the moon hangs over the capital;
Ten thousand washing-mallets are pounding;
And the autumn wind is blowing my heart
For ever and ever toward the Jade Pass....
Oh, when will the Tartar troops be conquered,
And my husband come back from the long campaign!

Young Adult Literature

Young Adult literature (YA), whether in the form of novels or short stories, has distinct attributes that distinguish it from the other age categories of fiction: Adult fiction, Middle Grade Fiction, and Children's Fiction. The vast majority of YA stories portray an adolescent as the protagonist, rather than an adult. The subject matter and story lines are typically consistent with the age and experience of the main character, but beyond that YA stories span the entire spectrum of fiction genres. The settings of YA stories are limited only by the imagination and skill of the author. Themes in YA stories often focus on the challenges of youth, so much so that the entire age category is sometimes referred to as problem novels or coming-of-age novels. Writing styles of YA stories range widely, from the richness of literary style to the clarity and speed of the unobtrusive and even free verse. Despite its unique characteristics, YA literature shares the fundamental elements of fiction with other stories: character, plot, setting, theme, and style (http://www.ala.org; www.ncrel.org/litweb/young/add.htm).

Most novels are 125 pages in length and are easily read. Teachers may wish to pair classic literature with young-adult literature which addresses the same issue, particularly for low ability, struggling readers who need extra assistance in comprehending challenging prose. For example, Shakespeare's Romeo and Juliet can be paired with **Marie Lee's** young-adult novel **Finding My Voice** (www.ncrel.org).

The category of YA fiction continues to expand into new genres: graphic novels, light novels, manga, fantasy, mystery fiction, romance novels, and even subcategories such as cyberpunk, splatterpunk, techno-thrillers, and contemporary Christian fiction. New formats such as eBooks make it easy for teens to access these online (http://www.ala.org).

Coming-of-Age Novels
A coming-of-age story or novel is memorable because the character undergoes adventures and/or inner turmoil during growth and development. Some characters come to grips with the reality of cruelty in the world (war, violence, death, racism, and hatred) while others deal with family, friends, or community issues. See the web site: www.home.comcast.net/~antaylorl/alabestteens.html for a complete list of the 100 top books for young adult readers. Representative works and categories of popular YA works include the following:

Great Expectations is one of the most famous works by **Charles Dickens**. Philip (Pip) narrates

this novel years after the episodes occur; the novel contains some autobiographical elements. Pip, the main character, a boy around 13 years old, is easily frightened, and often sad. He is in love with Estella and wants her to return his love, but is shy and does not reveal his love to her. Pip meets an escaped convict, Magwitch, and gives him food in an encounter that is to haunt both their lives. After Pip receives riches from a mysterious benefactor, he snobbishly abandons his friends for London society and his 'great expectations.'

A Tree Grows in Brooklyn by **Betty Smith** is considered a classic, The novel consists of five stories, each covering a different period in the characters' lives. Much of the book is thought of as a thinly disguised autobiography. Many of the characters derive from actual inhabitants of Williamsburg where the author grew up. The metaphor of the book is the hardy Tree of Heaven, common in the vacant lots of Texas City. The New York Public Library has chosen this YA novel as one of the "Books of the Century."

To Kill a Mockingbird, by **Harper Lee**, depicts the story of a young girl, "Scout" Finch. The story takes place during three years of the Great Depression in Maycomb, Alabama. The narrator, six-year-old Scout, lives with her older brother Jem and their widowed father Atticus, a middle-aged lawyer. Jem and Scout befriend a boy named Dill who visits Maycomb to stay with

his aunt for the summer. The three children are terrified of their neighbor, the reclusive "Boo" Radley. Following two summers of friendship with Dill, Scout and Jem find that someone is leaving them small gifts in a tree. Several times, the mysterious Boo makes gestures of affection to the children, but, to their disappointment, never appears in person. Atticus is appointed by the court to defend Tom Robinson, a black man who has been accused of raping a young white woman. Although many of Maycomb's citizens disapprove, Atticus agrees to defend Tom to the best of his ability. Other children taunt Jem and Scout for Atticus' actions and Scout is tempted to stand up for her father's honor by fighting. Atticus faces a group of men intent on lynching Tom, but this danger is averted when Scout, Jem, and Dill shame the mob by forcing them to view the situation from Atticus' and Tom's points of view. Although popular, this novel has encountered censorship battles. Librarians voted this book the best novel of the 20th century www.ncrel.org/litweb/young/add.htm.

The Red Badge of Courage, published in 1895 by struggling American writer, 23 year-old **Stephen Crane**, describes a young man who is traumatized by his experience in the Civil War. It's the story of a young man growing up in the midst of death and destruction, with his whole world turned upside down.

The Member of the Wedding was written in 1945 by **Carson McCullers** and tells the story of a young, motherless girl, who struggles with growing up.

Portrait of the Artist as a Young Man was first published in *The Egoist* in 1914. The story describes the early childhood of Stephen Dedalus while growing up in Ireland. The novel is one of the earliest works to employ **stream of consciousness** - though the novel is not as revolutionary as **Joyce's** later masterpiece, *Ulysses*.

Charlotte Bronte's *Jane Eyre*, gothic romance tells the story of a young orphaned girl who grows up to become a governess and teacher. She eventually finds love and a home for herself.

The Adventures of Huckleberry Finn was originally published in 1884. **Mark Twain's** young adult novel describes the journey of a young boy (Huck Finn) as he traveled down the Mississippi River. Huck encountered thieves, murderers, and various adventures along the way. Although popular, this novel has encountered years of censorship for language as Twain describes Huck's friendship with Jim, a runaway slave. It is important to note that this book was recently reprinted with the offensive terms removed (www.ncrel.org/litweb/young/add.htm).

The Problem Novel

Problem novel is a term used to refer to a sub-genre of young adult literature that deals exclusively with an adolescent's first confrontation with a social or personal problem. The term was first used in the late 1960s to differentiate contemporary works like *The Outsiders* from earlier fiction for adolescents. Notable problem novels include: *The Catcher in the Rye (1951)*, *The Outsiders* (1967), and *The Pigman* (1968) (www.ncrel.org/litweb/young/add.htm).

The Outsiders is a coming-of-age (also categorized as a problem novel) by S. E. Hinton. First published in 1967 by Viking Press, Hinton was 15 when she started writing the novel, and 18 when it was published. The book follows two rival groups, the Greasers and the Socs (pronounced by the author as "so-shez," short for *Socials*), who are divided by their socioeconomic status.

The Pigman (1968) ,by **Paul Zindel**, tells the story of two dispossessed young people who find a

surrogate parent in Angelo Pignati, an Italian widower who has never had children. The main characters, fifteen-year-olds John and Lorraine, feel that the world is meaningless and that nothing is important. They can't please their parents, attending school is difficult; and to pass the time, they play pranks on unsuspecting people. They meet the Pigman in the process and Pignati shares his joy for life with them.

The Catcher in the Rye written in 1951 by **J.D. Salinger**, details 48 hours in the life of Holden Caulfield as he encounters a prostitute and her pimp, his girlfriend who refuses to marry him, his gay English teacher, and his younger sister who considers him a hero. The novel is the only novel-length work by J.D. Salinger, and its popularity has been colorful and controversial. J. D. Salinger died in 2010.

Other Popular Young Adult Authors

Secondary language arts and reading teachers should be able to demonstrate knowledge of a substantial body of young adult literature. See the web site: www.home.comcast.net/~antaylorl/alabestteens.html for a complete list of the 100 top books for young adult readers.

Robert Cormier, *Fade* (1988)

While growing up in the Great Depression of the 1930s, Paul discovers that he is a "fader," able to disappear at will. However, Paul finds this gift has a hidden curse. The fade, as well as his undying love for his Aunt Rosanna, hinders Paul's chance of ever being a normal and happy adult. Progressive generations possessing the gift of "fade" become increasingly unhappy,until the climactic showdown between Paul and his uncontrollable nephew, Ozzie, occurs (www.ncrel.org/litweb/young/add.htm).

Maya Angelou, *I Know Why the Caged Bird Sings* (1970 - 2014)

This novel is Maya Angelou's autobiographical story of survival in a harsh, racist world. Maya is very young when she and her brother are sent from their parents' house to live with their grandmother and uncle in Stamps, Arkansas. Life in Stamps is not easy. Grandmother (Momma) is a religious fundamentalist and harsh authoritarian who does not show love to her granddaughter.

Life in Stamps, Arkansas is full of racism and struggle. Maya's life becomes even more of a struggle when she goes to live with her mother in Texas. Maya's beautiful mother, Vivian, makes Maya feel ugly and awkward. Because of Vivian's lack of protectiveness, Mr. Freeman, who is Vivian's live-in boyfriend, rapes Maya at the age of eight. When Maya's uncles learn about the rape, they beat Freeman to death. After this double tragedy, Maya goes into a state of silence and emotional exile and is soon sent back to Stamps to live with Momma. In Arkansas, Maya finds that her color and her gender complicate her life, for she is treated as a second-class citizen. To prove her worth, she buries herself in books and graduates from high school with honors.

Chris Crutcher, *Ironman* (1996)

Bo Brewster constantly fights with his father and the conflict manifests in angry outbursts towards his football coach. Bo turns to the only adult he believes will listen-Larry King, the talk-show host. In his letters to Larry, Bo describes his quest for excellence on his own terms. "No more coaches for me," he tells the talk show icon, "no more dads. I'm going to be a triathlete, an Ironman." Bo is assigned to Mr. Nak's before-school anger management group in which he meets and falls in love with Shelly, a future American Gladiator, whose passion for physical challenge more than matches his.

Walter Dean Myers, *Hoops* (1981)

On the basketball court 17-year-old Greg "Slam" Harris is a winner. Off the court, however, his life is a mess. His grandmother is in the hospital on her death bed; his grades are bad, and his best friend is dealing drugs. Slam wants to go to college and then play for the NBA, so he gets help from Mtisha, who he begins to like. Slam's coach feels that he is a showoff, and does not play him. Slam befriends the old basketball coach at Latimer who not only gives him basketball tips but also gives him tips on life. Latimer high school must play Carver high school for first place team in the state tournament. It is a very tight game all the way but Latimer is victorious.

Gary Paulsen, *Woodsong* (1991)

Woodsong is an autobiographical story of Paulson's lifetime love of dog sledding and sled dogs. In the first part of the novel, Paulsen tells numerous accounts of the lessons about life he has learned from his dogs and the frozen land. The second part of the novel tells the story of a sled race across the Alaskan wilderness from Anchorage to Nome. The story is gripping with adventure and danger. Woodsong blends Paulsen's deep introspection with fast-paced action.

Science Fiction / Fantasy

Modern fantasy is rooted in traditional literature, and also has an identifiable author. Modern fantasy includes modern fairy tales like those from Hans Christian Andersen. In general, modern fantasy stories involve magic, the "quest," and/or "good versus evil." Fantasy creates an alternative universe, which operates within laws different than our own. Sub-genres of fantasy include animal fantasy, quest fantasy, machine fantasy, toy and doll fantasy, time fantasy, comic fantasy, high fantasy, and other world fantasy.

Harry Potter, a series of seven fantasy novels written by the British author **J. K. Rowling**, chronicle the adventures of the adolescent wizard Harry Potter and his best friends Ron Weasley and Hermione Granger, all of whom are students at Hogwarts School of Witchcraft and Wizardry.

The main theme concerns Harry's trials to overcome the evil wizard Lord Voldemort, who killed Harry's parents in a quest to conquer the wizarding world and subjugate non-magical people, the "Muggles."

Science fiction, or speculative fiction, speculates on what might happen in the future in our universe, so it has some basis in reality. The books in this genre address themes of love, justice, truth, loyalty, goodness, courage, wisdom, etc. Sometimes the line between fantasy and science fiction is blurred, with elements of both genres in the story.

The Twilight series by **Stephenie Meyer**, consists of three books: *Twilight*, Little, Brown, (2005), *New Moon*, (2006), and *Eclipse,* (2007), and is one of the most popular of the Young Adult genre, second only to Harry Potter.

The Hunger Games (2008) by American television writer and novelist **Suzanne Collins** is written in the voice of 16-year-old Katniss Everdeen, who lives in the post-apocalyptic nation of Panem, where the countries of North America once existed. The Capitol, a highly advanced metropolis, holds hegemony over the rest of the nation. The Hunger Games are an annual event in which one boy and one girl aged 12 to 18 from each of the twelve districts surrounding the Capitol are selected by lottery to compete in a televised battle to the death until only one person remains. *The Hunger Games* is the first novel in The Hunger Games trilogy, followed by *Catching Fire,* published in 2009, and *Mockingjay*, published in 2010.

Fairy Tales

Fairy tales are stories either created or strongly influenced by oral traditions. Their plots feature stark conflicts between good and evil, with magic and luck determining the usually happy endings. While each culture and geographic region of the world has its own body of folk tales and fairy tales that it considers "its own," certain themes and motifs tend to be repeated across many cultures and time periods. Universal human emotions such as love, hate, courage, kindness, and cruelty appear in bold, broad strokes on the canvas of fairy tales. In order for a work to be considered a fairy tale, it must contain most of the following characteristics:

- Begins with "Once Upon a Time," "Long, long ago," etc.
- Story setting is usually in a castle, forest, or town
- Story has good / nice characters and mean / bad characters
- Many of the characters are animals or members of royalty
- Story has an element of magic
  - Story has the numbers 3 or 7 in it
  - The main character has a problem which is solved in the story
  - Good wins and outsmarts bad
  - Ending is "happily ever after"

The Work of Hans Christian Anderson

The most well-known author of fairy tales is Danish writer, **Hans Christian Anderson.** Most of the world's fairy tales were told and retold for generations before they were written down, so now we can read fairy tales from almost any culture. When these stories are compared it is important to note the similar traits found in the stories from different parts of the world. From countries as distant and different as Egypt and Iceland similar fairy tales are told: Egypt, China, and Iceland have "Cinderella" stories, as do England, Korea, Siberia, France, and Vietnam. There are many versions of the Cinderella story, each with a unique telling which carries cultural information about the time and place the story was told. These popular stories appeal to everyone because truth prevails over deception, generosity is ultimately rewarded, hard work overcomes obstacles, and love, mercy and kindness are the greatest powers of all (www.kirjasto.sci.fi/hcanders.htm).

Hans Christian Andersen used informal language and style to disguise the didactic, moral teachings within his fairytales. Many of Andersen's fairy tales depict characters who gain happiness in life after suffering and conflict using some sort of magical element www.andersen.sdu.dk/index. Some of Anderson's best known fairy tales include *The Ugly Duckling, The Little Mermaid, Thumbelina, The Steadfast Tin Soldier, The Princess and the Pea, and The Emperor's New Clothes*.

References

Alverman, E. and Phelps, S. (1994). *Content Reading and Literacy: Succeeding in Today's Diverse Classrooms*. Allyn and Bacon: Boston.

Bradbury, M. & Ruland, R. (1992). *From Puritanism to Postmodernism: A History of American Literature*. Penguin, NY.

Coyle, M. & Peck, J. (2002). *A Brief History of English Literature*. Palgrave: London.
Coyle, M. & Peck, J. (2002). *A Brief History of English Literature*. Palgrave: London.

Davis, P, Harrison, G., Johnson, D., Smith, P , Crawford, J. (1995). *Western Literature in a World Context: The Ancient World through the Renaissance*. Volume One. St. Martin's Press: Texas.

Davis, et al. (1995). *Western Literature in a World Context: The Enlightenment through the Present*. Volume Two. St. Martin's Press: Texas.

Geok-lin Lim, S. (2000). Asian-American Literature: Leavening the Mosaic. U.S. Society and Values: Electronic *Journal of the Department of State*, Vol. 5, No.1, February. **http://www.usia.gov/journals/journals.htm**.

Graves, R. (1965). *Greek Gods and Hero*es. Random House: NY.

Hobson, G. (2000). Native American Literature: Remembrance Renewal. U.S. Society and Values: Electronic *Journal of the Department of State*, Vol. 5, No.1, February. http://www.usia.gov/journals/journals.htm.

Langer, J. (1995). *Envisioning Literature: Literary Understanding and Literature Instruction*. Teachers College Press: NY.

Miller, K. D. (2010). "Standing Up Naked and Turning Around Very Slowly." *Writers Talking*, Metcalf, J. & Wilkshire, C. (Ed). Porcupine's Quill.

Rosenblatt, L. M. (1983). The literary Transaction: Evocation and Response. *Theory into Practice*, V 21: 268-277.

Septo, R. B. (2000). Black American Literature at Year 2000: A New Presence. U.S. Society and Values: Electronic *Journal of the Department of State*, Vol. 5, No.1, February http://www.usia.gov/ journals/journals.htm.

Springer, C. B. (Ed.) (2000). U.S. Socie0J and values: Electronic Journal *of the Department of State*, Vol. 5, No.1, February. http://www.usia.gov/journals/ journals.htm.

Suarez, V. (2000) . Hispanic American Literature: Divergence and Commonality. U.S. Society and Values: Electronic *Journal of the Department of State*, Vol. 5, No.1, February. http://www.usia.gov/journals/journals.htm.

Tchudi, S. and Mitchell, D. (1999). *Exploring and Teaching the English Language Arts* (4th edition). Addison Wesley
Web Sites:
www.andersen.sdu.dk/index
www.ala.org
www.lnstar.com/literature/Pablo
www.nobelprize.org
www.plays.about.com/od/playwrights/a/brecht.htm.
www.home.comcast.net/~antaylorl/alabestteens.html
www.ncrel.org/litweb/young/add.htm
www.greekmythology.com
www.andersen.sdu.dk/index
www.readwritethink.org/.../fairy-tales
www.usc.edu/isd/archives/ethnicstudies/harlem.html
www.ac.wwu.edu
www.frederickdouglass.org
www.onlineliterature.com
http://www.cla.purdue.edu/

Practice Questions

1. Of the following, which group of writers popularized "existentialism"?

    a. Randall Jarrell, Richard Seridan, e.e. cummings
    b. Sartre, Franz Kafka, Fyodor Dostoyevsky
    c. Emily Dickinson, Charles Dickens, Langston Hughes
    d. Emily Bronte, Charlotte Bronte, Anne Bronte

B is correct.

2. Which of the following is the correct definition of the term "anachronism"?

    a. Having an unusual focus on time, clocks, and calendars
    b. Giving favors to one's political friends
    c. placing an event, person, or object out of its proper chronological place.
    d. placing events of a story out of correct time sequence.

C is correct.

3. Which of the following characteristic cannot be applied to the literary genre of "fairy tales"?
a. The story has an element of magic within the plot.
b. The main character has a problem or dilemma to solve.
c. Sometimes the story ends when evil triumphs over good.
d. The story always ends with a happy phrase such as: and they lived happily ever after.

C is correct. This is not a characteristic of a fairy tale. In fairy tales, good triumphs over evil.

4. Which of the following characteristics correctly describe young adult literature?

a. YA literature explores issues that can relate to the lives of young adults.
b. YA literature is often narrated in first person voice,
c. YA literature contains teen characters that are usually quite strong in beliefs and actions.
d. all of the above.

D is correct. This genre explores a wide range of societal issues that can relate to the lives of young adults. A good novel has the potential to illuminate concepts in history, science, mathematics, art, music, physical education, health, agriculture, or industrial arts. The works of fiction are often narrated in first person voice, and contain teen characters that are usually quite strong in beliefs and actions. Most novels run about 125 pages and are easily read.

5. Of the following, which contains a statement of "antithesis"?

    a. Many are called, but few are chosen.
    b. Abraham Lincoln was an extremely tall and gangly man.
    c. She spoke in a flattering manner, a true coquette.
    d. The old women, wrinkled and small, sat before the fire stirring the stew.

A is correct. Antithesis sets up a contrast; a thought is balanced with a contrasting thought.

6. A static character can be defined as _____.

    a. a character who changes in some way during the story.
    b. a character who exhibits few personality traits.
    c. a character who is very complex.
    d. a character who does not change during the course of the story.

D is correct.

7. Mr. White has selected works from the following set of authors to use in his 10th grade English / language arts class: Richard Rodriguez, N. Scott Momaday, Sandra Cisneros, and Toni Morrison. Of the following, which statement describes the best reason for selecting this set of authors?

    a. These works will help students identify with different authors from the various geographic regions of the United States.
    b. These works will help teach students to recognize resistance to government policies.
    c. These works will introduce students to the diversity of cultural experiences found within the United States.
    d. These works will help spark students' interest in the social changes that took place in the United States during the 1960s.

C is correct. An important reason for studying a wide variety of authors is to expose students to the diverse cultures found within the United States.

8. Read the following excerpt; then answer the question that follows:

> Lo, praise of the prowess of people-kings
> of spear-armed Danes, in days long sped,
> we have heard, and what honor the athelings won!
> Oft Scyld the Scefing from squadroned foes,
> from many a tribe, the mead-bench tore,
> awing the earls. Since erst he lay
> friendless, a foundling, fate repaid him:
> for he waxed under welkin, in wealth he throve,
> till before him the folk, both far and near,
> who house by the whale-path, heard his mandate,
> gave him gifts: a good king he!
> To him an heir was afterward born,
> a son in his halls, whom heaven sent
> to favor the folk, feeling their woe
> that erst they had lacked an earl for leader
> so long a while; the Lord endowed him,
> the Wielder of Wonder, with world's renown.
> Famed was this Beowulf: far flew the boast of him,
> son of Scyld, in the Scandian lands.
> So becomes it a youth to quit him well
> with his father's friends, by fee and gift,
> that to aid him, aged, in after days,
> come warriors willing, should war draw nigh,
> liegemen loyal: by lauded deeds
> shall an earl have honor in every clan.

The style and subject matter of this poem are most characteristic of works from which of the following movements in world literature?

    a. Classicism
    b. Romanticism
    c. Realism
    d. Modernism

A is correct. This is the prelude to the ancient epic, *Beowulf*.

9. Literary works by British writers of the romantic period such as William Wordsworth, William Blake, and Samuel Taylor Coleridge tend to share which of the following characteristics?

    a. a belief that many individuals are in turmoil between rational thought and emotional self-interest
    b. a belief that seeking one's inner truth and beauty will help ensure a deeper connection to others
    c. a belief that the natural world should be celebrated
    d. All of the above.

D is correct, all are characteristics of the romantic period of British literature.

10. Of the following writers, which is most closely associated with the "imagist" poetic movement?

a. Pablo Neruda
b. N. Scott Momaday
c. Ezra Pound
d. Ann Bradstreet

C is correct. During the Modern era of American literature, poets rebelled against the romanticized sentimentality found in works of previous decades. These poets expressed life in concrete terms using everyday language of the common man. Poets during this time presented new forms of writing using strong imagery. These poets were known as imagists. The leader of the imagist movement was Ezra Pound (1885-1972), *In a Station of the Metro, The River Merchant's Wife.*

11. Which of the following authors is best known for his "stream-of-consciousness" narrative combined with dialect to depict the conflict among tormented characters?

    a. Chinua Achebe
    b. William Carlos Williams
    c. Jonathan Edwards
    d. William Faulkner

D is correct. William Faulkner (1897-1962) used stream-of-consciousness narration along with dialect in his novels to depict the conflict among the tormented characters in his novels and short stories.

12. Read the following soliloquy from Shakespeare's *King Lear* spoken by Edmund and then choose the best interpretation of the passage:

> . . . Thou, nature, art my goddess; to thy law
> My services are bound. Wherefore should I
> Stand in the plague of custom, and permit
> The curiosity of nations to deprive me,
> For that I am some twelve or fourteen moonshines
>
> Lag of a brother? Why bastard? wherefore base?
> …Legitimate Edgar, I must have your land.
> Our father's love is to the bastard Edmund
> As to the legitimate. Fine word—"legitimate"!
> Well, my legitimate, if this letter speed,
> And my invention thrive, Edmund the base
> Shall top the legitimate. I grow; I prosper.
> Now, gods, stand up for bastards!

a. Deprived by his bastard birth of the respect and rank that he believes to be rightfully his, Edmund sets about forging personal prosperity through treachery and betrayals.
b. The repeated use of the epithet "legitimate" in reference to Edmund reveals Edgar's obsession with his brother's enviable status as their father's rightful heir.
c. Edgar wants recognition from his mother and father more than anything else.
d. Edgar and Edmund work toward becoming brothers in the true sense and set about getting that recognition by any means necessary.

A is correct. Edmund is plotting to gain legitimate status in his family and in society.

13. The works of Gabriel Garcia Marquez, Bertold Brecht, and Sidonie Gabrielle Colette are associated with:

    a. works written for adolescents
    b. romantic works dealing with courtly love
    c. contemporary works originally written in languages other than English
    d. writers from the "kitchen sink" era

C is correct.

Use the following poem, "**The Onset,**" by **Robert Frost** to answer the questions which follow:

The Onset
Always the same, when on a fated night
At last the gathered snow lets down as white
As may be in dark woods, and with a song
It shall not make again all winter long
Of hissing on the yet uncovered ground,
I almost stumble looking up and round,
As one who overtaken by the end
Gives up his errand, and lets death descend
Upon him where he is, with nothing done
To evil, no important triumph won,
More than if life had never been begun.
Yet all the precedent is on my side:
I know that winter death has never tried
The earth but it has failed: the snow may heap
In long storms an undrifted four feet deep
As measured against maple, birch, and oak,
It cannot check the peeper's silver croak;
And I shall see the snow all go down hill
In water of a slender April rill
That flashes tail through last year's withered brake
And dead weeds, like a disappearing snake.
Nothing will be left white but here a birch,
And there a clump of houses with a church.
(www.americanpoems.com/poets/robertfrost)

14. Which of the following best explains Robert Frost's use of **analogy** in the poem?

    a. The good and evil forces within man and the universe are constantly at battle.
    b. Man must learn to appreciate the rebirth of the earth during spring, the season that follows the bleak winter days.
    c. The trees, birds, and flowers that appear in the spring are all signs of God's grace and goodness upon the earth.
    d. The cold, harsh winter cannot prevail over the earth because spring always comes to bring the warmth and rebirth of plant and trees just as evil and death cannot prevail over the spirit of man.

D is correct. This answer choice describes Frost's use of analogy comparing death and winter and birth and spring.

15. Which of the following offers the best interpretation of the simile "like a disappearing snake," found in the lines below from **Robert Frost's** poem, **"The Onset"**?

> And I shall see the snow all go down hill
> In water of a slender April rill
> That flashes tail through last year's withered brake
> And dead weeds, like a disappearing snake.

a. All of the weeds and the snakes are destroyed by the harsh coldness of winter.
b. The melting snow forms streams which flow down the mountain in small curving streams.
c. The mountain trails are all filled with snakes after the winter snow melts.
d. The dead trees and weeds all lie hidden under the melting snow.

B is correct. This explanation correctly describes the meaning of Frost's simile when he compares the small streams which flow down the mountain through the brush to a snake moving through tall weeds.

16. Read the first two lines from the poem, The Tide Rises, the Tide Falls, written by Henry Wadsworth Longfellow below:

> The tide rises, the tide falls,
> The twilight darkens, the curlew calls.

The lines contain which of the following literary elements?
a. assonance
b. simile
c. catharsis
d. euphemism

A is correct. Assonance is the repetition of vowel sounds in nearby words.

17. Read the following excerpt from Maya Angelou's autobiographical account, *I know Why the Caged Bird Sings,* and then choose the correct interpretation of the passage.

> . . . If growing up is painful for the Southern Black
> girl, being aware of her displacement is the rust on
> the razor that threatens the throat. It is an
> unnecessary insult.

    a. Southern Black girls are often assaulted by others using razors.
    b. The rusty razor in Angelou's house is a result of the extreme poverty found in the Southern United States.
    c. Angelou is afraid of being cut by a rusty razor.
    d. Angelou likens the experience of growing up black in the segregated American South as to having a razor at one's throat.

D is correct. The metaphor compares the harshness of living as a Black girl in the south with having her throat cut by a sharp razor.

18. Of the following, which sentence contains a **euphemism**?

    a. Mark is a tall, handsome man with a quick wit.
    b. Bill wanted to join the choir, but he was vocally challenged.
    c. Sue, the new charge nurse, walked the floor to inspect the care provided by the novice nurses.
    d. I can't tell you how happy I am that you have finally arrived!

B is correct. "vocally challenged" is a polite way of saying that Bill did not have a good singing voice.

19. Of the following, which sentence contains metonymy?

    a. Last night, Bill lounged lazily by the lipid pool.
    b. Hollywood presented the Golden Globe Awards in a televised ceremony.
    c. She, being brand new and all, was confused by the company's new employee booklet.
    d. During the storm, the ship creaked, rattled, and rolled in the high seas.

B is correct. The term "Hollywood" was used to represent the U. S. film industry.

Domain II: Chapter 7

Competency 7: Responding to Literature
The beginning teacher:

- Demonstrates knowledge of various types of responses to literary texts (e.g., experiential, aesthetic, pragmatic) and encourages a variety of responses in students. B. Knows strategies for motivating students to read literature and for promoting their appreciation of the value of literature.

- Knows how to draw from wide reading in American, British, world and young adult literature to guide students to explore and select independent reading based on their individual needs and interests.

- Knows how to promote students' interest in literature and facilitate their reading and understanding.

- Uses technology to promote students' engagement in and comprehension of literature.

- Knows strategies for creating communities of readers and for promoting conversations about literature and ideas.

- Understands and teaches students strategies to use for analyzing and evaluating a variety of literary texts, both classic and contemporary.

- Applies effective strategies for helping students view literature as a source for exploring and interpreting human experience.

- Applies effective strategies for engaging students in exploring and discovering the personal and societal relevance of literature.

- Promotes students' understanding of relationships among literary works from various times and cultures.

- Promotes students' ability to analyze how literary elements and devices contribute to meaning and to synthesize and evaluate interpretations of literary texts.

- Knows effective strategies for teaching students to formulate, express and support responses to various types of literary texts.

- Demonstrates an understanding of informal and formal procedures for monitoring and assessing students' comprehension of literary texts.

- Knows how to use assessment results to plan and adapt instruction that addresses students' strengths, needs and interests and that builds on students' current skills to increase their proficiency in comprehending literary texts.

Key Terms

Aesthetic
Cause / Effect
Compare / Contrast
Definition
Electronic Resources
Efferent
Historical Categorization
Literature Circles
Mimetic Approach
Objective (form or structural) Analysis
Pragmatic Analysis
Social and Historical Analysis
Time Order or Sequence
Verbal Representation Analysis

Literary Response

Reading and responding to literature presents an opportunity for students to explore life from different perspectives, thereby providing insight into a wide variety of human experiences. Students need opportunities to seek connections between the story and their personal experiences and need time for classroom discussion in order to reflect and make sense of the new information.

In exploring the world through good literature, a student's cognitive activity cannot be separated from emotional involvement. Louis Rosenblatt (1983) purported that a reader's thoughts and feelings in response to a literary selection should be considered very important components of literary interpretation. All texts, whether literary or informational, require affective as well as intellectual responses from its readers. Rosenblatt (1983) describes these two levels of response as **efferent** and **aesthetic** responses. When the reader is responding in an **efferent** way, the focus is on what has been learned from the ideas and information encountered in the text. When the reader is responding in an **aesthetic** way, the reader focuses on personal feelings and attitudes toward the reading selection.

It is important to remember when asking students to respond to a reading selection that a balance exist between practice and application of skills and the pleasurable, aesthetic enjoyment of reading a great work of literature. Most of us have experienced the heavy-handed use of literature in the classroom where great works are reduced to drudgery by teachers assigning questions and papers that wring the life out of a great work of literature. Teachers should encourage students to explore reading selections (both aesthetic and efferent) by requiring them to participate in a wide variety of student-centered lessons involving active learning and higher order thinking (Rosenblatt, 1983).

The five basic approaches to interpreting literature include: **verbal representation, social and historical analysis, pragmatic analysis, objective (form or structural) analysis,** and **historical categorization within the canon.**

Verbal Representation Analysis
The most basic way to think of literature is as a verbal representation of the real world (Guerin, 1999; http://www.rlwclarke.net). Literary works, especially prose fiction, are thought to be **realistic** if they hold a mirror up to 'life.' The realism of particular characters, their likeness to real human actions, is often at the crux of such concerns. In technical terms, this is called the **'mimetic'** approach to criticism. In order to encourage this type of analysis, the teacher may pose a question such as: In the short story, *Shooting an Elephant,* how would you describe George Orwell's depiction of the police officer's frustration under British colonial rule?

Social and Historical Analysis

When conducting a social and historical analysis of a work, students are asked to think about the literary work and determine what it reveals about the author, place, and time (the **social and historical context**) during which the author lived. Literature, from this point of view, is a form of self-expression and literary works (especially lyric poems) are seen as windows into the soul of their writers. Social and historical analysis is also known as the **expressive** approach to literary criticism (Guerin, 1999; http://www.rlwclarke.net). In order to encourage this type of analysis, the teacher may pose a question such as: In the poem, *The Rime of the Ancient Mariner*, how does Coleridge reveal his personal views as well as his views of the world in which he lived?

Pragmatic Analysis

When analyzing a work using the pragmatic approach, students are asked to ponder whether or not literature may have a positive or negative effect upon those who are exposed to it. Can literature corrupt the reader, resulting in anti-social or unlawful behavior? Does literature need to be censored? On the other hand, can literature also have a positive impact on the reader? This type of literary analysis, known as the **pragmatic** approach to criticism, requires students to look at a literary work with a broad perspective. In order to encourage this type of analysis, the teacher may pose a question such as: Should young adult novels such as J. D. Salinger's *Cather in the Rye* be banned? Could Salinger's work negatively influence the future actions of a reader?

Objective (form or structural) Analysis

When participating in objective (form or structural) analysis of a literary work, students are asked to focus on how a work is structured or arranged by the author. Questions may focus on the diction of the work (literary elements such as simile or metaphor), the structure of the plot, the genre (comedy, tragedy, prose, etc.), or the narration / point of view of the work.

Before most authors begin writing, they usually have a definitive **purpose** for writing and usually have chosen a structure or pattern of organization for their writing. They may wish to convey an opinion, explain an idea, describe an event, entertain, provide a sequence of events or steps, provide reasons or rational for an idea, etc. English / language arts teachers must be able to demonstrate knowledge of types of text structure and provide students with strategies to facilitate comprehension of these structures.

When conducting an objective analysis of a literary work, a student might wish to think of **organizational patterns** as the backbone or skeleton of a reading selection. The following are examples of the patterns of organization that are found most frequently in non-fiction writing (Smith, 1993):

> **Time order or Sequence** - the selection usually contains signal words such as *first, second, third, next, after, finally*, etc.

Compare / Contrast-the selection usually contains signal words such as *on the other hand, similarly, however, in the same way,* etc.

Definition - the entire selection is devoted to explaining a concept such as *beauty, freedom, democracy, terrorism, nuclear fission,* etc.

Cause/effect - the selection usually contains signal words such as *because, consequently,* etc.

In order to encourage this type of analysis, the teacher may pose a question such as: Describe the plot structure of the Charles Dickens's novel, *Great Expectations*. In Shakespeare's *King Lear*, how does the plot structure support the audience's emotional reaction of pity and fear?"

Historical Categorization Analysis

When participating in the historical or categorical analysis of a literary work, students are asked to analyze the works with regard to its place in literary history. That is, students are asked to analyze how and where the literary work fits within the canon. Literature has a history (in the sense that Chaucer precedes Shakespeare who precedes Wordsworth, and so on), and each writer works during a particular period of that history. Critics interested in literature from this angle try to historically categorize authors (e.g. Shakespeare is normally classified as a Renaissance writer while Wordsworth is deemed a Romantic), and study whether the literature produced during a given period shares certain characteristics (Guerin, 1999; http://www.rlwclarke.net). In order to encourage this type of analysis, the teacher may pose questions such as:

- What characteristics are seen in the poetry of a Shakespeare in order for it to be classified as Renaissance literature?

- What "romantic" characteristics are found within Wordsworth's poetry?"

- Chinua Achebe, (*Things Fall Apart*) purports that Joseph Conrad's THE HEART OF DARKNESS fails to grant full humanity to the Africans. This perspective is shaped by a postcolonial literary theory that presupposes a history of exploitation and racism. How does this post-colonial African writer, Achebe, resist the influence of the established canon?

Teaching Students to Respond Literature

Deciding the best strategies and methods to use when asking students to respond to literature is a difficult task. Rosenblatt (1983) suggests that reading is an interaction between the reader and the text and that the reader gains meaning from the text depending upon the stance or purpose that the reader chooses. Rosenblatt (1983) maintains that the act of reading literature requires both efferent and aesthetic responses. Teachers need to teach students to read for both efferent and aesthetic purposes; however, with literature, emphasis should be placed on aesthetic reading.

Judith Langer's (1995) research suggests that in order for students to engage with literature, they must envision the ideas and characters within a text. These images are subject to change as the ideas and characters unfold and new ideas are revealed within a story. These sense-making and meaning-making interactions between the reader and the text create true understanding. When students are involved with a piece of literature they want time to make sense of it, discuss its content, and connect it to their lives (Tchudi & Mitchell, 1999).

Criticism of literature is also a natural part of interacting with literature since students read, react to, and articulate their responses to literature. Criticism of literature is simply a part of the literary analysis process. Four stances that students can take when responding to literature include (Langer, 1995):

- **Initial responses to Literature-Gathering Ideas**
  During this lesson teachers can ask students to respond to their first impressions of the text and the characters. Do they feel they are beginning to like / dislike the character?

- **Interpreting literature-Being Immersed in the Text**
  During this lesson teachers can encourage students to continue to develop understanding and fill in the gaps for understanding. Teachers can ask students to think about the character's motives, how the character might be feeling, or which places in the story are hard to understand.

- **Relating to literature-Gaining Insight into the Text**
  During this lesson teachers can encourage students to focus on what they have learned about themselves from reading the text. Teachers can ask students to discuss whether they would do something that a character did, or explain if they agree or disagree with a character's view on an issue. They can write a letter to a character explaining what they learned from that character.

- **Analyzing Literature**
  During this lesson, students are usually ready to look at the bigger picture of analysis. Teachers may ask students why this piece of literature is significant. Why they agree or disagree with other interpretations? Which novel made a strong impact on them? What did the author do to make this kind of impact?

Teaching Strategies for Exploring Literature: Literature Circles

Literature circles have become a reliable, successful, instructional approach to engage high school readers with quality literature. A **literature circle** is a students' equivalent of an adult book club, but with greater structure, expectation and rigor. The aim is to encourage thoughtful discussion and a love of reading in young people. The true intent of literature circles is to allow students to practice and develop the skills and strategies of good readers (DaLie, 2001; https://secure.ncte.org/library).

Planning Literature Circles:
- Plan time for reading and discussing the book (4-5 weeks, 2-3 times each week)
- Select and have on hand enough titles and copies to support groups of 4-6 students
- Devise a check-out system for books and materials
- Quantify assignments (i.e. answer 5 discussion questions, create 2 illustrations, define 10 vocabulary words, etc.)

Prepare students for Literature Circles:
- Explain how literature circles work; preview selected three or four books (conduct a book talk for each)
- review student roles and responsibilities (discussion leader; illustrator; literary luminary; vocabulary enricher; connector; summarizer; travel tracer; investigator). Some teachers use a short story to "practice" the various roles
- Allow each student to select a book from those selected and discussion/ work group members
- Discuss appropriate group behavior and listening skills

First Meeting Day:
- Students meet in groups to select roles and discuss responsibilities
- Groups plan a reading schedule (number of pages per week). Record dates on bookmark index card
- Create and have students complete a "Literature Circle Responsibility Sheet" based on selected roles. Define the responsibilities of each role.

Monitoring Literature Circle Discussions: (teacher facilitates groups)
- Teacher circulates among groups and ask individuals about the work they have prepared for their group.
- If students are struggling, help them problem solve and negotiate issues
- Students must understand that no one is to dominate group discussions (practice listening skills and discuss appropriate group behavior)
- Allow students time to self-assess (responses to assignment sheets; survey questions, etc.)

Assessing Literature Circles:
- Varied assessments are appropriate: (i.e. group participation; group project; check

lists; peer assessment)
- Final assessment should be based on a combination of individual and group assignments.

Meeting the Needs of Diverse Students

English teachers must strive to broaden the selection of books in their curriculum in order to use books that represent cultural diversity. In fact, literature can complement the study of any content area. Many social studies teachers have included literature in their course requirements; literature complements the study of history and many contemporary social issues by dramatizing and personalizing issues and events.

Electronic Resources for Literary Analysis

In order to expand student knowledge of literary analysis and support research skills, numerous reference databases are easily found on the internet through major libraries across the state and nation (http://www.gale.cengage.com). These databases have been compiled for student use and are built on various author and literary criticism journals including:

Contemporary Authors
Contemporary Literary Criticism Select
Dictionary of Literary Terms
Children's Literature Review
Classical and Medieval Literature Criticism
Drama Criticism
Drama for Students
Literature from 1400 to 1800
Nineteenth-Century Literature Criticism
Literature of Developing Nations for Students
Literature and Its Times
Novels for Students
Poetry Criticism
Poetry for Students
Shakespearean Criticism
Shakespeare for Students
Short Story Criticism
Short Stories for Students
Twentieth-Century Literary Critics

Other Electronic Sources

In addition, Gale Publishing Service offers an easy-to-use source for librarians, teachers, students, and other researchers entitled, *Something about the Author*. This critically acclaimed series covers more than 12,000 individuals, ranging from established award winners to authors and illustrators who are just beginning their careers. Each volume in the series also provides illustrated biographical profiles of approximately 75 children's authors and artists. Entries typically cover: personal life, career, writings, works in progress, adaptations, and additional sources. A cumulative author index is included in each odd-numbered volume (http://*www.gale.cengage.com).*

References

DaLie, S. (2001). Students becoming real readers: Literature circles in high school English classes. In Ericson, B. (ed). *Teaching Reading in High School English Classes*. NCTE stock number 51868-3050.

Guerin, W. et. al. (1999). *Critical Approaches to Literature* (4th edition). Galaxy: Oxford University Press.

Langer, J. (1995). *Envisioning Literature: Literary Understanding and Literature Instruction*. Teachers College Press.

Rosenblatt, L. M. (1983). The Literary Transaction: Evocation and Response. *Theory into Practice*, V. 21: 268-277.

Tchudi, S. & Mitchell, D. (1999). *Exploring and Teaching the English Language Arts* (4th edition). Addison Wesley Longman, Inc.: NY.

Smith, B. D. (1993). *Bridging the Gap*. (4th Edition), Harper Collins, NY.

http://www.rlwclarke.net
http://www.gale.cengage.com
https://secure.ncte.org/library/NCTEFiles/Resources/Books/Sample/51868chap07.pdf

Practice Questions

1. Which of the following types of literary analysis would best be applied to gain a greater appreciation of Arthur Miller's play, *Death of a Salesman*?

a. Social and historical analysis
b. Form analysis
c. Structure analysis
d. Verbal representation analysis

A is correct. From the earliest plays Arthur Miller wrote as a student to his latest works in the 1990s, social and political pressures and their effects on human values and morality have remained Miller's central concern. His most effective exploration of these themes occurs in his play, *Death of a Salesman*, long recognized as a classic of American theater.

2. In addition to comprehension questions concerning main idea, details, inferences, and vocabulary,
Mrs. Garcia, an 11th grade English / language arts teacher, asks students to respond to reading selections in aesthetic ways. Which of the following statements best explains the primary reason this instructional strategy is effective in increasing student understanding and comprehension?

   a. Students of high school age should be allowed to express their opinions and ideas in order to ensure effective psychosocial maturation.
   b. A reader's thoughts and feelings in response to a literary selection are considered very important components of literary interpretation.
   c. Introducing the fine arts in response to good literature may accommodate students with diverse learning styles.
   d. It is important that students learn to interpret literature on varying levels: literal, interpretive and critical.

B is correct. This answer provides the rational for requiring aesthetic responses to reading.

3. Of the following, which best describes the mimetic approach to critical analysis?

    a. Students are asked to describe or determine the reasons for the character's actions as if they were in a real world setting.
    b. Students are asked to analyze how and where the literary work fits within the literary canon.
    c. Students are asked to analyze the structure of the plot within the work.
    d. Students are asked to determine the genre of the work.

A is correct. Literary works, especially prose fiction, are thought to be realistic if they hold a mirror up to 'life.' The realism of particular characters, their likeness to real human actions, is often at the crux of such concerns; this is called the 'mimetic' approach to criticism.

4. To gain a greater appreciation of *Anne Frank: The Diary of a Young Girl*, which of the following types of literary analysis / criticism would best be applied?

    a. Pragmatic Analysis
    b. Objective (form and structure) Analysis
    c. Social and Historical Analysis
    d. Time Order Analysis

C is correct. During social and historical analysis, students are asked to think about the literary work and determine what it reveals about the author and, in addition, the place and time (the social and historical context) during which the author lived. Literature, from this point of view, is a form of self-expression and literary works are seen as windows into the soul of their writers.

DOMAIN III:

Chapter 8: The Writing Process

Chapter 9: Writing Effectively

DOMAIN III — WRITTEN COMMUNICATION

Competency 008: The teacher understands and promotes writing as a recursive, developmental, integrative and ongoing process and provides students with opportunities to develop competence as writers.

- Understands recursive stages in the writing process (e.g., prewriting, drafting, conferencing, revising, editing, publishing) and provides students with explicit instruction, meaningful practice and effective feedback as they engage in all phases of the writing process.
- Understands writing as a process that allows students to construct meaning, examine thinking, reflect, develop perspective, acquire new learning and influence the world around them.
- Applies writing conventions, including sentence and paragraph construction, spelling, punctuation, usage and grammatical expression, and provides students with explicit instruction in using them during the writing process.
- Applies criteria for evaluating written work and teaches students effective strategies for evaluating their own writing and the writings of others.
- Structures peer conference opportunities that elicit constructive, specific responses and that promote students' writing development.
- Understands and promotes the use of technology in all phases of the writing process and in various types of writing, including writing for research and publication.
- Applies strategies for helping students develop voice and style in their writing.
- Demonstrates an understanding of informal and formal procedures for monitoring and assessing students' writing competence.
- Uses assessment results to plan and adapt instruction that addresses students' strengths, needs and interests and that builds on students' current skills to increase their writing proficiency.

Competency 009: The teacher understands effective writing and teaches students to write effectively in a variety of forms and for various audiences, purposes and contexts.

- Understands and teaches the distinguishing features of various forms of writing (e.g., reflective essay, autobiographical narrative, editorial, report, memorandum, summary/abstract, résumé, play, short story, poem).
- Applies and teaches skills and strategies for writing effectively in a variety of forms and for a variety of audiences, purposes and contexts.
- Understands and teaches how a writer's purpose and audience define appropriate language, writing style and text organization.
- Provides students with explicit instruction, meaningful practice opportunities and effective feedback as the students create different types of written works.

- Promotes students' ability to compose effectively (e.g., organizing ideas to ensure coherence, logical progression and support; using precise language to communicate ideas clearly and concisely; writing in a voice and style appropriate to audience and purpose).

- Provides students with professionally written, student-written and teacher- written models of writing.
- Demonstrates knowledge of factors that influence student writing (e.g., writer's experiences, situational context in which writing occurs, interactions within the learning/writing community, features of various written forms).
- Analyzes and teaches the use of literary devices (e.g., imagery, tone, dialogue, characterization, irony, figurative language) in writing.
- Teaches students skills and strategies for using writing as a tool for reflection, exploration, learning, problem solving and personal growth.
- Understands and teaches writing as a tool for inquiry, research and learning.
- Teaches students to evaluate critically the sources they use for their writing.
- Provides instruction about plagiarism, academic honesty and integrity as applied to students' written work and their presentation of information from different sources, including electronic sources.
- Understands and teaches students the importance of using acceptable formats for communicating research results and documenting sources (e.g., manuals of style such as the Modern Language Association Handbook [MLA style], the Publication Manual of the American Psychological Association [APA style], and The Chicago Manual of Style [Chicago style]).

Domain III: Chapter 8

Competency 008: The Writing Process

The beginning teacher:
- Understands recursive stages in the writing process (e.g., prewriting, drafting, conferencing, revising, editing, publishing) and provides students with explicit instruction, meaningful practice and effective feedback as they engage in all phases of the writing process.
- Understands writing as a process that allows students to construct meaning, examine thinking, reflect, develop perspective, acquire new learning and influence the world around them.
- Applies writing conventions, including sentence and paragraph construction, spelling, punctuation, usage and grammatical expression, and provides students with explicit instruction in using them during the writing process.
- Applies criteria for evaluating written work and teaches students effective strategies for evaluating their own writing and the writings of others.
- Structures peer conference opportunities that elicit constructive, specific responses and that promote students' writing development.
- Understands and promotes the use of technology in all phases of the writing process and in various types of writing, including writing for research and publication.
- Applies strategies for helping students develop voice and style in their writing.
- Demonstrates an understanding of informal and formal procedures for monitoring and assessing students' writing competence.
- Uses assessment results to plan and adapt instruction that addresses students' strengths, needs and interests and that builds on students' current skills to increase their writing proficiency.

Key Terms

Absolutes

Active Voice

Analytical evaluation

Appositive linking adverbials

APP

Ask.com

Checklists

Clausal modifier

Coherence

Cohesion

Colloquial style

Complex sentence

Complex subordinating conjunctions

Compound sentence

Concrete subjects

Conferences

Contrast / concession linking adverbials

Convergent

Coordinating conjunction

Dependent clause

Diction

Divergent

Editing

Enumerative linking adverbials

Evaluation

Formal style

Holistic evaluation

Idea List

Independent clause

Linking adverbials

Passive voice

Peer editing

Phrasal modifier

Portfolio

Prewriting

Research

Result / inference linking adverbials

Revising

Searchopolis

Self-evaluation

Semicolon

Simple sentence

Simple subordinating conjunctions

Style

Subordinate conjunction

Summative linking adverbials

Technology

Tone

Transition linking adverbials

Voice

Word processing software

Writer's workshop

Writing process

Yahooligans

Writing / Composing Processes

The philosophical approach of teaching writing as a process was influenced by the work of Donald Graves (1983). Graves (1983) defines the process of writing by referring to what students do during its occurrence. The stages of the writing process include: prewriting, drafting, revising / editing, and sharing / publishing. These stages do not necessarily occur in a set sequence for individual writers. Graves (1983) explains that writing is a recursive process; that is, writers do not always do things in the same order. For example, a student may create a great ending for a story first, and then be inspired to finish the rest of the work.

Most importantly, Graves (1983) suggests that students need to have multiple ways to start writing and must be led to realize that first drafts should be adaptable and flexible. Students should be provided opportunities to take chances with their writing through experimentation with ideas and words. Teachers should work to build a supportive environment in which creativity can flourish, instead of hosting a classroom with static, routine steps for writing development.

Writing is often a difficult task that involves risk-taking; students should be allowed to discover how to write about their world in a supportive environment. English / language arts teachers must understand that using the writing process in the classroom allows students to construct meaning, examine their thinking, reflect upon their work, develop perspectives, and acquire new learning.

The Classroom as a Writer's Workshop
Teachers have found that students benefit greatly from a classroom arranged as a writer's workshop. Recommended texts to help English / language arts transform their classrooms into writers' workshops include: ***The Art of Teaching Writing*** by **Lucy Calkins**, ***Writing: Teachers and Children at Work*** and ***A Fresh Look at Writing*** by **Donald Graves,** and **Nancie Atwell's** ***Reading and Writing In the Middle***. These books are filled with anecdotes, student writing samples, and classroom strategies for adapting and sustaining a writers' workshop model.

The writer's workshop classroom exemplifies the social constructivist approach to learning developed by Lev Vygotsky in the late 1800s. Vygotsky emphasized the importance of social interaction in learning. Teachers should be on hand to "**scaffold**" students to a higher level of learning through social interaction. Students should be allowed to interact with their peers when sharing their writing during the planning, revision, and editing stages. The student's role is to explore, discuss, and write about a topic of choice. It is through the exploration and practice of writing that students learn to develop their "writer's" voice.

The teacher's role also involves modeling and explaining the **metacognitive processes** involved in writing. Teacher-student and student-student interactions are frequent as students work together with others to rethink, revise, and edit their work. Finally, in the writers' workshop classroom, grammar and writing mechanics are taught in the context of the student's work when needed. For example, after grading a set of essays, a teacher discovers that many students in the class have made comma errors in their work. The next day, the teacher begins class with a mini-lesson on comma usage. The teacher uses examples from the student's work to emphasize the lesson's objective.

Organizing the Classroom as a Writer's Workshop

- The writing session begins with a mini lesson on grammar or mechanics, concept, or skill needed by the students.
- The workshop is followed by a brief planning period in which the students plan their day.
- The majority of time is reserved for writing; the teacher acts as facilitator.
- The teacher may hold brief conferences with individual students during this time.
- The end of the period is reserved for sharing of work with peers on idea development, revision, or editing.
- Assessment is usually ongoing (use of portfolio encouraged); students work to achieve their preset writing goals and conduct periodic self-assessment on how their work matches the goals.
- The writer's workshop works well in a heterogeneous group of students with varied abilities.

Stages of the Writing Process

Prewriting

The first stage of the writing process, prewriting, is more than giving instructions to students. It is any activity which motivates students to write or encourages creative thought before or during writing. Prewriting exercises can move writers from the thinking, brainstorming stage to the independent writing stage. During this stage of the writing process students may want to participate in "freewriting," a technique which allows students to write down ideas without interruption of the flow of thought. Another effective strategy during this stage is the use of "authors' circles," students sit together in small groups and discuss their ideas and receive feedback.

English / language arts teachers should choose writing prompts that are not convergent to one answer or one point, but rather encourage creative, divergent thinking and writing. Teachers should model the prewriting stage aloud for students and allow time for students to share prewriting ideas. During prewriting, teachers should use multiple strategies as they guide students in choosing a topic and then narrowing down the topic.

Prewriting involves:
- Choosing a topic
- Organizing thoughts
- Finding a direction
- Deciding on a form
- Redirecting writing
- Motivating writing
- Building self-confidence

Writing / Drafting

After the prewriting strategies, students move to the next stage of the writing process, the drafting or writing stage. During this stage, students should be encouraged to work independently and quietly with ample time allowed for thinking and writing. While writing their drafts, students should concentrate on the organization of their thoughts as they express their ideas on paper. The teacher should model this process by writing quietly during this time. Students should be encouraged to stay on task as they develop fluency, voice, style, and coherence in their writing.

During the drafting stage, students need to develop their own voice and style within their writing. Just like the spoken voice, a writer's voice and style change depending upon the situation or audience. Students would not speak to the school principal with the same voice and style they would speak to their friends at school. Similarly, when students are writing a narrative assignment, they do not use the same voice and style as when writing a research project. Choice of words, verb tense, sentence structure, and use of literary elements all contribute to a writer's voice and style. When helping students develop their own voice and style in their writing, English / language arts teachers can pose a variety of writing assignments in order to allow students opportunities to vary the style and voice of their writing to match the audience and purpose of the assignment.

Writing / drafting involves:
Drafting of ideas
Staying on task
Developing fluency and coherence
Developing voice and style

Revising / Editing

After students' drafts are written, students should have the opportunity to work with a partner or small group of peers to revise their work. This stage of the writing process requires that students look back at their work to ensure that the overall thoughts and ideas are coherent and orderly. Students can accomplish this task by reading their work out loud to check for clarity or by asking another student to read their work and offer suggestions for improvement.

It is important to note that a revision of ideas should take place before the editing stage. Several questions on the teacher certification exam will ask the examinee to clarify the difference between revision and editing.

During the revision stage the student is asked to examine the arrangement of ideas in the work or the relationship among the ideas presented. Editing involves checking the grammar and mechanics of the work for misusage or misspelled words. During the revision and editing stage of the writing process, teachers should provide a learning environment that is nonthreatening and risk-free, and should promote the attitude that revision and editing is a valid and important step in the writing process.

Routman (2000) found that teachers who have the strongest writing workshop classrooms produce the best spellers. That is, students best learn to spell when teachers concentrate on spelling not only as a component in the process of reading and writing, but also as a separate activity that takes into account students' needs, abilities and interests. When modeling editing, teachers should provide specific examples from student work whenever possible. After allowing time for students to complete their revisions and edits, students should then rewrite the final draft to get their work ready for sharing.

Conferences should take place during revision time; teachers and students can meet together briefly to talk about revision suggestions. During conferencing teachers are able to informally evaluate student progress using quick checklists or observation rubrics. Teachers should sit near or next to the student and engage the student in conversation, and the student should hold the composition while the teacher listens. Teachers should ask student-centered questions such as:

- **Do you think this part would be clearer if you . . .?**
- **Does this part lead the reader to the next part?**

A two or three minute personal conference between the teacher and student has been found to be very motivating for students to improve their work before they submit their final drafts.

Revision / Editing involves:
- Providing a risk-free environment
- Modeling correct revision and editing practices
- Revising for coherent, orderly meaning
- Revising for organization and clarity
- Editing and proofreading for mechanical errors
- Conferencing with the teacher or peers
- Using portfolio folder for work

Sharing / Publishing
Students should be encouraged to share their work in a variety of ways. Class newsletters, class books, journal entries, essays, and poetry can all be shared with others. Teachers should make every effort to encourage authentic writing assignments to enable students to link classroom learning to real-world assignments such as: submitting opinion and editorial letters to local government officials, researching family biographies, investigating causes for local environmental problems, conducting interview and opinion polls, and serving on the student newspaper staff.

Sharing / Publishing involves:
- Publishing and displaying finished work
- Evaluating and grading finished work

Using Technology to Enhance the Writing Process

English / language arts teachers must be able to demonstrate and promote the use of technology in all phases of the writing process. Computers and other technology tools help motivate students as writers. Julie Wood's (2000) article entitled, A *Marriage Waiting to Happen: Computers and Process Writing*, provides numerous suggestions for teachers who are interested in using computers in ways that enhance the process of writing.

During the prewriting stage, some students have had success recording their ideas into a computer as a way to rehearse before beginning to write. Then, students are able to listen to their own ideas and decide which ones to incorporate into their compositions (Wood, 2000).

Using art as an entry point for writing can be especially effective for writers. Students can get started on writing by creating art using computers. Vygotsky reminds us that students' drawings tap into their narrative impulses and can be translated into written pieces. Software with built-in art tools, such as **Apple Works**, can help students create artwork and write about it all in one document. Alternatively, students can scan in images that hold special meaning and use them as the centerpiece of their writing. Images might include a photograph from a family album, a postcard, or some other artifact that evokes a time or place (Wood, 2000).

Teachers who have access to **cameras** can send small groups of students off on a photographic "shoot." Students should be encouraged to capture images of their world that they can then transform into a photo essay. If a digital camera is used, the photo essay can be elegantly formatted using computer software (Wood, 2000).

Students might enjoy creating **graphic organizers** using **Inspiration Software**, a program that makes it easy to design and manipulate representations of ideas. An added plus is that with a single mouse click, Inspiration can convert a graphic organizer into a traditional outline (Wood, 2000; www.inspiration.com/diagrams/ed/ediagram.html).

During the writing / drafting stage students are better able to extend their writing if they have opportunities to organize their ideas. Writers' notebooks offer a way of doing this; in fact, notebooks can be used for all sorts of writing purposes to capture drawings and ideas for stories, or revise current work. In addition to notebooks, word processing software can lend an organizational framework to student's works in progress. Students can keep personalized electronic folders to accomplish the same goal. They can give their documents titles such as "ideas for stories, "cool facts to write about," and "writing right now." Then students can save their work either on a personal device or on a network workspace (Wood, 2000).

Using Technology to Aid Student Research

For research assignments that link the English / language arts classroom to the content areas, computers and the internet offer a wealth of information. For example, websites sponsored by National Geographic's *Picture Atlas of the World* offer rich resources-maps, facts, and video clips about countries all over the world.

The Internet vastly increases the number of resources students can utilize when exploring nonfiction topics. Careful investigations using student-friendly search engines such as **Yahooligans, Ask.com**, and **Searchopolis** can lead to appropriate content on topics from astronomy to quantum physics (Wood, 2000).

APPS for High School English / Language Arts Teachers

The term "app" is a shortening of the term "application software". It has become very popular and in 2010 was listed as "Word of the Year" by the American Dialect Society. In information technology, an application is a computer program designed to help people perform an activity. If you're a teacher with an iPad, you've probably already discovered lots of fun apps, as well as a few that can boost classroom productivity. Listed below find apps currently recommended for English teachers

- **Note Taker HD** - An app for writing handwritten notes, diagrams, etc.
- **CourseNotes** - Take notes in class and keep them organized by subject area.
- **MindNode** - Mind mapping, brainstorming, organization.
- **iThoughtsHD** - A mind map tool for the iPad
- **Inspiration Maps** - This App is ideal for brainstorming, analyzing, and organizing information. If you are familiar with the desktop version of Inspiration, this is a great port to the iPad
- **Evernote** - Evernote turns the iPad into an extension of your brain, helping you remember anything and everything that happens in your life.
- **Stick It – Sticky Notes with Bump™** - Sticky notes you can share with other iPad Users
- **WritePad for iPad** - WritePad lets you take notes in your own handwriting with an iPad stylus, pen, or even your finger
- **Writing Prompts** - This writing prompt generator app uses pictures, colors, words, genres and different types of writing to provide creative inspiration for writers and writing students. The app also includes a database of 600 creative writing prompts in the form of quotes, story openers and writing exercises that can be used to jump-start student writing projects.
- **iBooks** - an ereader book store
- **Book Creator** - Create your own iBooks right on the iPad. (Allows everything except video)
- **Free Books** – 23,469 Classics to Go
- **Reading Trainer** - This app teaches you how to train your eyes and brain to read and comprehend text faster. Think of it as exercise for your reading skills
- **Dictionary.com** – Dictionary & Thesaurus – A dictionary and a Thesaurus
- **Literary Analysis Guide** – Elements of literature are arranged graphically around three wheels (poetry, prose, and rhetoric)
- **Shakespeare Pro** – Complete works of Shakespeare. 41 plays, 154 sonnets, and 6 poems. All works can be cross searched for anything
- **Jules Verne Collection** – Sixteen of Jules Verne's books
- **MaxJournal** – A simple and elegant journal
- **Essay Grader** – Provide feedback on essays with this easy to use app
- **LitCharts** – Link to LitCharts website. Each of the LitCharts are available on the iPad

Conventions of Oral and Written Language

A Brief Guide to Grammar and Usage
The following outline serves to review the teacher candidate on basic grammar and usage terms needed for the certification exam. A secondary English teacher must know the rules of grammar, usage, sentence structure, punctuation and capitalization in Standard English and be able to edit non-standard usage in student writing.

Parts of Speech
Noun - names a person, place, thing or idea. Example: golf, freedom, theater. Note: Proper nouns name a particular place or person and are capitalized. Example: Don, Austin, Alley Theater.

Pronoun - used in place of a noun. Example: he, she, it, they, someone. A pronoun identifies people, places, things or ideas without renaming them. The noun that a pronoun replaces is the antecedent of the pronoun. If a pronoun is placed too far away from its antecedent it is considered unclear or vague in reference. The three types of pronouns include: simple (I, you, he, she, it, we, they, who, what); compound, (itself, myself, anybody, someone, everything; and phrasal (each other, one another).

Verb - expresses action or state of being. Types of verbs include: action verbs (Example: run, jump, memorize, crawl), linking / helping verbs (Example: be, is, was, were, may, might, shall).

Adjective- a word that modifies a noun or a pronoun and answers the question: Which one? What kind? How many? Example: *western* civilization, *unorthodox* service, *twenty thousand* people.

Adverb - a word that modifies a verb, adjective or another adverb and answers the question: How? When? Where? How often? To what extent? Example: Though injured, Joanna walked the last mile of the race *courageously.*

Preposition - expresses a relationship between a noun or pronoun and another word in a sentence. Example: The designer *from* Paris visited our showroom and restructured our display cases. Note: A preposition is usually followed by a noun or a pronoun, which is called the object of the preposition. Together, the preposition, the object and the modifiers form a prepositional phrase.

Conjunction - a word that connects words or groups of words. Three types of conjunctions include:
> **Coordinating conjunction**: Example: and, but, for, nor, or, so and yet. The biologist, hoping to find a good specimen, *but* not expecting to find one, traveled to the rainforest.

Correlative conjunction: Example: either ... or; not only ... but also; neither ... nor; whether . .. or. Jon stated that he had *neither* watched the video *nor* read the novel before the English test.

Subordinating conjunction: introduces a subordinate clause that cannot stand by itself as a complete sentence. Example: *As* the weeks and months passed, the young woman's health problems began to diminish.

Gerund – is made up of a present participle (a verb ending in –ing) and always functions as a noun. Example: *Snorkeling* is Michael's hobby.

Infinitive – is made up of the word "*to*" and the base form of a verb, such as *to show* or *to love*. It can function as an adjective, adverb, or noun.

Interjection - an exclamatory word or phrase that usually expresses strong emotion. Example: *Wow!* I love this Italian food.

Participle – is a verb form that usually ends in –ing or –ed. Participles operates as adjectives but also maintain the characteristics of verbs. Examples: the *dancing bear* or *baked goods*.

Parts of Sentences

Subject - tells who or what the sentence is about. **Subject complement**-follows the linking verb and describes or identifies the subject. Example: **Dr. Bhattacharjee** is a professor. Dr. Bhattacharjee is efficient.

Predicate - the verb or verb phrase that describes the action or state of being of the subject.

Direct Object - a noun or pronoun that follows a verb and answers the question: what? or whom?

Indirect Object - a noun or pronoun that follows a verb and answers the question: to whom? For whom? to what? for what?

Phrase - a group of related words that functions as a single part of speech but lacks a subject, a predicate, or both.

Prepositional phrase-Example: *in the house, under the table, for the last two decades*

Appositive phrase-explains the noun. Example: Joanna Williams, *vice-president of marketing,* presented the new business plan to the board of directors.

Participle phrase-functions as an adjective in the sentence. Example: There is Jonathan, *walking across the parking lot to his car.*

Gerund phrase-a verb that ends in "ing" and functions as a noun in the sentence. Example: *According to Joanna,* shopping at the mall eases her stress level.

Infinitive phrase-a verb usually proceeded by "to" that functions as a noun, adjective, or adverb in the sentence. Example: The best way *to prepare for a career* is to attend college.

Clause-a group of related words that contains both a subject and a predicate.

Independent clause-can stand by itself as a complete sentence. Example: *I love this beautiful day.* Connect two independent clauses with a coordinating conjunction (and, or, but) or a semi-colon. Example: *I love this beautiful day; I am going to play outside.*

Subordinate clause (dependent clause)-is not a complete sentence and is connected to an independent clause by a comma. Example: *Although the day was cold,* Don played a complete round of golf.

Adjective clause-functions as an adjective and usually begins with a relative pronoun: that, which, who, whom or whose. Example: Jon often dresses in jeans and a western shirt, *which is typical attire for a Texas man.*

Adverb clause-functions as an adjective in the sentence. Example: *After twelve weeks of exercise in the gym,* I began to see a difference in the muscle tone of my body.

Noun clause-functions as a noun in the sentence. Example: *Whether or not to sell the house* was a concern for all of us.

Sentence Structure

Declarative Sentence -makes a statement and ends with a period. Example: My boat is moored at the Seabrook Marina.

Interrogative Sentence -asks a question. Example: What do women want?

Exclamatory Sentence -reveals strong emotion and ends with an exclamation point. Example: I need more money!

Imperative Sentence -gives an order or makes a request. Example: Please sign the divorce decree.

Simple Sentence -expresses a complete thought. Example: My father is visiting me for the week.

Compound Sentence -contains two or more independent clauses. Connect two independent clauses with a coordinating conjunction (and, or, but) or a semi-colon. Example: *My father is visiting me for the week; we are going fishing.*

Complex Sentence -contains one independent clause and one or more subordinate clauses. Example: *When Jon tired of his position at the ship brokerage firm, he interviewed for a new job.*

Compound-Complex Sentence -contains two or more independent clauses and one or more subordinate clauses. Example: *Ever since the women's movement in the 1970s, the employment opportunities for educated women proliferated, but recent developments, which include a downturn in the economy and rising child care costs, have changed the business climate to one of high unemployment and frustration for American women.*

Writing Complete Sentences
A complete sentence is a group of words that has a subject and a predicate and expresses a complete thought.

Fragment-a group of words that is not a complete sentence. Example: *Planning to graduate from college.*

Run-on sentence-consists of two or more sentences written as one sentence. Several ways exists to correct run-on sentences: (1) separate the run-on sentence into two sentences, (2) use a coordinating conjunction, (3) use a semicolon, (4) turn one of the independent clauses into a subordinate clause, or (5) use a semicolon and a conjunctive adverb (however, therefore).

Parallel structure: similarity of structure in a pair or series of related words, phrases, or clauses. By convention, items in a series should appear in parallel grammatical form: a noun is listed with other nouns, an *-ing* form with other *-ing* forms, and so on. Failure to express such items in similar grammatical form is called **faulty parallelism.**
Examples:
He ate, ran, and showered before going to work. (correct)
He purchased the blender on Friday, used it on Saturday, and broke it on Sunday. (correct)
He exercised while I watch television. (Incorrect…."watch" should be "watched")

Usage and Agreement in Sentences

Subject-Verb Agreement -a subject and verb must agree in number; that is, if a subject is singular, the verb should also be singular. Likewise, if the subject is plural, the verb should also be plural. Example: *Joanna has* traveled all over the world. *Joanna and Jonathan have* traveled the world.

Count nouns refer to items which can be counted, meaning that there can be more than one of them. Also, when a count noun is singular and indefinite, the article "a/an" is often used with it. Thus, the real meaning of "a" is "one". Example: "There are two books on the table." "There is a strange odor in my car."

Non-count nouns (or uncounted nouns) name items which cannot be counted, such as rice or water. Non-count nouns are treated as grammatically singular, but when they are indefinite, the writer should use the word "some" (or nothing at all) instead of an article. Example: "May I have some rice please?" "I'd like water with my meal."

Pronoun-Antecedent Agreement - a pronoun must agree with its antecedent in number (singular or plural), gender (masculine or feminine), and person (first person, second person or third person).

Consistency in Verb Tense -use of verb tense by the writer indicates whether an action or condition takes place in the present, past or future. The writer should stay consistent with verb tense. Example: Jonathan *lifted* the box while his mother *swept* the floor under it.

Correct Use of Modifiers -misplacement of modifiers (subordinate clauses) can create misunderstanding. Faulty sentence example: *Hanging on the wall, Joanna examined the beautiful paintings by Remington.* Correct by moving the modifier closer to the noun that it modifies. Example: *Joanna examined the beautiful paintings by Remington that hung on the wall.*

Capitalization
- first word in a sentence
- proper nouns
- official titles (Dr., Dean, Mr.)
- gods of mythology
- heavenly bodies
- names of peoples and nationalities
- titles of books, newspapers, poems, etc.
- names of academic subjects and languages
- names of organizations, government bodies, clubs, schools
- proper adjectives (Example: Russian wolfhound)
- both letters in abbreviations
- states, cities, counties

Punctuation:
Commas
- Separate three or more words or phrases in a series.
- After introductory phrases. Example: *After the trip to Hawaii, Joanna felt rested and ready to return to work.*
- Separate sentence parts that may be misread or confused. Example: *Whenever possible, alternative ideas should be offered by each member of the group.*
- To distinguish non-essential phrases. Example: *The new employees, who did not understand the insurance benefits, attended an additional information meeting.*

Pronunciation Overview

Modern English displays a vast inconsistency between sound and spelling, and so a dictionary of English must devote considerable attention to the pronunciation of the language. The English lexicon contains numerous "eye rhymes" such as *love, move,* and *rove,* words which do not sound alike despite their similar spellings. On the other hand, English also contains rhyming words such as *breeze, cheese, ease, frieze,* and *sleaze* whose rhymes are all spelled differently http://www.merriam-webster.com).

English Vowels

English vowels present different complexities of sound and spelling, due in large part to the fact that William Caxton introduced printing to England in 1476, many decades before the sound change known as the Great Vowel Shift had run its course. With the rise of printing came an increasingly fixed set of spelling conventions, but the conventionalized spellings soon lost the connection to pronunciation as the vowel shift continued. The stressed vowels of *sane* and *sanity* are therefore identical in spelling though now quite different in quality. For the trained observer the vagaries of English orthography contain a wealth of linguistic history; for most others, however, this disparity between sound and spelling is just a continual nuisance at school or work (http://www.merriam-webster.com).

Variant Pronunciations

Readers often turn to the dictionary wanting to learn the exact pronunciation of a word, only to discover that the word may have several pronunciations, as is the case for *deity, economic, envelope,* and *greasy,* among many others. The inclusion of variant pronunciations disappoints those who want their dictionary to list one "correct" pronunciation (http://www.merriam-webster.com).

Intonation is the rise and fall of the voice pitch when speaking and is the name given to sentence stress, or what is sometimes called the "music of the language." Just as words have stressed syllables, sentences contain regular patterns of stressed words. In addition, the voice tends to rise, fall or remain flat in various different types of phrases and sentences.

Conventional forms of spelling:

The value of correct spelling is that it gives writing credibility and therefore helps writers communicate effectively. Recent developments in technology, such as spell-check software, have not replaced the need for writers to understand how to spell words correctly. Such technology assists in proofreading, but is not a substitute for spelling knowledge (McCrum, et al, 1987; Bear, et al, 2008).

In the early stages of their language and spelling development, students often use spellings that approximate conventional forms. Students typically move from approximation to correct spelling during their education. During these stages, in particular, it is important that teachers give students support and encouragement about how to spell unfamiliar words correctly.

The early form of English (or Anglo-Saxon) was more phonetically regular than Modern English. In the original English, grammatical meaning was heavily dependent on word endings and word order was less important. Some of these original features still remain (e.g. *ox–oxen, man–men; mouse– mice*). Over time, as word order assumed greater importance, many of the word endings dropped off. The silent *e* at the end of many English words is due to this change (McCrum, et al, 1987).

After the introduction of Christianity and the Norman invasion, large numbers of Latin and French words entered the language. Because the Anglo-Saxon language had many sounds that were not found in French, and also because French handwriting was different from that used by the Anglo-Saxons, some spelling compromises had to be made when writing the language.
For example, the latter phenomenon led to the introduction of the letter *o* in words like *love, son,* and *women.*

Consistency in spelling is a comparatively recent phenomenon. For example, as Anglo-Saxon moved towards Middle English and into Elizabethan times, many words with *i* and *e* vowels and the *ae* diphthongs changed.

In Shakespeare's time, for example, the word *reason* was pronounced "raisin" (as it still is in parts of the United Kingdom today), which is why Shakespeare indulges in a play on words with *reasons* and *blackberries* in *Henry IV* (McCrum, et al, 1987).

Since medieval times, English has acquired thousands of new words from a variety of sources. Many of these were derived from Latin and Greek, during the Renaissance. Other words were derived from the languages of communities colonized by Britain. Following the industrial revolution, additional words had to be invented. Moreover, when scientific knowledge was growing in the early modern age, Greek words were used as the basis for coining new scientific words. The Greek alphabet has some letter sounds that the English alphabet does not have, such as *phi, chi,* and *psi.* This accounts for the non-phonetic spelling of a host of English words, such as *telephone, trachea,* and *psychology* (McCrum, et al, 1987).

Understanding English spelling

Within the context of meaningful written language experiences, students need explicit teaching about the phonological, visual, morphemic, and etymological aspects of spelling that are relevant to their stage of spelling development. When they have access to this knowledge, students will be better able to spell unfamiliar words accurately for a variety of social and academic purposes (Bear, et al, 2008).

Basic Spelling Rules

One of the most common spelling rules is "I before E, except after C, unless it sounds like A as in neighbor and weigh." However, there are a number of other rules that you can use to help decode the spelling of an unfamiliar word (http://grammar.about.com/od/words/tp/spellrules.htm). For example:

- The letter Q is always followed by U. In this case, the U is not considered to be a vowel.

- The letter S never follows X.

- The letter Y, not I, is used at the end of English words. Examples of this rule include my, by, shy, and why.

- To spell a short vowel sound, only one letter is needed. Examples of this rule include at, red, it, hot, and up.

- Drop the E. When a word ends with a silent final E, it should be written without the E when adding an ending that begins with a vowel. In this way, come becomes coming and hope becomes hoping.

- When adding an ending to a word that ends with Y, change the Y to I if it is preceded by a consonant. In this way, supply becomes supplies and worry becomes worried.

- All, written alone, has two L's. When used as a prefix, however, only one L is written. Examples of this rule include also and almost.

- Generally, adding a prefix to a word does not change the correct spelling.

- Words ending in a vowel and Y can add the suffix -ed or -ing without making any other change.

Morphemes are the smallest units of language that carry meaning. The **phonemes** /b/, /a/ and /t/ together form the morpheme /bat/. While the word *bat* carries some meaning, its particular meaning depends on the context of its use. For example, its meaning is different in each of the following sentences:

> I bought a baseball bat.
> She went to bat for him.
> The bat spread its wings.

The ending *-ing* is also a morpheme, even though it carries meaning only when it is bound to a word like *bat*, to make *batting*. As you see, adding the *-ing* morpheme causes a change to the other morpheme, in this case the doubling of the end consonant. Fortunately, such morphemic changes are fairly regular in English, which is why understanding morphemic patterns is another important aspect of spelling knowledge. This is often the point of spelling "rules" (Bear, et al, 2008).

Understanding these features of the English language helps writers spell, because it is useful to remember that many of the words that are difficult to spell have non-phonetic spellings for a variety of reasons; their present spelling might reflect the way they were pronounced many years ago (the word *knight*), or they might be borrowed from a foreign language (the French word *charade*).

Most of these features must be learned as individual cases. There is no consistent approach to what the English language does with words borrowed from other languages. Either visual knowledge or etymological knowledge is used in these instances (http://grammar.about.com/od/words/tp/spellrules.htm).

Phonological, visual, morphemic, and etymological knowledge

The knowledge that students need if they are to become proficient spellers takes four different forms:

- **phonological knowledge**: how words and letter combinations sound
- **visual knowledge**: the way words and letter combinations look
- **morphemic knowledge**: the meaning of words and the way words take different spellings when they change form
- **etymological knowledge**: word origin; the derivations of words

Phonological knowledge focuses on how sounds correspond to letters.

It includes teaching students:

- **the names of letters**, the sounds they represent and the ways in which letters can be grouped to make different sounds e.g. vowels, consonants, consonant blends, and word families like *ound, itch, ock*
- **the concept of onset and rime**, e.g. in the word *pink*, *p* is onset and *ink* is rime
- **how to segment the sounds** in words into "chunks" of sound (phonemic awareness): cat, has three phonemes or sounds

Visual knowledge focuses on how words look.

It includes teaching students:

- **to recall and compare the appearance** of words, particularly those which they have seen or learned before or those which are commonly used
- **to recognize what letters look like** and how to write them
- **to recognize** that **letters can be grouped** in particular ways, e.g. endings that frequently occur in words

Morphemic knowledge focuses on the meaning of words and how they change when they take on different grammatical forms.

It includes teaching students:

- how to use morphemes to assist them to spell words
- how **compound words** are constructed (examples: hotdog, bathroom, football)
- knowledge of **suffixes and prefixes** and the generalizations that can be made and the rules that can be generated about adding them to words

Etymological knowledge focuses on the origins and meaning of non-phonetic words.
It includes teaching students:

- about the roots of words and word meanings
- particular clusters of letters that appear in words not only look the same, but also are related in meaning, often because of their root, e.g. *aquatic, aquatint, aquarium.*

Writing Conventions

Types of Sentences:
Simple Sentence: A complete sentence that expresses a single thought and contains a subject and a verb.

Independent Clause: A simple sentence which is combined with another simple sentence or a dependent clause to form either a compound or complex sentence.

Dependent Clause: A group of words that adds information to or modifies an independent clause. It is not a complete sentence and cannot stand by itself as a sentence.

Compound Sentence: A sentence formed by the joining of two independent clauses using a coordinating conjunction, a semicolon, or a conjunctive adverb.

Complex Sentence: A sentence composed of an independent clause and one or more dependent clauses joined by subordinating conjunctions.

Compound-Complex Sentences: A sentence containing two or more independent clauses and one or more dependent clauses. The methods of joining these clauses may include any of the options below.

Techniques for Creating Sentence Variety
The Coordinating Conjunction
The most common way to join two simple sentences (independent clauses) is with a coordinating conjunction (and, or, but, nor, for, yet, so). Example: I went to China, **but** Michael went to Mexico. I went to China **(independent clause), (comma)** but **(conjunction)** Michael went to Mexico **(independent clause)**.

The Semicolon
To join two closely related simple sentences (independent clauses), you may use a semicolon without a conjunction. Example: I went to China; Michael went with me. I went to China **(independent clause); (semicolon)** Michael went with me **(independent clause)**.

The Semicolon and a Conjunctive Adverb
To combine two simple sentences (independent clauses), you may use a semicolon and a conjunctive adverb (however, therefore, indeed, moreover, consequently, etc.). Conjunctive adverbs carry the thought of the first independent clause to the related independent clause.
Example: I wanted to become a professor; **therefore**, I complete a doctorate degree. I wanted to become a professor **(independent clause); (semicolon)** therefore **(conjunctive adverb), (comma)** I completed a doctorate degree **(independent clause)**.

Subordinate Conjunction

Another method of joining two simple sentences is the use of subordinating conjunctions (after, although, as, as if, before, because, if, since, unless, when, whenever, until, while, etc.). The example below contains a common subordinating conjunction. The main point of the sentence is considered an independent clause and the dependent clause contains the subordinate conjunction. Example: **Although** I recently recovered from a bad cold, I continued with my vacation plans. Although **(subordinating conjunction)** I recently recovered from a bad cold **(dependent clause),** I continued with my vacation plans **(independent clause)**.

Clausal and phrasal modifiers

Clausal modifier: a phrase with an adjective or adverb that adds detail to the sentence
Examples:
The dog ran after the ball **that bounced across the road**.
I love broccoli **which is a very healthy vegetable**.
The little boy, **who wanted his Mother to buy the new toy,** was throwing a tantrum in the store.

Phrasal modifier: a phrase, joined by hyphens, that is used to modify a noun; the noun is singular
Examples:
We have a **three-day weekend** coming up.
My **ten-speed bicycle** broke down.
I need a roommate for my **two-bedroom apartment**.

Devices to control focus in sentences and paragraphs

Concrete language refers to experiences related directly through the senses. Specific language refers directly to particular cases, not generalizations about many cases.   For example, the name of an individual person, "Mr. Downs," is both specific and concrete. A larger group, "the teachers at Labay Middle School," is concrete but more general. "Teachers" is even more general. Whenever possible, a writer should use concrete, specific language. The best way to do this is to write about specific individuals and events rather than abstract concepts (**http://dpalomar.edu/handbook/specific.htm**).

Active and Passive Voice

In sentences using the active voice, the subject of the sentence does the action. In sentences using the passive voice, the object of the sentence does the action, which weakens the sentence's subject. Active sentences are more emphatic and vigorous, although there are instances in which the passive voice may be preferred. In order to correct passive voice.
1. Find the verb in the sentence.
2. Ask who or what is performing the action in order to identify the actor in the sentence.
3. Construct the sentence so the actor performs the action.

Examples:
Passive: The poisonous spider was caught by Cooper.
Active: Cooper caught the poisonous spider.

Passive: The house was struck by lightning, plunging us into darkness.
Active: Lightning struck the house, plunging us into darkness.

Passive: The apartment building was destroyed by years of neglect.
Active: Years of neglect destroyed the apartment building.

Transitional Words and Phrases

Transitions are words or phrases that specify a relationship between sentences (or paragraph) which help direct the reader from one idea to another. Common transitions include:

10. **To specify sequence**: again, also, and, and then, besides, finally, first, second, third, furthermore, last, moreover, next, still, too

11. To specify time: after a few days, after a while, afterward, as long as, as soon as, at last, at that time, before, earlier, immediately, in the meantime, in the past, lately, later, meanwhile, now, presently, simultaneously, since, so far, soon, then, thereafter, until, when

12. **To specify comparison**: again, also, in the same way, likewise, once more, similarly

13. **To specify contrast**: although, but, despite, even though, however, in contrast, in spite of, instead, nevertheless, nonetheless, on the contrary, on the one hand, on the other hand, regardless, still, though, yet

14. **To specify examples**: after all, for example, for instance, indeed, in fact, of course, specifically, such as, the following example, to illustrate

15. **To specify cause and effect**: accordingly, as a result, because, consequently, for this reason, hence, if, then, since, so, then, therefore, thereupon, thus, to this end

16. **To specify place**: above, adjacent to, below, beyond, closer to elsewhere, far, farther on, here, near, nearby, opposite to, there, to the left, to the right

17. **To specify concession**: although it is true that, granted that, I admit that, it may appear that, naturally, of course

18. **To specify summary, repetition, or conclusion**: as a result, as has been noted, as I have said, as mentioned earlier, as we have seen, in any event, in conclusion, in other words, in short, on the whole, therefore, to summarize

Cohesion and Coherence

Cohesion: Readers must feel that they move easily from one sentence to the next; a group of sentences "go together." **Coherence:** Readers must feel that sentences are not just individually clear, but constitute a unified passage focused on a coherent set of ideas.

Cohesive Devices
1. Linking Adverbials
The writer may use linking adverbials to explicitly state relationships between sentences, paragraphs, and ideas. The result is increased cohesion of text (*www.webenglishteacher.com).* Linking adverbials can show six different categories of relationships:

- Enumeration and addition
- Summation
- Apposition
- Result/Inference
- Contrast/concession
- Transition

2. Enumerative Linking Adverbials
Enumerative linking adverbials can be used to show the order of pieces of information. Enumeration can follow logical or time sequences, or can be used to move to the next point:
- ordinal numbers: first, second, third, etc.
- adverbs: finally, lastly
- phrases: for one thing, to begin with, next

3. Additive Linking Adverbials
Similar to enumerative linking adverbials, additive linking adverbials link items together. Additive linking adverbials state explicitly that two items are similar to each other:
- also
- similarly
- by the same token
- further(more)
- likewise
- moreover

4. Summative Linking Adverbials
Summative linking adverbials explicitly state that the text is concluding. They signal that the author is summarizing the information already presented:
- in sum
- in conclusion
- to conclude
- all in all
- overall
- to summarize

5. Appositive Linking Adverbials

Appositive linking adverbials signal a restatement of the previous information which will be expressed in a slightly different manner to make it more explicit:

- which is to say
- in other words
- that is

In addition, appositives may introduce an example that is the equivalent of the first piece of information:

- for example
- for instance
- namely
- specifically

6. Result/Inference Linking Adverbials

Result/inference linking adverbials demonstrate to readers that the following textual element is the result or consequence of the previous information:

- consequently
- thus
- as a result
- hence
- so
- therefore

7. Contrast/Concession Linking Adverbials

Contrast linking adverbials signal differences or alternatives between two pieces of information:

- on the other hand
- in contrast
- alternatively
- conversely
- by comparison
- instead

Linking adverbs of concession demonstrate that the following information signals a reservation concerning the previous information:

- though
- anyway
- however
- nevertheless
- in any case
- in spite of that

8. Transition Linking Adverbials

Transition linking adverbials signal that the following item will not directly follow the previous item. However, this does not mean that the information is not related, just that is not directly related:

- now
- meanwhile

Cohesive Devices: Coordinating Conjunctions

Writers use coordinators (also called coordinating conjunctions) to stack elements of a sentence. These coordinators indicate that the elements have the same syntactic role, meaning that they are on an equal level. The three main coordinators are:

- and
- but
- or (and negative nor)

Cohesive Devices: Subordinating Conjunctions

The use of subordinators (also called subordinating conjunctions) contributes greatly to the cohesion of a text. Unlike coordinators, these words and phrases introduce ideas that are dependent to the main clause in a sentence. There are three types of subordinators include:

- simple
- complex
- correlative

Simple Subordinating Conjunctions

Simple subordinators consist of single words that introduce dependent clauses.
Simple subordinators can belong to three classes:

- adverbial clauses: after, as, because, if, since, although, whether, while
- degree clauses: as, than, that
- complement clauses: if, that, whether

Adverbial and degree clauses signal a particular relationship between the clauses. On the other hand, complement clauses signal structural dependency.

Complex Subordinating Conjunctions

Complex subordinators are phrases of two or more words. Complex subordinators perform the same function as simple subordinators. Examples of complex subordinators include:

- as far as
- as long as
- given that
- on condition that
- provided that
- supposing that
- now that
- except that
- so that
- even though
- in case
- even if

Using "Image Grammar" to enhance writing

The writer must learn to literally and metaphorically "see" with a visual eye and the writer must learn to write using details and color to tease the reader's visual appetite. The writer must learn to "paint pictures with words," which should appear in the imagination of the reader. The qualities of a writer's images – the details, colors, shapes, movement – derive from visual perception (Noden, 1999).

A well-described fiction or nonfiction work creates the mental equivalent of a film, leading readers through a visual journey of endless images with close-ups, action scenes, and angle shots. Creating art that "shows," requires more than visual awareness; it requires a knowledge of techniques - the ability to select words like colors on a palette and apply sentence structures like brush strokes to a verbal canvas (Noden, 1999). The five techniques for creating images include:

1. **Participles:** An "ing" verb phrases tagged on to the beginning, end or middle of a sentence. (Note: "ed" forms can also be used).
   Original example sentence: **The diamond-scaled snakes attacked their prey.**
   The writer could add a participial phrase at the beginning of the sentence:
   Hissing, slithering, and coiling, the diamond-scaled snakes attacked their prey.
   The writer could also add participial phrases along with any modifiers that complete the image.
   Hissing their forked red tongues and coiling their cold bodies, the diamond-scales snakes attacked their prey.

2. **Absolutes** – a two-word combination – a noun and an "ing" or "ed" verb added onto a sentence. Original example sentence: **The cat climbed the tree.**
   The writer could add (absolutes) two-word combinations to the original sentence:
   Claws digging, feet kicking, the cat climbed the tree.

3. **Appositives** - a noun that adds a second image to a preceding noun.
   Original example sentence: **The raccoon enjoys eating turtle eggs**.
   The writer could add an appositive phrase to the sentence.
   The raccoon, **a midnight scavenger who roams lake shorelines in search of food,** enjoys eating turtle eggs.

4. **Adjectives** – shifted from their usual placement in a sentence - shifted to other parts of the sentence. Examples: And then, suddenly, in the very dead of the night, there came a sound to my ears, **clear, resonant, and unmistakable.** Beulah was a simple city, **long and rectangular.**

5. **Action Verbs / Detailed Verbs** - reducing "be" verbs and selecting action verbs.
   Writers can strengthen sentences in which "be" verbs link vague noun complements. For example, in the sentence: The meal was wonderful. The "be" verb spotlights wonderful, a word that tells instead of shows. Because of this quality, most "be" verbs are effectively passive, functioning like passive voice. Most leading software programs will highlight passive voice for a writer. With a little time spent eliminating "be" verbs, writers can bring descriptive images to life. However, if the "be" verb cannot be easily replaced, it may belong in the sentence. Some being verbs function to define and others can convey a mood of passivity when a passage requires it for effect.

Evaluating Student Work

Teachers should use a variety of formal and informal measures to evaluate student work.
Student **portfolios** work well for evaluation and assessment of student writing. Periodic conferences should be held between teachers and students to review the portfolio's contents. Portfolios can be very effective for teacher-parent conferences as well. The portfolio should contain a balance of assignments. Specifically, there should be a collection of work in the portfolio reflecting both **aesthetic** and **efferent** assignments.

Rosenblatt (1983) describes the two levels of response as **efferent** and **aesthetic**. When the reader is responding in an efferent way, the focus is on what has been learned from the ideas and information encountered in the text. When the reader is responding in an aesthetic way, the focus is on his feelings or emotions about the work.

Moreover, teachers can use student **portfolios** to discover consistent patterns in the work that reflect strengths or weaknesses. English / language arts teachers should use assessment results to plan and adapt instruction that addresses students' strengths, needs, and interests.

During periodic conferences, the teacher and student can discuss the goals that need to be met to improve reading and writing skills. Portfolios can also be used by students to **self-evaluate** their growth and set their own goals for learning. **Self-evaluation** activities help students reflect upon their own writing and take ownership of the learning process.

Peer editing can be used during the writer's workshop to help students improve their writing, not only during class, but when writing future assignments. Students are assigned to work with a partner or small group as they discuss and share their writing. The teacher facilitates the classroom while listening to peer discussions, and is available for assistance when needed. Peer editing provides students the opportunity to help their peers in a positive and critically constructive manner, as well as receive feedback on their own writing. Prior to the **peer-editing** session, the teacher provides guidance and models ways for students to help their peers through the use of positive statements, focus check-lists, and helpful resources.

Holistic Evaluation vs. Analytical Evaluation

Holistic evaluation assesses student's writing as a whole instead of examining each part.
When grading a writing assignment **holistically**, teachers should read the paper once to get an impression of the work as a whole. The writing is then graded according to the impression of the whole work rather than in parts. The use of a **grading rubric**, that establishes the overall criteria for a certain score, is very effective when grading work holistically. **Holistic scoring** is very subjective. "Holistic rubrics are the quickest way to score papers in any content area, requiring a teacher to read a paper only once. Teachers can develop rubrics by basing them on the content they've taught and practiced; assess papers based on established criteria agreed upon by students and teachers; and give a single holistic score that indicates the quality level of the writing, ranging from deficient to competent to outstanding (Urquhart & McIver, 2005)."

Example Holistic Rubric:
4. Above Average: The audience is able to easily identify the focus of the work and is engaged by its clear focus and relevant details. Information is presented logically and naturally. There are no more than two mechanical errors or misspelled words to distract the reader.
3. Sufficient: The audience is easily able to identify the focus of the student work which is supported by relevant ideas and supporting details. Information is presented in a logical manner that is easily followed. There is minimal interruption to the work due to misspellings and/or mechanical errors.
2. Developing: The audience can identify the central purpose of the student work without little difficulty and supporting ideas are present and clear. The information is presented in an orderly fashion that can be followed with little difficulty. There are some misspellings and/or mechanical errors, but they do not seriously distract from the work.
1. Needs Improvement: The audience cannot clearly or easily identify the central ideas or purpose of the student work. Information is presented in a disorganized fashion causing the audience to have difficulty following the author's ideas. There are many misspellings and/or mechanical errors that negatively affect the audience's ability to read the work.

Advantages to Holistic Rubrics
- Emphasis on what the learner is able to demonstrate, rather than what s/he cannot do.
- Saves time by minimizing the number of decisions raters make.
- Can be applied consistently by trained raters increasing reliability.

Disadvantages for Holistic Rubrics
- Do not provide specific feedback for improvement.
- When student work is at varying levels spanning the criteria points, it can be difficult to select the single best description.
- Criteria cannot be weighted.

Analytical evaluation, on the other hand, is a more objective method of evaluating student work. **Analytical evaluation** specifies the criteria and quality for success and provides a point value for each criterion. Some students prefer this type of evaluation system since it is objective and outlines specific strengths and weaknesses. The disadvantage of **analytical evaluation** is that it places great emphasis on the parts of a writing assignment rather than the whole.

In sum, the writing process helps develop fluency in writing, builds self-confidence and promotes **self-expression**, with the added benefit of helping students to take ownership of learning through **self-evaluation**. The writing process also provides a means through which language arts and reading skills can be taught within the context of assignments that have personal meaning to the students.

Using the writer's workshop model of instruction, teachers can also explicitly teach the use of correct writing conventions: sentence and paragraph construction, spelling, punctuation, usage, and grammatical expression. Each week, students should be given independent as well as guided writing assignments and should be allowed time to write for a variety of purposes and audiences in different formats. These opportunities allow students time for developing oral and written language skills through authentic use rather than through skill practice exercises. Teachers should model all stages of the process to ensure that students experience the metacognitive processes involved in writing. During the writer's workshop, teachers should allow students time for revising and sharing so students can receive input from many sources: peers, specialized dictionaries, teacher, computer research, etc. (Routman, 2000).

References

Graves, D. (1983). *Writing: Teachers and Children at Work*, Heinemann: Portsmouth, NH.

Bear, D; Invernizzi, M; Templeton, S; Johnston, F. (2008). *Words Their Way*. Pearson, Upper Saddle River, NJ.

McCrum, R; Cran, W. & MacNeil, R. (1987). *The Story of English*. Penguin: New York, NY.

Noden, H. (1999). *Using grammatical structures to teach Writing*. Heinemann: Portsmouth, NH.

Rosenblatt, L.M. (1983). The literary Transaction: Evocation and Response. *Theory into Practice*. V 21: 268-277.

Routman, R. (2000). Conversations: Strategies for Teaching, Learning, and Evaluating. Heinemann: Portsmouth, NH.

Urquhart, V. & McIver,M. (2005). *Teaching Writing in the Content Areas*. ASCD

Wood, J. (2000). A Marriage Waiting to Happen: Computers and Process Writing. *Education Development Center, Inc.* (EDC). http://www.edtechleaders .org

http://www.inspiration.com/diagrams/ed/ediagram.html
http://www.calstatela.edu/faculty/lgarret/paragraphs.htm.
http://dpalomar.edu/handbook/specific.htm
http://*www.webenglishteacher.com*
http://www.grammarforteachers.com
http://grammar.about.com/od/words/tp/spellrules.htm.
http://www.merriam-webster.com

Practice Questions

1. A teaching strategy used during a writer's workshop to encourage students to write without interruption of the flow of thoughts is called:
    a. Brainstorming
    b. Freewriting
    c. Portfolio writing
    d. Authors' circle

B is correct. Freewriting allows students to write without interruption.

2. Of the following, which is the most important advantage of using portfolios for developing writers?

    a. Keeping a large amount of their work in one place provides students with additional writing opportunities.
    b. A portfolio can be used during teacher-student conferences.
    c. A portfolio can provide evidence of growth and change in a student's writing skills.
    d. A portfolio contains goals for writing improvement.

C is correct. Portfolios can reveal growth and change in writing skills over time

3. Of the following, which is the major advantage of using a holistic evaluation method when assessing student writing assignments?

    a. Holistic grading utilizes a subjective method of grading.
    b. Holistic grading is concrete and highlights specific strengths and weaknesses.
    c. In holistic grading the student's grade is determined by the point total which makes it fair and objective.
    d. Holistic grading places emphasis on the whole paper rather than parts.

D is correct. This is a major advantage of holistic grading practices.

4. Which of the following changes could be made in order to revise the following paragraph for coherence?

(1) An indoor grill is a useful kitchen tool to solve the problems presented by lengthy meal preparation time demanded by traditional cooking. (2)America is always on the forefront of new discoveries. (3) Most American women work outside the home and have little time to cook a full meal using traditional means. (4) Indoor grill cooking can provide a quick, tasty, nutritious main dish in a matter of minutes.

    a. Reorder the paragraph as follows: 2, 1, 3, 4
    b. Reorder the paragraph as follows: 3,1,4 (omit sentence 2)
    c. Reorder the paragraph as follows: 1,2,4,3
    d. No changes needed.

B is correct.

5. Which of the following paragraphs is written in informal style?

    a. The enthusiastic English teacher gratefully acknowledged her students' efforts and thanked them effusively. She then walked to the podium to present the prizes for the winning debate team.

    b. His mother was tall, with long soft hair and a face that was gentle and thin. She read a lot. She read a lot to him. His father said of her, "She is just like Arthur Junior. She never argued. She was quiet, easygoing and kindhearted." (Excerpt from *Arthur Ashe Remembered*, by John McPhee).

    c. There was once a town in the heart of America where all life seemed to live in harmony with its surroundings. The town lay in the midst of a checkerboard of prosperous farms, with fields of grain and hillsides of orchards where, in spring, white clouds of bloom drifted above the green fields. In autumn, oak and maple and birch set up a blaze of color that flamed and flickered across a backdrop of pines. Then foxes barked in the hills and deer silently crossed the fields, half hidden in the mists of the fall mornings. (Excerpt from *Silent Spring* by Rachel Carson)

    d. The oldest form of mass communication – the printing press – is less than six hundred years old. In 1440, German inventor Johannes Gutenberg invented a printing press process that, with refinements and increased mechanization, remained the principal means of printing until the late 20th century. The inventor's method of printing from movable type, including the use of metal molds and alloys, a special press, and oil-based inks, allowed for the first time the mass production of printed books.

B is correct.

6. Which of the following sentences is written in "active" voice?
 a. The breakfast was eaten by my daughter.
 b. My daughter was eating breakfast.
 c. The earrings were lost.
 d. I lost 10 pounds.

D is correct.

7. Identify the underlined part of the following sentence.

<u>In conclusion,</u> I hope that everyone here will enjoy the freedom America has offered by voting during every election.

 a. summative linking adverbial
 b. subordinating conjunction
 c. appositive linking adverbial
 d. concession linking adverbial

A is correct. Summative linking adverbials explicitly state that the text is concluding. They signal that the author is summarizing the information already presented.

8. Which of the following sentences contains two independent clauses?

 a. After lunch, we drove down the coast to enjoy the scenery.
 b. We waited for Jules for two hours.
 c. We drove down the coastal highway; I wanted to see the area.
 d. Can you please direct me to the nearest drugstore?

C is correct. An independent clause contains a subject and a verb. In this sentence, the two independent clauses are joined by a semi-colon.

9. Of the following which is the best rationale for students to self-evaluate their own work?

   a. Self-evaluation allows students time for developing oral and written language skills through authentic assessment.
   b. Self-evaluation places emphasis on subjective measures.
   c. Self-evaluation is a non-threatening and risk-free form of evaluation that promotes the attitude that evaluation is a valid, useful step in the writing process.
   d. Self-evaluation helps students reflect upon their own writing and take ownership of the learning process.

D is correct. This is the best answer choice; students should take ownership of the development of their personal writing skills.

10. Which of the following sentences contains an error in punctuation?

   a. As the rain pelted down upon him, he walked hurriedly down the street.
   b. My mother is a terrible listener, she always interrupts when I am talking.
   c. I need to investigate the cost of the new sailboat; the price needs to fall within my budget.
   d. Hurry up, shouted the train conductor.

B contains a comma splice error. A semicolon should follow the word, listener instead of a comma. A semicolon is used to join two independent clauses.

11. Mr. Kuzmick notices that many of his 10th grade students have an inadequate working vocabulary. He hopes to incorporate effective lessons to increase his students' vocabulary. Which of the following strategies would be the *most* effective way for Mr. Kuzmick to help his students increase the number of words in their working vocabulary?

 a. Ask students to work in groups to complete "word family" lessons in order to create new words with common root words and affixes.
 b. After reading an assigned novel, ask students to work in groups and use the dictionary to define unknown words they encountered during the reading assignment.
 c. Require that students make journal entries about new words and definitions that they come into contact with over the next two weeks.
 d. Ask students to create an individual glossary and write each new word and its definition in the glossary.

A is correct. Having students build word knowledge by working with a known Latin root is a very effective method of building students' vocabulary. This teaching strategy builds upon a student's prior knowledge.

12. Which of the following sentences contains an error?

 a. She felt that the classroom contained an adequate amount of instructional materials.
 b. The principal walked over to the new teacher to discuss the new lunchroom rules.
 c. Mr. Bloomberg skulked behind the gang members until he determined that they meant no harm.
 d. He know that each of the students needs a book, pencil, and paper.

 .

D has an error in subject / verb agreement. The sentence should read as follows: He knows that each of the students needs a book, pencil, and paper.

13. Which of the following is the best way to punctuate an inserted phrase within a quote?

 a. Use brackets to punctuate the phrase.
 b. No punctuation is needed for the inserted phrase.
 c. Use ellipses to set off the inserted phrase from the quoted material.
 d. Add a subscript notation immediately following the phrase.

C is correct.

14. A **morpheme** can be defined as:

      a. the smallest unit of sound in a word
      b. the smallest unit of meaning in a word
      c. a letter or symbol representing a sound
      d. a schwa sound

B is correct. A morpheme is the smallest unit of meaning in a word. For example, the word "unfaithful" contains three morphemes: un = not, faith = a belief that does not rest on logical proof or material evidence, and full = having a great deal or many.

Domain III: Chapter 9

Competency 009: Writing Effectively

The beginning teacher:

- Understands and teaches the distinguishing features of various forms of writing (e.g., reflective essay, autobiographical narrative, editorial, report, memorandum, summary/abstract, résumé, play, short story, poem).
- Applies and teaches skills and strategies for writing effectively in a variety of forms and for a variety of audiences, purposes and contexts.
- Understands and teaches how a writer's purpose and audience define appropriate language, writing style and text organization.
- Provides students with explicit instruction, meaningful practice opportunities and effective feedback as the students create different types of written works.
- Promotes students' ability to compose effectively (e.g., organizing ideas to ensure coherence, logical progression and support; using precise language to communicate ideas clearly and concisely; writing in a voice and style appropriate to audience and purpose).
- Provides students with professionally written, student-written and teacher- written models of writing.
- Demonstrates knowledge of factors that influence student writing (e.g., writer's experiences, situational context in which writing occurs, interactions within the learning/writing community, features of various written forms).
- Analyzes and teaches the use of literary devices (e.g., imagery, tone, dialogue, characterization, irony, figurative language) in writing.
- Teaches students skills and strategies for using writing as a tool for reflection, exploration, learning, problem solving and personal growth.
- Understands and teaches writing as a tool for inquiry, research and learning.
- Teaches students to evaluate critically the sources they use for their writing.
- Provides instruction about plagiarism, academic honesty and integrity as applied to students' written work and their presentation of information from different sources, including electronic sources.
- Understands and teaches students the importance of using acceptable formats for communicating research results and documenting sources (e.g., manuals of style such as the Modern Language Association Handbook [MLA style], the Publication Manual of the American Psychological Association [APA style], and The Chicago Manual of Style [Chicago style]).

Key Terms

Acknowledgement letter
Adjustment letter
Ad hominem
Ad populum
Advertising techniques
Appeal to emotion
Appeal to morality
Appeal to reason
Audience
Begging the claim
Body of a business letter
Business letter
Business writing
Circular argument (reasoning)
Classical argument
Complaint letter
Closing of a business letter
Deductive reasoning
Descriptive writing
Emotional appeal
Enthymeme
Ethos
Expository writing
Fallacies of argument
Hasty generalities
Historical investigation
Inquiry letter

Logical arguments
Logos
Narrative writing
Narrative poetry
Non-narrative poetry
Order letter
Pathos
Proposition of fact
Purpose
Persuasive writing
Poetic writing
Questions of policy
Questions of value
Red herring
Refutation
Register
Response letter
Rhetorical strategies of persuasion
Salutation
Slippery slope
Subject matter
Syllogism
Technical writing
Toulmin method
Types of persuasive speeches
Weak analogy

Effective Writing

Teacher candidates must recognize and be able to teach a variety of writing applications and rhetorical features of texts. The analysis of different types of literature promotes cognitive development, giving the student opportunity to apply similar skills and strategies, such as identifying themes discussed in one genre (i.e fiction) to other genres (i.e. poetry, reports, descriptive pieces, and plays). Smith (1994) explains that the more experience students have in reading different genres, the more successful they will be in writing in different genres.

Descriptive Writing:
Descriptive writing vividly portrays a person, place, or thing in such a way that the reader can visualize the topic and enter into the writer's experience. The general characteristics of descriptive writing include (http://www.thewritingsite.org/resources/genre/technical.asp):

- Elaborate use of sensory language
- Rich, vivid, and lively detail
- Figurative language such as simile, hyperbole, metaphor, symbolism and personification
- *Showing*, rather than *telling* through the use of active verbs and precise modifiers

Expository Writing
Expository writing seeks to inform, explain, clarify, define, or instruct. The goal of this genre is to give information such as an explanation or directions. Expository writing appears in letters, newsletters, definitions, instructions, guidebooks, catalogues, newspaper articles, magazine articles, manuals, pamphlets, reports, and research papers (http://www.thewritingsite.org/resources/genre/technical.asp). The general characteristics of expository writing include:

- Focus on main topic
- Logical supporting facts
- Details, explanations, and examples
- Strong organization
- Clarity
- Unity and coherence
- Logical order
- Smooth transitions

Historical Investigation
When planning, researching, and organizing an historical investigation, the writer must investigate the topic and surrounding issues thoroughly. To conduct an historical investigation, the writer should:
- Narrow the Topic: Once a topic has been identified, the writer should gather background information in order to identify and create a list of possible issues surrounding the topic. When writing a historical investigation, it is best to choose issues that are controversial and arguable.

- Research & Gather Evidence: When investigating this topic, a thorough investigation may reveal a multitude of accounts that enable the writer to successfully research the topic. The writer then focuses research in an area in order to develop a working thesis question. With the working thesis in mind, begin to construct a pro and con argument by gathering evidence from all points of view. It is important to gather a full scope of evidence that addresses all sides of the argument so that the writer may analyze these sources in terms of what argument is most reliable.

- Select Relevant Evidence: It is important that the evidence selected is relevant to the investigation. Be sure to exclude all background information that is not relevant to the question. Keep in mind; rather, that an analytical paper examines the facts in order to obtain a critical view.

- Develop a Research Question: Once evidence is gathered, the writer will develop the research question. This is best achieved by focusing on what evidence is most convincing. An important process of developing a good question is to be sure the conclusion of the historical investigation answers the research question.

Narrative writing

The goal of this genre is to tell a story of an experience, event, or sequence of events while holding the reader's interest. Narrative writing appears in short stories, biographies, autobiographies, historical accounts, essays, poems, and plays (http://www.thewritingsite.org/resources/genre/technical.asp). The general characteristics of narrative writing include:

- Plot Structure
    - introduction
    - rising action
    - climax
    - falling action
    - resolution
- Conflict
- Characterization
- Setting
- Theme
- Point of view
- Sequencing
- Transitions

Persuasive writing

The goal of persuasive writing is to give an opinion in an attempt to convince the reader that this point of view is valid. This type of writing tries to persuade the reader to take a specific action. Persuasive writing appears in speeches, letters to the editor, editorials, advertisements, award nominations, pamphlets, petitions, scholarly writing, and opinion pieces. (http://www.thewritingsite.org/resources/genre/technical.asp). The general characteristics of persuasive writing include:

- Stated position or belief
- Factual supports
- Persuasive techniques
- Logical argument
- A call to action

Writing Poetry

Poetic writing is a written art form that helps the writer express an imaginative awareness and is arranged to create a specific emotional response, sometimes employing the use of repetition, meter, and rhyme. Poetry is an art form that uses language and form to communicate an idea or an experience, because it is highly individual, the structure and elements are varied and unlimited in scope (http://www.thewritingsite.org/resources/genre/technical.asp). Poetry appears almost everywhere, and examples include haiku, couplet, tercet, quatrain, cinquain, limerick, ballad, lyrics, sonnet, etc. The general characteristics of poetry may include:

- Figurative language
- Rhyme and euphony

- Meter
- Poetic devices
- Free verse
- Blank verse

On the basis of subject matter, style or literary characteristics, poetry is classified in two genres: narrative and non-narrative poetry.

Narrative Poetry

Narrative poetry is the oldest genre of poetry which tells a story with regular rhyme scheme and meter. Narrative poetry can be short or long. Very often, narrative poetry reveals tradition and culture of a particular group of people (epics and ballads). This kind of poetry dates back to ancient time and many scholars believe that narrative poetry was recited as the evening entertainment. For example, Scottish and English ballads, adventurous tales such as *Robin Hood,* and Baltic and Slavic heroic poems have an oral tradition.

Sometimes, narrative poetry consists of a number of short narrative poems relating individual episodes. Greek poet Homer's famous epics *Iliad and Odyssey* are prominent examples of this kind of narrative poetry.

Narrative poetry may have an historical link based on historical fact. For instance, Alfred Lord Tennyson's *Charge of the Light Brigade* is based on the incident that occurred at the Battle of Balaclava during the Crimean War. However, sometimes the story might come from a poet's imagination or ancient mythology like Mahabharata or Ramayana of ancient India.

Non-narrative Poetry

Unlike narrative poetry, non-narrative poetry does not tell any story. This kind of poetry reveals the speaker's feelings, beliefs, and experiences. Poets of non-narrative poetry directly address the reader, without describing the characters and their actions. Non-narrative poems are focused on the writer's inner thoughts. Some of the popular forms of non-narrative poetry are Lyric, Sonnet, and Ode.

Business and Technical Writing

The goal of technical writing is to clearly communicate a select piece of information to a targeted reader or group of readers for a particular purpose in such a way that the subject can readily be understood. Technical writing appears in business and industry in the form of reports, manuals, evaluation forms and questionnaires, and business letters. (http://www.thewritingsite.org/resources/genre/technical.asp). The general characteristics of technical writing may include:

- Objective point of view
- Clear, concise language
- Factual information

- Uncomplicated structure
- Logical order
- Identified audience

Writing a Business Letter

A business letter is a formal means of communication between two people, a person and a corporation, or two corporations. Business letters differ from personal letters because they follow set rules for composition.

Common Types of Business Letters

There are many types of business letters. The key to writing a business letter is to know what type of letter is to be written. The different types of letters include: **acknowledgement, adjustment, complaint, inquiry, order, and response letter.**

- **Acknowledgement letter** -used to thank or acknowledge someone.
- **Adjustment Letter** - used in response to a written complaint against someone or something. The purpose of it is to inform the reader that actions are being taken to correct the problem and it serves as a legal document acknowledging the complaint.
- **Complaint Letter** - The complaint letter is similar to the adjustment letter; this letter let the reader know that an error as been found and needs to be corrected as soon as possible. This letter is considered a legal document.
- **Inquiry Letter** - An inquiry letter is written as a request or in response to a request made by someone. The object of the inquiry letter is to get the object or material requested in the letter.
- **Order Letter** - Order letters are exactly as they sound, they are used to order material that is running low and will be needed soon. This type of letter is commonly known as a PO (purchase order). This letter is also a legal document showing a transaction between a business and a vendor.
- **Response Letter** - The purpose of this letter is to respond to a request.

Business Letter Formatting

1. Salutation

The salutation is followed by a comma or a colon; the colon is considered more formal of the two.

2. Body

In a business letter, paragraphs are not indented, but instead designated by extra spaces, with one inch margins all around, including after the letterhead, if space permits. The letter should be centered on the page, based on its total length, including the complimentary close and any instructions like "cc:" or "encl." Paragraphs are brief, clear, and to the point. The first paragraph should answer all the journalistic W's: why, when, where, who, what, and how. The subsequent paragraphs provide details, or the solutions to the situations presented.

Business letters should be formal in nature; informal correspondence should be reserved for memos. Business letters are usually kept as records.

3. Closing

A business letter is closed with an appropriate complimentary close. "Sincerely," "Very truly yours," "Best wishes," or "Regards." A business letter ends with the sender's name (typed, with the signature above the sender's title), cc: or encl: (if appropriate).

Purpose, Audience, and Register

Students must acknowledge the myriad of purposes for communication. Thus, students must consider **purpose, audience, subject matter,** and **register** (formality of language) and how each of these affects discourse.

An important feature of writing is the major purpose or aim of the writer. The four basic purposes of writing can be categorized as follows:

- Convey information (to convey knowledge, to describe a scene, to give instructions, etc.)
- Persuade (to inspire, to express a desire or need, to prove a point, etc.)
- Express the self (to express beliefs, to express emotions, to react to an event, etc.)
- Create literature (to tell a story, to amuse, to reveal the human condition, etc.)

The strategies a writer uses for **informing** the reader about a subject are vastly different from those a writer uses when trying to persuade the reader. The writer who is trying to inform conveys his or her message while providing subject knowledge, while the writer who is trying to persuade concentrates on having an effect on the reader (Hunt, 1991).

Moreover, the strategies and skills for writing literature are equally specialized from those used when writing for **self-expression**. The writer who is creating literature places emphasis on literary characteristics such as plot, characterization, rhythm, symbolism, and dialogue, while the writer who writes for self-expression focuses on his or her inner feelings and expressions. Most writing does not attempt to achieve all of these aims, but rather conveys a single, dominant purpose while subordinating the others (Hunt, 1991).

A writer must also consider **register**, the formality or informality of language, when writing. **Formal English** utilizes words, expressions, grammar, and standards of usage used for serious occasions when writing essays, research papers, scholarly works, literary criticism, and speeches. The syntax of formal language is often long and precisely structured with extensive use of vocabulary, few contractions, and little or no use of slang or colloquial expression (Hunt, 1991). Conversely, **informal English** is the Standard English used in oral conversations and broadcasting as well as in newspapers, magazines, and trade books. The syntax and vocabulary of informal English reflect more relaxed standards than those used in formal English and also include the use of contractions, colloquial expressions, and slang (Hunt, 1991).

Using Rhetorical Strategies for Persuasion

Three types of rhetorical appeals, or persuasive strategies, most often used in arguments to support claims and respond to opposing arguments include:

- **appeal to reason (logos);**
- **appeal to morality (ethos); and**
- **appeal to emotion (pathos).**

1. Appeal to reason (logos)

Logos, or the appeal to reason, relies on logic to make a point. Logos often depends on the use of **inductive** or **deductive reasoning**.

Inductive reasoning takes a specific representative case or facts and then draws generalizations or conclusions from them. Inductive reasoning must be based on sufficient, reliable evidence. In other words, the facts drawn upon must fairly represent the larger situation or population.

For example: Fair trade agreements have raised the quality of life for coffee producers, so fair trade agreements could be used to help other farmers as well. In this example the specific case of fair trade agreements with coffee producers is being used as the starting point for the claim. Because these agreements have worked, the author concludes that it could work for other farmers too.

Deductive reasoning begins with a generalization and then applies it to a specific case. The generalization at the beginning of the paper or speech must also be based on sufficient, reliable evidence.

For example: Genetically modified seeds have caused poverty, hunger, and a decline in bio-diversity everywhere they have been introduced, so the same thing will occur when genetically modified corn seeds are introduced in Mexico. In this example the author starts with a large claim, that genetically modified seeds have been problematic everywhere, and from this draws the more localized or specific conclusion that Mexico will be affected in the same way.

2. Appeal to morality (ethos)

Ethos, or the ethical appeal, is based on the character, credibility, or reliability of the information. In order to establish good character and credibility an author or speaker should:

- Use only credible, reliable sources to build the argument and cite those sources properly.

- Respect the reader by stating the opposing position accurately.

- Establish common ground with the audience. Most of the time, this can be accomplished by acknowledging values and beliefs shared by those on both sides of the argument.

- If appropriate for the assignment, disclose the reasons for interest in this topic or personal experiences which support the topic.

The argument should be organized in a logical, easy to follow manner such as the **Toulmin Method** of logic or should follow a simple pattern: chronological order, general to detailed, earliest to most recent, etc. Using the Toulmin Method is an effective way of getting to the HOW and WHY levels of the arguments. It is a type of textual "dissection" that allows the writer or speaker to break an argument into its different parts (such as claim, reasons, and evidence) so that judgments can be made on how well the different parts work together. To respond analytically to an argument is to do much more than state a basic agreement or disagreement with it; it is to determine the BASIS of one's agreement or disagreement. In other words, analysis is a process of discovering how the argumentative strategies an author employs (the HOW and WHY levels of an argument) lead the reader to respond to the content (the WHAT level) of that argument in a specific way.

3. Appeal to emotion (pathos)
Pathos, or emotional appeal, appeals to an audience's needs, values, and emotional sensibilities. Argument emphasizes reason, but used properly there is often a place for emotion as well.

Emotional appeals can use sources such as interviews and individual stories to paint a more legitimate and moving picture of reality or illuminate the truth. For example, telling the story of a particular child who has been abused may make for a more persuasive argument than simply stating the number of children abused each year because it would give a human face to the numbers.

An emotional appeal should only be used if it truly supports the claim being made, not as a way to distract from the real issues of debate. An argument should never use emotion to misrepresent the topic or frighten people.

Types of persuasive arguments
The three main types of persuasive arguments are: proposition of fact, questions of value, and questions of policy.

1. Proposition of fact - refers to something that is known to be either true or false, and the writer chooses to argue about it.

> Examples include historical controversy, predictions, or questions of existence:
> *To persuade the audience that California should succeed from the Union.*
> *To persuade the audience that the purchase of a home is a good financial investment.*

2. Questions of value - the writer argues whether or not a topic is right or wrong, moral or immoral, or better or worse than another.

> Examples include:
> *To persuade the audience that it is wrong to drive when drinking.*
> *To persuade the audience that an Apple computer is better than a PC computer.*

3. Questions of policy - the writer argues that some action should or should not be taken. The form is always: To persuade the audience that X should do Y.

> Examples include:
> *To persuade the audience that the U.S. military should leave Iraq and Afghanistan.*
> *To persuade the audience that they should get a flu shot every year.*

Fallacies of Argument

Common errors in reasoning that undermine the logic of a speaker's or writer's argument are fallacies of argument. An informed reader must be aware of fallacies in an argument (http://www.fallacyfiles.org/wanalogy.html). Examples of errors in reasoning may include:

Slippery slope: This is a conclusion based on the premise that if A happens, then eventually through a series of small steps, through B, C,..., X, Y, Z will happen, too, basically equating A and Z. So, if we don't want Z to occur, A must not be allowed to occur either.

Example: "If we ban assault rifles because they are capable of killing multiple people eventually the government will ban all guns, so we should not ban assault rifles." In this example the author is equating banning assault rifles with banning all guns, which is not the same thing.

Hasty Generalities: This is a conclusion based on insufficient or biased evidence. In other words, the speaker is rushing to a conclusion before he or she has obtained all the relevant facts.

Example: "Even though it's only my first day of my vacation to France, I can tell this is going to be a terrible summer."

Begging the Claim: The conclusion that the writer is trying to prove is already validated within the claim.

Example: "Filthy and polluting coal should be banned." Arguing that coal pollutes the earth and thus should be banned would be logical. But the very conclusion that should be proved, that coal causes enough pollution to warrant banning its use, is already assumed in the claim by referring to it as "filthy and polluting."

Circular Argument: This restates the argument rather than actually proving it.

Example: "President Obama is a good communicator because he speaks effectively." In this example the conclusion that Obama is a "good communicator" and the evidence used to prove it "he speaks effectively" are basically the same idea.

Either/or: This is a conclusion that oversimplifies the argument by reducing it to only two sides or choices.

Example: "We can either stop using oil or destroy the earth." In this example where two choices are presented as the only options, the author ignores a range of choices in between such as developing alternative energy or cutting oil usage.

Ad hominem: This is an attack on the character of a person rather than their opinions or arguments.

Example: "Green Peace's strategies aren't effective because they are all dirty, lazy hippies." In this example the author doesn't name particular strategies Green Peace has suggested, much less evaluate those strategies on their merits. Instead, the author attacks the character of the individuals in the group.

Emotional Appeal (Ad populum): This is an emotional appeal that speaks to positive (such as patriotism, religion, democracy) or negative (such as terrorism or fascism) concepts rather than the real issue at hand.

Example: If you were a true American you would support the rights of people to choose whatever gun they want. In this example the author equates being a "true American," a concept that people want to be associated with, particularly in a time of war, with allowing people to buy any gun they want even though there is no inherent connection between the two.

Red Herring: This is a diversionary tactic that avoids the key issues, often by avoiding opposing arguments rather than addressing them.

Example: Growing and selling poppies to produce opium is unsafe, but what will poor farmers in third world countries do to support their families? In this example the author switches the discussion away from the illegalities of growing opium and talks instead about an economic issue, the livelihood of those growing poppies to produce opium. While one issue may affect the other, it does not mean we should ignore illegal drug issues because of possible economic consequences to a few individuals.

Weak Analogy – a weak comparison. Arguments by analogy rest on a comparison between two cases. Students would examine a known case, and extend their findings to an unknown case. This kind of argument relies on the cases compared being similar. The argument is only as strong as that comparison. If the two cases are dissimilar in important respects, then the argument commits the weak analogy fallacy. For example: In an Associated Press news article, *Efforts to ban chlordane assailed*, a weak comparison is presented:

WASHINGTON (AP)--The only exterminator in Congress told his colleagues Wednesday that it would be a short-sighted move to ban use of chlordane and related termiticides that cause cancer in laboratory animals. Supporters of the bill, however, claimed that the Environmental Protection Agency was "dragging its feet" on a chemical that could cause 300,000 cancers in the American population in 70 years. "This bill reminds me of legislation that ought to be introduced to outlaw automobiles" on the grounds that cars kill people, said Rep. Tom DeLay, R-Texas, who owns an exterminating business. EPA banned use of the chemicals on crops in 1974, but permitted use against termites because the agency did not believe humans were exposed. Chlordane does not kill termites but rather drives them away (Associated Press, June 25th, 1987).

Logical Argument

However, the appeal to reason is often complicated in terms of rhetoric, because rhetorical reasoning is not exactly the same as logical reasoning. Logic operates in fully developed and articulated **syllogisms**, while rhetoric often employs a truncated syllogism—called an **enthymeme**.

A **syllogism** consists of three parts: a major premise, a minor premise, and a conclusion. While the tests for valid logic are quite complicated, the basic idea of a **syllogism** is the logical argument that if:

- All x are y, and
- Z is an x,
- Therefore, z is a y.

In logic, **a syllogism** uses a form of deductive reasoning consisting of a major premise, a minor premise, and a conclusion.

> Major premise: All mammals are warm-blooded.
> Minor premise: All black dogs are mammals.
> Conclusion: Therefore, all black dogs are warm-blooded.

In rhetoric, an **enthymeme** is an informally stated **syllogism**. Several examples include:
> George Bush is not a wimp; he's a military hero.
> She's a girl; she can't throw the ball.
> He's a man, of course he wouldn't stop to ask directions.

In rhetoric, though, we rarely spell out the full **syllogism**; instead, we argue through the use of **enthymemes**—a **syllogism** in which one premise (usually the minor premise) is not stated. The writer assumes the omitted premise. It makes the logic harder to test, because the whole argument is not spelled out, however, the reasoning in an **enthymeme** is usually easy enough to follow, and a bad premise is easily found and disputed.

Classical Argument

Since the days when Greek peasants learned strategies for appealing their cases to Greek courts in the fifth century B.C., the **classical argument** has stood as a model for writers who believe their case can be argued logically and plausibly to an open-minded audience. In its simplest form, the classical argument has five main parts:

1. The **introduction**, which warms up the audience, establishes goodwill and rapport with the readers, and announces the general theme or thesis of the argument.

2. The **narration**, which summarizes relevant background material, provides any information the audience needs to know about the environment and circumstances that produce the argument, and set up the stakes–what's at risk in this question.

3. The **confirmation**, which lays out in a logical order (usually strongest to weakest or most obvious to most subtle) the claims that support the thesis, providing evidence for each claim.

4. The **refutation and concession**, which looks at opposing viewpoints to the writer's claims, anticipating objections from the audience, and allowing as much of the opposing viewpoints as possible without weakening the thesis.

5. The **summation**, which provides a strong conclusion, amplifying the force of the argument, and showing the readers that this solution is the best at meeting the circumstances.

Academic Honesty / Citing Sources

It is essential that students understand and apply the fair use / copyright rules that protect copyrighted information. The first place to begin this endeavor is by teaching students about fair use / copyright law.

Critiquing Sources

Once students have gathered their sources for their research paper, they must then evaluate the material found. This is especially true of resources found on the Internet.

The articles in scientific publications are previously scrutinized by scientific evaluation before being published. Scientific journals have a system called peer review, which means that all articles are reviewed by researchers within the field before publication to guarantee scientific quality. In contrast, anyone can publish anything on the Internet so there is no safeguard for evaluation. Students must therefore develop the skills to judge the quality of information found on the Internet.

Considering this, evaluation is mostly about judging the quality of webpages. By asking a number of questions students can ascertain if the information can be used for their research paper (www.libraryresources.com).

Author - Who is the author? Can you find any information about him/her? Can this information be verified?

Subject and perspective- How does the material cover the subject? Sometimes all that is needed is an overview of the subject; sometimes specific aspects of a subject are needed. The material chosen should suit the student's information needs.

Facts & Details – Is the material correct? Are the facts right? It is naturally easier to be certain as to what is correct when dealing with a known subject. However, encyclopedias can be used to compare facts with the material found.

Is the text objective or does the author put forward his or her own views?

Is the material unique or are you finding similar or better information from other sources?

Purpose and target groups - What is the purpose of the text? What does the author want to achieve by it? Does he want to inform, provoke, or persuade?

Audience - Who is the intended audience: researchers, school students or the public?

Is the material relevant and up to date?

Publisher - Which organization is responsible for the information?

References - Which other articles and so on has the author used or quoted? Does the author reference the sources in a bibliography?

Citing Sources

Students may be surprised to learn that the myriad of media materials and electronic information found online are not only subject to critical evaluation, but also must be cited as reference sources when integrated into class work. Students must be taught to assume that everything found online is copyrighted and protected.

Fair use is the most significant limitation on the copyright holder's exclusive rights (United States Copyright Office, 2010, para. 1). The individual who wants to use a copyrighted work must weigh four factors:

The purpose and character of the use:
- Is the new work merely a copy of the original? If it is simply a copy, it is not as likely to be considered fair use.
- Does the new work offer something above and beyond the original? Does it transform the original work in some way? If the work is altered significantly, used for another purpose, appeals to a different audience, it more likely to be considered fair use (NOLO, 2010). Recent case law has increasingly focused on transformative use to make fair use determinations
- Is the use of the copyrighted work for nonprofit or educational purposes? The use of copyrighted works for nonprofit or educational purposes is more likely to be considered fair use (NOLO, 2010).

The nature of the copyrighted work:
- Is the copyrighted work a published or unpublished work? Unpublished works are less likely to be considered fair use.

- Is the copyrighted work out of print? If it is, it is more likely to be considered fair use.
- Is the work factual or artistic? The more a work tends toward artistic expression, the less likely it will be considered fair use (NOLO, 2010).

The amount and substantiality of the portion used:
- The more you use, the less likely it will be considered fair use.
- Does the amount you use exceed a reasonable expectation? If it approaches 50 percent of the entire work, it is not likely to be considered a fair use of the copyrighted work.
- Is the particular portion used likely to adversely affect the author's economic gain? If you use the "heart" or "essence" of a work, it is less likely your use will be considered fair (NOLO, 2010).

The effect of use on the potential market for the copyrighted work:
- The more the new work differs from the original, the less likely it will be considered an infringement.
- Does the work appeal to the same audience as the original? If the answer is yes, it will likely be considered an infringement.
- Does the new work contain anything original? If it does, it is more likely the use of the copyrighted material will be seen as fair use (NOLO, 2010).

Works Cited: Documentation Formats
Students should understand the importance of using acceptable formats for communicating the various forms of discourse. The three most common formats for documentation include: The Modern Language Association (MLA), The American Psychological Association (APA), and the Chicago Manual of Style. (A specific review of the MLA style is presented in previous chapters.)

MLA, **APA,** and the **Chicago Citation Style** are all style guides intended for use in research papers. The purpose of a style guide is to standardize formatting and style used in a document. Each of the common style guides has different guidelines when it comes to article preparation.

MLA was created in 1985 and is used mostly in academic papers in high school and undergraduate universities. MLA is particularly dominant as a citation format in the humanities because of the emphasis on the source's author and the specific page of reference. This makes it easy for a reader to locate the original quotation.

The American Psychological Association's (APA) style differs from MLA in its handling of citations, and is primarily used for research papers in the field of psychology and the related social sciences. It is notable for specific instructions to reduce bias in writing about gender, race, and other areas where discrimination is possible. APA citations bring focus to the year the source was published. This helps readers understand whether the research study is current, or an example of an "earlier theory."

The Chicago Manual of Style originated in 1906 and is used primarily in historical journals and some of the social sciences and has been relatively consistent since its inception. Chicago style is dependent on footnotes, which makes it ideal for historical topics. Historians often cite multiple sources in rapid succession, so lean, uncluttered citations are important to keep the reader engaged.

References

Beale, W. H. (1986). Real Writing. Scott Foresman: NY

Bruner, J.S. (1967). On knowing: Essays for the left hand. Cambridge, Mass: Harvard University Press.

Colburn, A. (2010). *What Teacher Educators Need to Know about Inquiry-Based Instruction*, http://www.csulb.edu/~acolburn/AETS.htm.

Copyright and Fair Use Guidelines for Teachers: www.mediafestival.org/downloads.html

Edward P. J. (2001). *Classical Rhetoric for the Modern Student* Oxford Press: UK

Hunt, D. (1991). The *Riverside Guide to Writing*. Houghton Mifflin Company: Boston.

NOLO. (2010). The Fair Use Rule: When use of Copyrighted Material is Acceptable. http://www.nolo.com/legal-encyclopedia/article-30100.html

Smith, C. B. (1994). *Helping Children Understand Literary Genres*. Bloomington, IN: ERIC Clearinghouse on Reading English and Communication

Wood, J. (2000). A Marriage Waiting to Happen: Computers and Process Writing, Education Development Center, Inc. (EDC). http ://www.edtechleaders.org

http://www.benedict.com
www.halldavidson.net/downloads.html
http://www.libraryresources.com
http://www.mediafestival.org
http://www.nolo.com/legal-encyclopedia/article-30100.html
http://www.writing.colostate.edu/guides/processes/topic/pop15c.cfm.
http://www.thewritesource.com
http://www.thewritingsite.org/resources/genre/technical.asp
http://history_How_to_Write_a_Historical_Essay.html

Practice Questions

The following excerpt is from a speech by Robert Kennedy delivered April 4, 1968 in which he announces the death of Martin Luther King and then answer the questions which follow.

. . . Martin Luther King dedicated his life to love and to justice between fellow human beings. He died in the cause of that effort. In this difficult day, in this difficult time for the United States, it's perhaps well to ask what kind of a nation we are and what direction we want to move in. For those of you who are black -- considering the evidence evidently is that there were white people who were responsible -- you can be filled with bitterness, and with hatred, and a desire for revenge.

We can move in that direction as a country, in greater polarization -- black people amongst blacks, and white amongst whites, filled with hatred toward one another. Or we can make an effort, as Martin Luther King did, to understand, and to comprehend, and replace that violence, that stain of bloodshed that has spread across our land, with an effort to understand, compassion, and love.

For those of you who are black and are tempted to fill with -- be filled with hatred and mistrust of the injustice of such an act, against all white people, I would only say that I can also feel in my own heart the same kind of feeling. I had a member of my family killed, but he was killed by a white man.

But we have to make an effort in the United States. We have to make an effort to understand, to get beyond, or go beyond these rather difficult times.

My favorite poem, -- my favorite poet was Aeschylus. And he once wrote:

> *Even in our sleep, pain which cannot forget*
> *falls drop by drop upon the heart,*
> *until, in our own despair,*
> *against our will,*
> *comes wisdom*
> *through the awful grace of God.*

What we need in the United States is not division; what we need in the United States is not hatred; what we need in the United States is not violence and lawlessness, but is love, and wisdom, and compassion toward one another, and a feeling of justice toward those who still suffer within our country, whether they be white or whether they be black.

So I ask you tonight to return home, to say a prayer for the family of Martin Luther King -- yeah, it's true -- but more importantly to say a prayer for our own country, which all of us love -- a prayer for understanding and that compassion of which I spoke.

We can do well in this country. We will have difficult times. We've had difficult times in the past, but we -- and we will have difficult times in the future. It is not the end of violence; it is not the end of lawlessness; and it's not the end of disorder.

But the vast majority of white people and the vast majority of black people in this country want to live together, want to improve the quality of our life, and want justice for all human beings that abide in our land.

And let's dedicate ourselves to what the Greeks wrote so many years ago: to tame the savageness of man and make gentle the life of this world. Let us dedicate ourselves to that, and say a prayer for our country and for our people (http://www.americanrhetoric.com/speeches/rfkonmlkdeath.html).

1. Which of the following strategies is Robert Kennedy using in his speech?
   a. Appeal to reason
   b. Appeal to authority
   c. Appeal to emotion
   d. The literary device of personification

A is correct.

2. Which of the following is the main theme of Kennedy's speech?
   a. This country is bountiful and will overcome all of its problems.
   b. All Americans must give up violence and work together toward a better future together.
   c. We are in difficult time and this will not be the last of the violence we see.
   d. It is difficult to overcome the tragedy of violence.

B is correct.

3. Of the following, which literary device is used in the first two lines of the poem that Kennedy quotes?
   Even in our sleep, pain which cannot forget
   falls drop by drop upon the heart,
   a. extended metaphor
   b. alliteration
   c. internal rhyme
   d. personification

D is correct.

4. Which of the following is an example of **syllogism**?

    a. We can either stop using oil or destroy the earth.
    b. Having a funeral without the body is like having a wedding without the bride.
    c. In mist or cloud, on mast or shroud, while all the night through fog-smoke moved.
    d. All books from that store are new. These books are from that store. Therefore, these books are new.

D is correct. In logic, **a syllogism** uses a form of deductive reasoning consisting of a major premise, a minor premise, and a conclusion.

5. Which of the following types of argument is presented in the sentence below?
President Reagan was a great communicator because he had the knack of talking effectively to the people.

    a. Red herring
    b. Hasty generalization
    c. Circular argument
    d. Either/or

C is correct.

DOMAIN IV:

Chapter 10: Oral Communication

Chapter 11: Media Literacy

DOMAIN IV — ORAL COMMUNICATION AND MEDIA LITERACY

Competency 010: The teacher understands principles of oral communication and promotes students' development of listening and speaking skills.

The beginning teacher:

- Understands similarities and differences between oral and written language and promotes students' awareness of these similarities and differences.
- Understands and helps students understand the role of cultural factors in oral communication.
- Facilitates effective student interaction and oral communication, including group discussions and individual presentations.
- Understands and teaches various forms of oral discourses (e.g., conversation, group discussion, formal presentation) and their characteristics and provides effective opportunities for practice.
- Understands and teaches skills for speaking to diverse audiences for various purposes and provides students with effective opportunities to apply these skills in a variety of contexts.
- Understands and teaches strategies for preparing, organizing and delivering different types of oral presentations, including informative and persuasive messages and literary interpretations.
- Understands and teaches skills and strategies for using technology in oral presentations.
- Understands and teaches strategies for evaluating the content and effectiveness of spoken messages and provides effective opportunities for practice.
- Understands and teaches skills for active, purposeful listening in various situations (e.g., skills for note taking, for critically evaluating a speaker's message, for appreciating an oral performance) and provides effective opportunities for practice.
- Demonstrates an understanding of informal and formal procedures for monitoring and assessing students' oral communication skills.
- Uses assessment results to plan and adapt instruction that addresses students' strengths, needs and interests and that builds on students' current skills to increase proficiency in oral communication.

Competency 011: The teacher understands and teaches basic principles of media literacy and provides students with opportunities to apply these principles in interactions with media.

The beginning teacher:

- Understands different types and purposes of media.
- Analyzes and teaches about the influence of the media and the power of visual images.
- Demonstrates awareness of ethical and legal factors (e.g., copyright, fair use, liability) to consider in the use and creation of media products.

- Applies and teaches skills for responding to, interpreting, analyzing and critiquing a variety of media (e.g., advertising, visual images, propaganda, documentaries).
- Understands and facilitates the production of media messages (e.g., illustrations, charts, graphs, videos, multimedia presentations).
- Guides students to evaluate their own and others' media productions.
- Demonstrates an understanding of informal and formal procedures for monitoring and assessing students' media literacy.
- Uses assessment results to plan and adapt instruction that addresses students' strengths, needs and interests and that builds on students' current skills to increase their media literacy.

Domain IV: Chapter 10
Competency 010: Oral Communication

The beginning teacher:
- Understands similarities and differences between oral and written language and promotes students' awareness of these similarities and differences.
- Understands and helps students understand the role of cultural factors in oral communication.
- Facilitates effective student interaction and oral communication, including group discussions and individual presentations.
- Understands and teaches various forms of oral discourses (e.g., conversation, group discussion, formal presentation) and their characteristics and provides effective opportunities for practice.
- Understands and teaches skills for speaking to diverse audiences for various purposes and provides students with effective opportunities to apply these skills in a variety of contexts.
- Understands and teaches strategies for preparing, organizing and delivering different types of oral presentations, including informative and persuasive messages and literary interpretations.
- Understands and teaches skills and strategies for using technology in oral presentations.
- Understands and teaches strategies for evaluating the content and effectiveness of spoken messages and provides effective opportunities for practice.
- Understands and teaches skills for active, purposeful listening in various situations (e.g., skills for note taking, for critically evaluating a speaker's message, for appreciating an oral performance) and provides effective opportunities for practice.
- Demonstrates an understanding of informal and formal procedures for monitoring and assessing students' oral communication skills.
- Uses assessment results to plan and adapt instruction that addresses students' strengths, needs and interests and that builds on students' current skills to increase proficiency in oral communication.

Key Terms

Active listening
Debate
Evaluation
Flow chart
Idea list
Informative speaking
Graphic organizer
Group discussion
Impromptu speaking
Kinesics
Literary interpretation
Nonverbal messages
One-on-one communication
Open ended questions
Oral discourse
Persuasive speaking
Pitch
Proximity
Rehearsal
Speaking rate
Spider cluster
Stress
T-chart
Teams Policy Debate
Transitions
Venn diagram
Visual aids
Volume

Oral Communication Processes

Oral communication is essential in the classroom for sharing ideas, and supporting learning, thinking, and decision-making in all areas of the curriculum. Oral communication is enjoyable and plays an important role in personal and professional life (Cox, 1999).

Principles of Oral Communication

Communication is the process people use to understand one another. In order to communicate effectively, students must learn to speak and listen carefully in order to convey their ideas or understand the ideas of others. When preparing to speak in front of an audience, students must plan their presentations carefully. Students must first learn to define and limit their topic and identify the purpose of their communication. Second, they must be able to show concern for their audience by understanding the type and needs of the listeners in order to match their message to the audience's needs. Third, when researching their topic, students must select and organize their information to be presented, and then select the appropriate media and timing options for delivery. Also, students must learn to present themselves and their message confidently. (Bienvenu & Timm, 2002) Finally, when giving an oral presentation, students should:

- Provide sufficient introductory information.
- Use transitions from one main part to the next and between points of the speech.
- Use summary statements and restatements.
- Make the main ideas of the report clearly distinguishable from one another.

Developing Communication Skills

In order to develop communication skills, students in English / language arts classrooms are required to participate in a variety of interpersonal and group communication settings. Students are required to develop effective one-on-one communication, group discussion, and public speaking skills (Bienvenu & Timm, 2002). During one-to-one communication, students must be able to:

- Choose words carefully in order to ensure that the listener will understand the message.
- Present ideas in a logical order to ensure that the listener will be able to follow the conclusion.
- Become careful listeners when conversing by concentrating on the speaker's message.
- Understand that effective conversations involve taking turns and showing respect for other speakers, even during disagreement.
- Use effective body language when speaking and listening.

People actually communicate on various levels, both verbally and nonverbally. In order for communication to succeed, a common language must be shared and the **nonverbal messages** of the speaker must be understood by the listener. **Nonverbal** communication through body language can send signals to listeners through a variety of ways. **Kinesics** is the understanding of body language or motion during communication. Rolling one's eyes, frowning, staring, laughing, gesturing, crossing one's arms, or any other similar body movement are all examples of kinesics or body language that will convey a message to the listener by supporting or discrediting the speaker's words. For example, eye contact can indicate a listener's interest in the speaker; however, too little eye contact can indicate a lack of interest, while too much eye contact can be distracting.

Proximity involves the use of space to communicate and is often related to cultural mores or conventions. The way people arrange the distance between themselves and the listener conveys a message. The way the space is arranged in the classroom or office often determines the type of communication between speaker and listener. Intimate conversations are usually conducted in very close proximity between the speaker and listener, while impersonal business or public speaking is conducted at much greater distances. Emotional closeness is often conveyed through proximity; however, it is important to remember that spatial comfort zones vary according to custom and individual preference (Bienvenu & Timm, 2002).

Active Listening Skills
In the English / language arts classroom emphasis must be placed on all aspects of communication because communication involves not talking, but listening as well. Listening involves understanding and interpretation of the speaker's message. Research reveals that most people are not very good listeners; therefore, it is important that students learn the skills of active, purposeful listening in a variety of situations. Teaching students to become active listeners will help them avoid misunderstandings, learn more about the world, and become more successful in school and in the business world (Cox, 1999).

A good listener should be an active listener; therefore, students must be taught the skills of critically evaluating the speaker's message, and appreciating an oral performance. As active listeners, students should be prepared to listen "actively" in order to gain the most from the speaker's message. This involves investigating the background of the topic to build prior knowledge, and staying engaged with the speaker (through note taking) in order to identify and understand the main idea or message.

During classroom discussion, teachers can promote active listening skills by focusing lessons on the construction of meaning rather than just the acquisition of information. Students must be taught to find the central idea the speaker is conveying and then be able to respond to the message through creative and critical thinking activities. Teachers help develop critical listening skills by providing opportunities for students to listen actively and respond orally as they analyze the speaker's message (Cox, 1999).

Teachers should pose open-ended questions which have a variety of answers and encourage critical and creative thinking-questions which help students discover their own ideas and sharpen critical thinking skills. For example: What is your response to the speaker's key points? What other solutions or answers do you wish to investigate? Teachers should encourage brain-storming when students discuss their responses in large or small groups. Brainstorming encourages students' imagination as they explore the facts, ideas, problems, and solutions related to the presentation. Students can then use clustering or webbing to record their ideas during discussions (Cox, 1999).

Strategies for Active Listening

Students should participate in lessons which require evidence of active listening. Teachers may ask students to create any number of graphic organizers while they listen to the concepts or ideas the speaker is communicating (Cox, 1999):

- Spider cluster-a graphic aid that connects supporting ideas to a main idea or point.
- T-chart-a graphic aid used to compare and contrast two subjects.
- Idea list or chronological list-a graphic aid using ideas which occur in a specific order.
- Flowchart-a graphic aid used to visualize the flow of ideas or steps in a solution.
- Main Idea - Supporting Evidence
- Venn diagram-a graphic aid used to visualize the relationship or overlap of characteristics of two or more concepts.

Teaching Strategies for Oral Communication

During whole-group or small group lessons, students should participate in lessons that require them to explore ideas and concepts orally in order to solve problems in pairs or small groups, conduct interviews, report on research findings, or participate in a read-aloud of their favorite play or short story. When teaching strategies for oral communication, it is important to note that group size, physical environment, and seating arrangements may affect learning outcomes. While participating in group discussion, students must be able to determine and manage the task, cooperate with others while working, solve conflicts within the group, and participate in decision-making in order to complete the task.

Oral Discourse

In order to build communication skills, students must learn to **plan and deliver speeches** in class by first focusing on a particular topic that would be of interest to the audience, and then researching the topic for supporting ideas in order to organize and outline the speech in a logical, easily-understood format. Before delivering a formal speech, students should prepare by rehearsing, either to themselves or to family members, in order to build confidence.

During **rehearsal**, consideration should be given to the physical aspects of the speaker which support communication including: **volume**-how loud or soft the speaker is speaking; **pitch**-the high or low sounds of the voice; **speaking rate**-how fast or slow the person is speaking; and **stress**-the amount of emphasis a speaker places on certain words (Bienvenu & Timm, 2002).

Types of Oral Discourse

Speeches can be delivered for a myriad of purposes: to entertain an audience, to introduce someone, to accept an honor or to eulogize a person. However, the majority of speeches are given to inform or provide others with information they do not already have, or to persuade or sway someone's opinion about a topic (Bienvenu & Timm, 2002).

Informative speaking

The purpose of an informative speech is to provide the audience with new knowledge or more knowledge than they previously had. The topics of informative speeches can vary from explaining a concept which involves theories, beliefs, or principles, to explaining an event or description of circumstances that led to an event. Most informative speeches begin with an introduction, impart a message and then conclude with a summary or restatement of the main point. Often in business settings, informative speakers use visual aids to clarify a point.

Demonstrative Speeches The demonstrative speech is closely related to the informative speech because it centers on providing the audience with information. The main difference, however, is that the demonstrative speech is considered a "how-to" lecture. Rather than passing on raw information to the audience, the speaker is explaining or teaching a concept or idea. The best way to prepare a demonstrative speech is to ask *how* and *why* questions. "How does a computer work?" "Why should I pay off my mortgage debt?" The speaker would answer those questions through a practical demonstration or visual aids, such as charts or diagrams, which explain the processes that cannot be observed easily by the audience.

Persuasive speaking

The purpose of a persuasive speech is to sway or influence an audiences' opinion about a topic. A successful persuasive speaker must appeal to the audiences' needs and logic while at the same time emphasizing his own expertise on the subject. Effective persuasive speakers are seen as competent and sincere, make frequent reference to facts and evidence, and are considered acting in the best interest of the audience. The persuasive speaker must appeal to the listeners' logic through reasoning. Thus, an effective persuasive speaker puts evidence together in a seemingly logical way in order to convince the audience of the main points. The 4th century Greek philosopher, Aristotle, described the three basic ways in which a speaker persuades an audience:

- **Ethos:** credibility, image, public reputation, perceived expertise
- **Logos:** words, concepts, logic
- **Pathos:** emotions, feelings, gut reactions

Literary Interpretation

Students may also participate in oral interpretation of literature. Oral interpretation allows students to practice oral speaking skills when retelling a favorite story, dramatically interpreting a scene or event, creating a life-like interpretation of a character, or reading a favorite poem. Oral and dramatic interpretation will be enhanced if students are asked to use props and costumes. Interviews and oral histories can also be enhanced by asking students to develop protocol questions before the interview, and then use the questions to organize the oral report when presenting their findings to the class.

Effective oral interpretation requires that students choose literature that has universal appeal, know the meaning and pronunciation of every word in the selection, and prepare for the audience by working carefully on every aspect of the delivery including: vocal flexibility, clear articulation, correct pronunciation, and appropriate hand and body gestures (Bienvenu & Timm, 2002). When adapting a written work or essay for an oral presentation, students should rewrite the passage using shorter, less complex sentences. Students should reinforce the author's main ideas through repetition.

Debate

A debate is a structured discussion or contest in which two or more people or teams present their arguments trying to persuade an audience or judge. Although debates vary in formats, often one side takes the affirmative position, supporting the resolution, while the other person (or team) gives the negative view, opposing it.

Debating Formats - Debating formats used in high schools and colleges differ, but most debates have common features. For example, all formats include both a proposition side and an opposition side. While the proposition side advocates adopting the resolution, the opposition side argues to refute it. Usually the resolution is a simple statement or policy such as "The United States federal government should go to war." Besides an audience, there's usually is a judge who declares a winner in the debate.

High School Debate format - The Lincoln-Douglas debate (L-D) is a popular high-school debating format inspired after the noted 1850s senatorial debates between Abraham Lincoln and Stephen A. Douglas. This format includes five speeches and two periods of cross-examination. Opposing teams take on affirmative and negative positions.

The Teams Policy Debate is the oldest debating format used in American high schools and is probably the most popular debating format. Teams of two debaters on each side argue affirmative and negative positions on an issue. The format consists of eight speeches. Because the first four speeches present the most important arguments, they are referred to as constructive speeches. Once a debate begins, debaters have two primary tasks: present their case in the most favorable light and to refute the arguments of the opposition. During the debate, students must take careful notes on a flow sheet to determine how the arguments on each issue are progressing. Following the constructive speeches are the rebuttals, which are the last four speeches that argue points already made instead of giving new arguments.

Impromptu speaking

Impromptu speaking is used when one is called upon to speak with no advance notice and with only a moment or two for preparation. The first rule of impromptu speaking is: "Don't panic!" Audiences do not expect impromptu speeches to be polished orations. They just want to hear the speaker's thoughts. They also do not expect a lengthy speech.

Using Visual Aids

Students should use visual aids only to clarify and support a main point. Students must also learn to choose the appropriate visual aid to support their message. Visual aids must be easily seen and read by audience members. Students should rehearse their speech using their visual aid. Caution should be used when relying upon technology as a visual aid support; a back-up plan may be needed if the computer enhanced visual aid does not work. Many effective speakers have been at a loss when equipment fails (Bienvenu & Timm, 2002).

Types of Visual Aids may include:

        Charts / Pictures
        Graphs / Three-dimensional objects
        Diagrams / Models
        Maps / Cutaways
        Posters / Handouts
        Cartoons

Delivery techniques

Proper breathing: Breathing properly is the key to a loud and powerful voice. If your shoulders move, you are only breathing from a small portion of your lungs. Instead, force your abdomen to do the work by breathing from the diaphragm. Do not move your shoulders.

Tone quality: For clarity, pay special attention to the distinctness of words. One way is to tape the speech in order to hear the clarity of the sound is, or practice with a peer. For articulation, practice reading tongue twisters, first slowly, then gradually increasing the pace to a normal rate of speaking.

Volume: Lacking volume makes a speaker appear weak, greatly diminishing the persuasiveness of the message. It is important to note that debating should not be related to arguing and quarrelling. The speaker should not give the audience a wrong impression by looking angry as if in a battle. Smile, when possible.

Pace: Speakers should also vary the rate of speaking, especially when debating, and trying to emphasize an important point. The speaker should not speak too quickly or slowly; speaking too fast and breathlessly makes the speaker appear nervous and inexperienced. Debaters tend to rush when emphasizing a point; it is better to have less information than to:

- Run words together
- Drop endings
- Unreasonably increase the pitch of one's voice

Rhythm: Words have a specific rhythm. For example, some words have short, snappy sounds, others have a flowing rhythm. The speaker should speak slowly and let the voice rise and fall naturally; thus, bringing the speech alive.

Intonation: Speakers have a certain rhythm (intonation) when speaking, sometimes not realizing it at all. Many of today's high school students exhibit the common flaw of ending every sentence with an upward intonation, making the sentence sound like a question. This should be avoided.

Emphasis: When debating, the speaker should place emphasis on the most important points in the argument; therefore, the strongest arguments are remembered by the audience.

Pauses - Mark Twain said, "The right word may be effective, but no word was ever as effective as a rightly timed pause." Students should learn to use pauses in their speech:

- To emphasize a particular point or idea
- After rhetorical questions
- After a humorous content, joke or anecdote.

Body language: Body movements and gestures should not be stilted or artificial; instead, they should originate naturally as the speech unfolds.

Style: Speakers should use a conversational tone and speak with strength and conviction, automatically raising and lowering the pitch of the voice, and increasing or decreasing the pace as needed.

Evaluating the Speaker's Message

English / Language arts teachers should use effective methods for evaluation of oral communication. Effective forms of evaluation can range from informal (self-evaluation, peers, teachers, audiences, or family members) to formal (debate contests).

Evaluation of oral presentations should align closely with the objectives of the project. Evaluation checklists and grading rubrics should be developed for each type of project (one-on-one communication, informational speech, persuasive speech, small group presentation, literary interpretation, etc.) in order to ensure that students are aware of the presentation and grading requirements.

An effective evaluation tool that supports the development of oral communication skills occurs when students practice their presentations in front of a small group of peers. The following guidelines may be implemented during the practice session for students to follow (Cox, 1999):

- Be open and receptive to feedback.
- Listen carefully to comments and take notes.
- Ask for specific information and examples.
- Look for nonverbal messages from the audience.
- Don't overreact in a defensive manner
- Accept responsibility for any needs or changes.
- Recognize that whatever the rehearsal audience perceives is real to them may represent what the real audience will see.

Delivering Speeches - A speech is a performance and effective speech delivery consists of the verbal, physical, and psychological factors that work together to constitute a performance. The following factors and questions may be used in a grading rubric for evaluation:

1. Verbal Factors

Vocal clarity - Did the speaker clearly enunciate / pronounce his/her words?
Adequate volume - Could the speaker be easily heard?
Fluency - Did the speaker's voice appear to "flow" throughout the speech? Did the speaker consistently avoid the use of "vocalized pauses"-- the *umms* and *eerrs* that can prove distracting to listeners and cause the speaker to appear less confident?

Tone - Was the speaker's manner of speaking consistent with the type of speech to be delivered?

2. Physical Factors

Presence - Did the speaker demonstrate an openness toward the audience?

Eye Contact - Did the speaker keep his/her eyes focused primarily upon the audience throughout the speech?

Effective Nonverbal Communication - Did the speaker use gestures and body language to reinforce the message?

3. Psychological Factors

Confidence - Did the speaker appear confident and in control of the message?

Connection - Was the speaker able to "connect" with his/her audience in a meaningful way?

Audience-centeredness - Were the speaker's goals and objectives focused on the audience's concerns?

References

Bienvenu, S. and Timm, P. (2002). *Business Communication: Discovering Strategy, Developing Skills*. Prentice Hall, Upper Saddle River, NJ.

Cox, C. (1999). *Teaching Language Arts: A Student and Response Centered Classroom*. Allyn and Bacon: Boston.

Lucas, S. (1998). *The Art of Public Speaking: Sixth Edition*. McGraw-Hill, Boston.

Practice Questions

1. Mr. Downs knows that when giving a persuasive speech, students should make every effort to show a genuine interest and good will toward the audience. He feels that it is important for his students to understand ways in which a speaker can persuade or convince an audience to think or act in a certain way. Of the following, which strategy would provide students the opportunity to apply their knowledge of effective persuasive communication?

   a. Have students work in small groups to view videos of the persuasive tactics of television news commentators, and then report their findings back to the class.
   b. Ask students to write a reflective response in their personal journal about the last time they were persuaded by another person.
   c. Ask students to work in small groups to write a skit about two people having a conversation; the skit should include effective persuasive communication between the speaker and listener.
   d. Have students work in small groups to read persuasive speeches presented previously by famous people.

C is correct. This answer choice asks that students apply their knowledge of effective persuasive communication.

2. Students should be aware of effective methods for evaluation of oral communication. An effective evaluation tool that supports the development of oral communication skills occurs when students are allowed to practice their presentations in front of a small group of peers. Before students present their speeches in front of their groups, Mr. Chen discusses the following guidelines:
   • Be open and receptive to feedback.
   • Look for nonverbal messages from the audience.
   • Don't overreact or defend yourself with the reasons why you said something.
   • Accept responsibility for any needs or changes.
   • Recognize that whatever your rehearsal audience perceives is real to them may represent what your real audience will see.

Which of the following additional guidelines (for evaluating oral presentations) would be **most important** for Mr. Chen to include on this list?

a. Begin and end your speech with your main points using a strong voice for emphasis.

b. At the end of your speech, thank your audience for their help in this evaluation.

c. Listen carefully to comments, take notes, and ask for specific information and examples.

d. Hand out a written summary of your speech to audience members.

C is correct. In order to gain the most from the peer evaluation process, it is important that students take notes on the evaluators' comments and ask for specific suggestions for improvement.

3. Mrs. Garcia knows that it is important for his students to practice their delivery skills for their speeches. During rehearsal, she tells the students to focus on the physical aspects of their delivery which support communication, including: volume: how loud or soft the speaker is speaking; pitch: the high or low sounds of the voice; speaking rate: how fast or slow the person is speaking; and stress: the amount of emphasis a speaker places on certain words. Of the following, which would be the best strategy to use in order to emphasize the physical aspects of speech delivery?

a. Place students with a partner and then have each student record his or her speech into a tape recorder. Students then work together with a partner to provide feedback on each other's delivery skills.

b. Ask students to view videos of professional speakers. Students then work in small groups to analyze the speakers' delivery skills.

c. Ask students to give their speeches in front of the class; when finished, ask students to provide a critique for each speech using a grading rubric.

d. Ask students to give their speeches in front of the class; when finished, Mrs. Garcia meets with each student in order to critique the delivery skills privately.

A is correct. Having each student listen to their own speaking and then working with a peer will help each student focus on the physical aspects of speech delivery.

4. Which of the following teaching strategies would be most effective in increasing student awareness of nonverbal elements when delivering a speech?

a. Ask students to take notes on a character's actions and emotions while viewing a video clip of a television show with the sound muted.

b. Ask students to take notes on a speaker's use of nonverbal expression and body language while viewing a video clip of a political speech with the sound muted.

c. Ask students to listen to previous speeches given by students.

d. Ask students to observe the teacher reading a popular poem. Students then meet in small groups to discuss their observations.

B is the correct answer. Asking students to focus only on the nonverbal elements of a speech would be an effective way to increase their awareness of this skill.

5. Which of the following lists the elements that an introduction to an oral interpretation should include?

    a. Title of the work, the author, background information, and summary
    b. Universal appeal, insight, beauty and technical excellence.
    c. Use of gestures, the nature of the work, the setting
    d. Voice, gestures, tone and clarity

A is correct. Introductions to an oral interpretation should include the title of the work, the author's name, some background information, and a summary of the work.

6. What should debaters focus on during a debate in order to prepare to meet the opposition during a rebuttal or cross-examination?

    a. Look for weak arguments and faulty reasoning, and keep a flow sheet.
    b. Prepare to prove that a problem exists and restate your side's solution.
    c. Prepare a list of short questions and demands to present to the other side.
    d. Prepare to debate the issues that are stated in the proposition.

A is correct. When preparing to meet the opposition during rebuttal or cross-examination, debaters should look for weak arguments and faulty reasoning and keep a flow sheet.

7. How does impromptu speaking differ from other types of speeches?
    a. Impromptu speaking is a type of formal speech given to a military or royal audience.
    b. Impromptu speaking requires the speaker to speak for 15 to 20 minutes on a chosen subject.
    c. Impromptu speaking requires that the speaker relax (Don't panic) and just offer his or her thoughts on a subject in a short speech.
    d. Impromptu speaking may vary in purpose depending on the synthesized and evaluated ideas presented by the opposing side.

C is correct. Impromptu speaking is used when one is called upon to speak with no advance notice and with only a moment or two for preparation. Audiences do not expect impromptu speeches to be polished orations. They just want to hear the speaker's thoughts. They also do not expect a lengthy speech.

Domain IV: Chapter 11
Competency 011: Media Literacy

The beginning teacher:

- Understands different types and purposes of media.
- Analyzes and teaches about the influence of the media and the power of visual images.
- Demonstrates awareness of ethical and legal factors (e.g., copyright, fair use, liability) to consider in the use and creation of media products.
- Applies and teaches skills for responding to, interpreting, analyzing and critiquing a variety of media (e.g., advertising, visual images, propaganda, documentaries).
- Understands and facilitates the production of media messages (e.g., illustrations, charts, graphs, videos, multimedia presentations).
- Guides students to evaluate their own and others' media productions.
- Demonstrates an understanding of informal and formal procedures for monitoring and assessing students' media literacy.
- Uses assessment results to plan and adapt instruction that addresses students' strengths, needs and interests and that builds on students' current skills to increase their media literacy.

Key Terms

Adobe page maker
Aesthetic considerations
Agenda setting theory
Catalytic theory
Critical thinking
Cultural impact of media
Cultivation theory
Desensitizing theory
Desktop publishing
Ethical factors
Excitation transfer theory
Graphic Design
Graphics
Hypodermic syringe theory
InDesign
Influence of media
Information pollution
Legal factors
Manipulation
Mass communication
Mass media
Media evaluation
Media induced passivity theory
Media literacy
Media messages
Media system dependency theory
Media types
Multimedia projects
Media purposes
Noncriticizing dysfunction theory
Opinion leader
Parasocial interaction
Persuade
QuarkXPress
Responding to media
Role model
Selective participation theory
Selective retention theory
Social impact of media
Special promotions
Spiral of silence theory
Television
Two-step flow theory

Media Analysis and Journalistic Applications

The convergence of media and technology within our global society has changed the way students learn about the world. This change has challenged the very foundations of education. In an age when most Americans get their information from television and electronic sources instead of printed texts, a need exists for a wider definition of what it means to be literate. These changes within modern society have produced a necessity for students to become media literate in order to understand and respond to an increasingly complex, technological society and world.

Students are constantly bombarded with a deluge of visual, auditory, and multimedia messages from television programs, commercials, newspapers, billboards, radio announcements, sales catalogs and social media of the Internet such as blogs, twitter, and Facebook. Media literacy requires that students interact with this growing body of information through the development of information-age communication skills. A media literate individual should be able to produce, create, and critique information in all its forms, in addition to print. In order to become media literate, students must develop an informed and critical understanding of the nature of media as it is used to transmit information. Media literacy requires that students not only recognize and comprehend information, but also think critically about the implicit meaning of media messages through questioning, analyzing and evaluating information as it is received. Students must understand that messages from the media must be examined for values, motives, and intent (Christ, 2004; Frechette, 2002).

Media Types and Purposes

The term media can be defined as a vehicle that conveys a message. A wide variety of media occur in daily life as individuals interact with their world through the use of textbooks, newspapers, television, photographs, audio / visuals, posters, graphics, billboards, music, radio programs, social media internet sites, etc. Individuals are bombarded with messages intended for worldwide audiences. Newspapers, magazines, television, radio, DVDs and video games are but a few examples of mass media.

Frechette (2002) explains that mass media have a powerful place and serve an important role in a democracy. The public's vision of the world and society are shaped by words and images projected by mass media. It is important that students understand that the exercise of democracy is affected by constraints on mass media such as high production and advertising costs. Since print and electronic media are supported primarily from sponsors through advertising, the choice of images and messages portrayed by the mass media is often pre-determined through these limitations.

Radio and television have become very effective means of mass communication, simply because of their capacity to reach a large amount of people. Most Americans have at least one television set in their home, many have multiple sets. The development of radio and television made it possible for large numbers of people to share a single experience (i.e. President John F. Kennedy's assassination; the men landing on the moon; the explosion of the Space Shuttle; the World Trade Center tragedy of 911). The global television audience for World Cup Soccer games number in the billions.

Radio and television can communicate events worldwide within a few moments. However, the audience has some control over radio and television, as they are not part of a captive audience such as a group of people in a theatre. With a push of a button, anyone can simply "turn the channel" to hear a different station or turn the medium off completely.

History of Television

Vladimir Kosma Zworykin is sometimes hailed as 'the father of modern television. He filed two patents in 1923 which formed the basis of what became "television." The Radio Corporation of America (RCA) unveiled a display of its first TV sets for sale to the American public at the World's Fair. For nearly all Americans in 1939, seeing pictures in motion on a small screen was a novelty, and a source of wonder. Some people just stared at the screen of the TV set on display. Others seeing TV for the first time that day, exclaimed, "I never thought it would be like this. Why, it's beyond conception, and here it is." (http://www.fcc.gov/omd/history/tv/1930-1959.html).

This first TV audience next saw a parade marching through the World's Fair center court. TV viewers saw New York's Mayor Fiorello LaGuardia walks up to the platform and look directly into the lens of the camera. Apparently, LaGuardia looked good on TV. The next day's New York Times called him "the most telegenic man" in the city, describing "the violent emphasis in the toss of his head and the dramatic facial expressions" that the Times reporter had watched on TV   in   Manhattan.

President Franklin D. Roosevelt also appeared on live TV that afternoon; he was the first President to do so. He rode a limousine into the Fair after the parade and later gave the speech that officially opened the Fair to the public.

It was in the years immediately preceding WWII that the television industry we know today was born. RCA's David Sarnoff used his company's exhibit at the 1939 World's Fair as a showcase for the first Presidential speech on television and to introduce RCA's new line of television receivers – some of which had to be coupled with a radio to hear sound. In addition, anybody visiting the Fair could go into the RCA pavilion and step before the cameras themselves.

The excitement about television generated by the 1939 World's Fair carried the interest in television through WWII when development of the medium took a back seat. By the time the war was over, the electronic system of television had clearly proven its greater capacity and a period of intense growth took place. Between 1945 and 1948 the number of commercial (as opposed to experimental) television stations grew from 9 to 48 and the number of cities having commercial service went from 8 to 23. Sales of television sets increased 500%, and by 1960 there were 440 commercial VHF stations, 75 UHF stations, and 85% of U.S. households had a television set (http://www.fcc.gov/omd/history/tv/1930-1959.html).

This "Golden Age" of television also saw the establishment of several significant technological standards. These included the National Television Standards Committee (NTSC) standards for black and white (1941) and color television (1953). Thus the "Golden Age" was a period of intense growth and expansion, introducing many of the television accessories and methods of distribution that we take for granted today. But the revolution – technological and cultural – that television was to introduce to America and the world was just beginning (http://www.fcc.gov/omd/history/tv/1930-1959.html).

The History of the Radio
Inventor Ernst Alexanderson was the General Electric Company engineer whose high-frequency alternator gave America its start in the field of **radio communication**. In 1904, Alexanderson was assigned to build a high-frequency machine that would operate at high speeds and produce a continuous-wave commission.

Before the invention of this alternator, radio was an affair only of dots and dashes transmitted by inefficient crashing spark machines. After two years of experimentation, Alexanderson finally constructed a two-kilowatt, 100,000-cycle machine. It was installed in the Fessenden station at Brant Rock, Massachusetts, on Christmas Eve 1906. It enabled that station to transmit a radio broadcast which included a voice and a violin solo.

The first **commercial** radio station was KDKA Pittsburgh in 1920. Since then the radio industry has enjoyed tremendous popularity, provided listeners with endless hours of entertainment and information, and played a valuable role in the making of history (http://www.fcc.gov/omd/history/tv/1930-1959.html).

The Development of Electronic Media
Mass communication in written forms has been available for hundreds of years. More recent technological advancement have made possible the development of electronic forms of mass communication. The growth from dependency on wires (telegraph, telephone) to "wireless" communication marked the beginning of important changes.

History of the World Wide Web / Internet

Tim Berners-Lee invented the World Wide Web in 1989, about 20 years after the first connection was established over what is today known as the Internet. At the time, Tim was a software engineer at CERN, the large particle physics laboratory near Geneva, Switzerland.

Many scientists participated in experiments at CERN for extended periods of time, then returned to their laboratories around the world. These scientists were eager to exchange data and results, but had difficulties doing so. Tim understood this need, and understood the unrealized potential of millions of computers connected together through the Internet. Tim documented what was to become the World Wide Web with the submission of a proposal to his management at CERN, in late 1989. This proposal specified a set of technologies that would make the Internet truly accessible and useful to people. Tim's initial proposal was not immediately accepted. However, by October of 1990, he had specified the three fundamental technologies that remain the foundation of today's Web:

- **HTML**: HyperText Markup Language. The publishing format for the Web, including the ability to format documents and link to other documents and resources.
- **URI**: Uniform Resource Identifier. A kind of "address" that is unique to each resource on the Web.
- **HTTP**: Hypertext Transfer Protocol. Allows for the retrieval of linked resources from across the Web.

Tim also wrote the first Web page editor/browser ("WorldWideWeb") and the first Web server ("httpd"). By the end of 1990, the first Web page was served. By 1991, people outside of CERN joined the new Web community. Very important to the growth of the Web, CERN announced in April 1993 that the World Wide Web technology would be available for anyone to use on a royalty-free basis. Since that time, the Web has changed the world https://webfoundation.org/about/vision/history-of-the-web.

The Growing Influence of the Media

The invention of the printing press by Gutenberg in the 15th century created a huge impact on mankind in that the printed word, in the form of newspapers, books, and flyers was used to convey messages and influence the public. The post-World War II era also brought about an unprecedented change in the rate and volume of communication to the general public. The onset of television, computers, and newer forms of electronic and social media as well as the widespread coverage of newspapers and magazines now shape every facet of American society (Vincent, 2005).

It is important that students become critical consumers of information and persuasive media in order to become critically engaged citizens in modern American society. Students must understand that media messages are created with specific purposes in mind. Each form of media (i.e., television, newspapers, posters, magazines, photographs, graphics, audio messages, video messages, etc.) may contain visual images or text that are manipulated to create the message.

Media's purpose may be to **inform, entertain,** or **persuade** an intended audience. Media messages have myriad purposes that can be singular or a combination of reasons to:
  • argue
  • condemn
  • describe
  • entertain
  • explain
  • enlighten
  • inform
  • persuade
  • ridicule
  • shock

These powerful messages often have an effect upon individuals and society as a whole. It is important that students understand that media messages are often a representation of reality, rather than actual reality, and that these messages affect the behaviors and actions of people every day.

In order to become effective information users, students must become aware of media and its effect and influence upon everyday life in America. Students must understand the nature of media as it is used to transmit information, how the various media work to influence people, and must develop an informed / critical understanding of media and its power to influence the behavior of people (Vincent, 2000). Teachers must conduct lessons that require students to think critically about who creates media messages and the purposes of the messages created.

Media/Communications Theories
Media has a strong **social and cultural impact** upon society. This is predicated upon their ability to reach a wide audience with a strong and influential message. Marshall McLuhan uses the phrase "the medium is the message" as a means of explaining how the distribution of a message can often be more important than the content of the message itself. Students must learn to critically analyze the implied meaning of the message in order to look beyond what is directly stated and understand the suggested meaning of the message and its impact upon society. Several theories exist to explain the impact of mass media upon society including:

Media Systems Dependency Theory (MSDT): Microscopic (personal) macroscopic (societal) analyses of how we depend on the media to shape our beliefs, attitudes, shared meanings and social organizations. This theory postulates that in a dependent relationship the satisfaction of one party's needs is contingent on the resources of the other. It also finds that dependency on the media increases during times of change.

Agenda-Setting Theory- Holds that the mass media determine what we think and worry about. It's **not** that various media tell us **what to think**, it's that they tell us **what to think about** by giving more exposure to some topics than others. In order for this cause-and-effect relationship to work, a lag between media priorities and public priorities must be observed.

Cultivation Theory- Suggests that repeated intense exposure to deviant definitions of reality can lead to the perception that that the deviant reality is "normal." This works particularly well in situations involving the social world -- and leads to the perception of the world as a hostile and frightening place. Cultivation Theory also suggests that TV viewers do not actually choose specific programs to watch.

Uses and Gratifications Theory- States that we all have different uses for the media and make specific choices about what to watch (exactly the opposite of Cultivation Theory). In other words, that we are not just watching mindlessly, that we expect to get something out of what we're watching: information, a sense of personal identity, social interaction, or entertainment.

Consistency Theory: Suggests that we choose media messages consistent with our pre-existing views and values.

Selective Participation Theory: States that we tend to hear what we want and expect to hear.

Selective Retention Theory: Suggests that we subconsciously retain some events and messages and not others.

Hypodermic Syringe Theory: Purports that the media is a "syringe" and strongly injects ideas, attitudes and beliefs into an audience which, as a powerless mass, has little choice but to be accept them.

Two-Step Flow Theory: Suggests that we are likely to discuss our media experiences with others and that if we respect them (and consider them opinion leaders) we may abandon our own opinions and switch to theirs.

Excitation Transfer Theory: Suggests that arousal or excitement caused by the media can be readily transferred to other situations (including non-media situations); that similar emotions or stimuli need not be involved.

Spiral of Silence Theory: Connects the areas of social psychology, mass media, and interpersonal communications. Elisabeth Noelle-Neumann, founder of Germany's Allensbach Institute purports that we all have the ability to judge the climate of public opinion and that we are likely to withhold our views if we think that they differ from those of the majority.

Narcoticizing Dysfunction: This theory suggests that media makes us believe we are personally involved in something when actually we have just heard or read about it.

Parasocial Interaction: This theory suggests that media gives us a false sense of participating in public dialogue.

Catalytic Theory: This highly controversial theory suggests that media violence is one of the factors that encourages violence in real life.

Desensitizing Theory: This theory supports that tolerance of real-life violence has grown because of media-depicted violence.

Information Pollution- This theory postulates that people are overwhelmed with information, which is delivered with no sense of order or priority.

Media-Induced Passivity Theory: This theory states that media is constantly experience on an individual level, and the individual is enticed away from social involvement.

Media Literate Students
The **National Communication Association** suggests the following competencies that media literate students should be able to understand and apply to their lives (www.natcom.org/instruction/K-12/standards):

• Media does not reflect the world, but instead is a construction of the world through the use of media effects.
• Media portrays a constructed reality instead of an actual reality.
• Media messages are interpreted individually; no two people will interpret a given message the same way.
• Media messages are commercially produced. Sponsors and underwriters usually promote their own agendas.
• Media images often portray ideological and value-laden messages.
• Media messages have powerful social and political impact.
• The form and content of media messages are closely related. Even though various media cover the same stories or events, interpretations of these events are often directly related to the media form.

Responding to Media
In order to develop media literacy, students must understand how to access, analyze, evaluate and produce communication in a variety of forms. To become effective information users, students must have frequent opportunities to work with a variety of media forms. Students must also learn to select the media most appropriate for their specific needs (Swain, 2000).

Students who are media literate will be able to obtain and assess information, process and communicate information, and think critically and evaluate media messages. Media literacy is concerned with helping students develop an informed, critical understanding of the nature of the media used in a message, how the media message produces meaning, how the message is organized, and how reality is constructed by the message. Students must learn to analyze media messages using higher order thinking, by answering critical questions about the message (Swain, 2000).

- What type of message is this?
- Who created the message?
- Who is the intended audience for the message?
- How are the images, language, or sound manipulated to influence the audience?
- Are there stereotypes evident in this message?
- How does this message connect with your experiences or the real world?
- Is there another side to the argument or other important details left out of the message?

Evaluation and Production of Media Messages
Media education is most effective when it includes both media analysis and production. Therefore, students should be given frequent opportunities to **analyze messages**, and also design and create their own media messages. Students need to understand the techniques and strategies necessary to create effective media messages and how to apply those strategies to their own media productions.

Media evaluation and production should offer students opportunities to develop skills such as: identifying point of view, distinguishing between fact and fiction, distinguishing main idea and details, and interpreting data. The National Research Center on English Learning and Achievement provides many suggestions for cross-content media lessons that blend content areas and media literacy. Listed below are a few Study lesson ideas (http://albany.edu/cela):

1. Health: Problem Solving in the Media
Examine how problems are solved in the media, use examples from TV; advertising and other formats. How are concerns resolved (i.e., buying a product, using violence, being dishonest, taking drugs)? What are some ways that the problems in question could have been worked out? In what time frame were they resolved (i.e., a 30 minute episode)? How does this compare with how long it takes to solve problems in real life?

2. Language Arts: Compare Media Forms

Some movies, television series or programs are based on a book or other literary work. Choose an example and have students compare the printed form of the work with the media production. List the similarities and differences. Which of the works presents the most accurate picture of the author's intent? Have students apply what they have learned by documenting a school event.

3. Math: Interpretation / Misrepresentation of Data

Help students discover how the same set of data can be represented differently in order to emphasize a particular message. Use a political poll or a research study as a data source and instruct students to manipulate scale and otherwise alter visual messages of tables and graphs in order to favor a certain point of view. Discuss the potential consequences of presenting data with a particular bias.

4. Science: Connotation of Words

Connect language arts and earth science by studying how natural disasters are covered in the news. After an introduction to connotation and denotation, explore word choice in natural disaster news stories. Ask students to pick out words with particularly strong connotations, and discuss. How accurate is the coverage? Introduce the idea of anthropomorphism: to what extent does news coverage of natural disasters anthropomorphize nature?

5. Social Studies: Manipulation of the Media

Discuss the relationship between media and terrorism. How do terrorists manipulate the news into communicating their messages and furthering their causes? In recent years have terrorists used self-produced web sites and video to achieve their objectives? How dependent are terrorists on media messages about their activities? How is terrorism different from other forms of combat?

Using Media in the Classroom: Word Processing - Graphic Design - Desktop Publishing

The term desktop publishing is often confused with the concept of word processing. Desktop publishing historically means organizing images and text together for display on a page. This distinguishes such work from simple word processing which is generally thought of as a text only process. However, newer versions of word processors now include many features that were once reserved for desktop publishing software (Williams, 2003). Often the document never is seen on paper, just on a computer screen.

It is now a routine in some schools for even one page assignment to contain a complex mix of main story text and sidebar text with a related story. Within this text will also be a range of **artwork, photographs**, **graphs, and charts**. **Page layout** and **image/graphic control** are the two critical features that distinguish desktop publishing software from basic-text word processors:

The **Page layout** feature allows the user to place different fonts of text and image objects on the same page without being forced into continuous columns. The image/graphics control features of most desktop publishing software allowing the user to resize, rotate, crop, and otherwise shape an image are superior to basic-text word processors.

Graphic design jobs involve the process of creating designs for concepts and ideas and then being able to arrange the design on the page in order to visually communicate a specific message (Lupton, 2004). Graphic designers use desktop publishing software and techniques to create the print materials they envision. Desktop publishing is the process that the designer and the non-designer use to turn their ideas for newsletters, brochures, ads, posters, greeting cards, and other projects into digital files for printing. Non-designers also use desktop publishing software and techniques to create print projects for business or pleasure. The amount of creative design that goes into these projects varies greatly. While desktop publishing does require a certain amount of creativity, it is more production-oriented than design-oriented. In reality, the two are separate but intertwined disciplines. Not everyone who works with desktop publishing is involved with graphic design, but most graphic designers are involved in desktop publishing, the production side of design (Williams, 2003).

Aesthetic Considerations for Desktop Publishing Software

Just as the **aesthetics** of a table setting makes the meal taste better, so **aesthetically** pleasing page design may not only make reading more pleasant, but can effect whether the message is read or even understood. A central issue in desktop publishing can be summarized in one word: design. In word processing and desktop publishing, **page layout programs** enable users to format pages of text and graphics. Many word-processing systems support their own page layout functions, but professional page layout applications generally give users more control over fine points such as text flow, kerning, and positioning of graphics.

The computerized **desktop publishing** software aids in the creative process by allowing the designer to easily try out various page layouts, fonts, colors, and other elements. Desktop publishing is important as a tool that can enhance communication by making it possible to quickly and efficiently produce printed and electronic documents. Desktop publishing software allows the user to rearrange text and graphics on screen, change typefaces easily, and resize graphics, before finally committing a design to paper.

Some applications provide a "fast-publish" newsletter assistant, wizard or procedure. **Appleworks, ClarisWorks**, and **MS Works** are the currently popular. However, new software programs are produced rapidly, so a complete list is difficult to produce. Programs such as MS Publisher provide a basic template for further modification and are gaining users in education. There are many more challenging and more powerful desktop programs such as **QuarkXPress, Adobe PageMaker,** and **InDesign.** However, even with **Appleworks, ClarisWorks, MS Works, or MS Publisher**, some additional skills generally have to be learned to use the template system effectively. Learning curves, software costs, compatibility issues, output file sizes, formats, software features, and dissemination methods are all factors to consider while choosing desktop publishing software.

In sum, **desktop publishing** products often have many visual elements: columns of text, headlines, photos, illustrations, pull-quotes, etc. These elements aid readers' understanding and readers often expect to find sidebars, informational text, and other oft-repeated elements in the same place from page to page. The elements of arts, words, paragraphs, and pages interact together on a well-designed, aesthetically pleasing page (Lupton, 2004). To make desktop publishing products easy to read and **aesthetically** pleasing, the user should consider color contrast, legible typefaces, balance of graphics, etc.

Assessing Media Assignments

There are important steps to creating objective, comprehensive and meaningful assessment and evaluation tools for media literacy work. The first is to use an evaluation tool such as a **rubric** that allows the teacher to assess the work in more than one way, along with making expectations clear to students. In general, media literacy work can be evaluated in three ways:

- Based on how well the student **understands** the key concepts of media literacy and the specific concepts and ideas being explored in the lesson or assignment.
- Based on the depth and quality of the student's **inquiry** and **analysis** of the questions raised in the lesson or assignment, as well as the student's thoughtfulness in **identifying issues and questions** to examine.
- Based on how well the student **applies specific technical skills** associated with either the medium being studied (movies, TV, video games, etc.), the medium used in the evaluation tool, or both.

Specific traits that teachers should look for in different components of student work include:
1. ideas and content of the piece,
2. its organization and structure,
3. how effectively the piece uses the language and rhetoric of its medium,
4. how the author's voice is present in the piece and how it connects with the audience,
5. and, technical competence; how well the author has handled the conventions and the technology of the genre or technology.

Example Media Project Grading Rubric

Level 5: Consistently Exceeds Expectations
The piece demonstrates a confident command and integration of all elements...it is often strikingly complete, insightful, creative and/or imaginative.

Level 4: Consistently Meets and Sometime Exceeds Expectations
The piece shows an effective control and integration of all elements; the content is thoughtful and thorough.

Level 3: Usually Meets Expectations
The pieces shows control of the elements...is generally integrated, clear and complete.

Level 2: Inconsistently Meets Expectations

Some control of most of the elements but it may be simple, unoriginal and/or incomplete.

Level 1: Does not Meet Expectations
Shows elementary grasp of some of the basic elements...simple or unfinished. Work that is plagiarized is assigned to this level.

References

Christ, W. G. (2004). Assessment, Media Literacy Standards and Higher Education. *American Behavioral Scientist*. (Sept., 2004). Vol. 48, No.1, Sage Publications.

Frechette, J. D. (2002). *Developing Media Literacy in Cyberspace: Pedagogy and Critical Learning for the Twenty-first Century Classroom*. Westport, CT: Greenwood Publishing Group, Inc.

Glossary of Desktop Publishing Terms. (n.d.). Retrieved May 16, 2006, from *http://www.edison.cc.oh.us/dtp/dtpgloss.html*

Lupton, E. (2004). *Thinking with type: A critical guide for designers, writers, editors, & students*. New York, NY: Princeton Arch.

Swain, K. (2000). Nonprint Media and Technology Literacy Standards for Assessing Technology Integration. *Journal of Educational Computing Research*, Vol. 23, No 1.

Vincent, T. (2005). Meaning and Mass Culture: The Search for a New Literacy. *Journal of Communication Inquiry Meaning and Mass Culture*. V. 162.

Williams, R. (2003). *The Non-Designer's Design Book* (2nd Ed). Berkeley, CA: Peachpit Press.
http://albany.edu/cela
http://www.medialit.org/reading-room/workshop
http://www.ukans.edu
http://www.natcom.org/instruction/K-12/standards
http://www.hall@cccd.edu
http://www.natcom.org/instruction/K-12/standards
http://mediasmarts.ca/digital-media-literacy-fundamentals
https://webfoundation.org/about/vision/history-of-the-web/

Practice Questions

1. Mr. Holmes, an 11 th grade English / language arts teacher, is planning a media literacy unit to promote student understanding of the ways people use television as an information medium in their public and daily lives. Of the following, which teaching strategy would best promote this concept?

> a. Require that students work in cooperative groups to compose and conduct a school-wide survey about the information gained from the media during public and daily life. Students then report their findings to the class.
> b. Require that students work in cooperative groups to create a list of various types of visual media (such as television, film, billboard advertising, etc.) found in their daily lives. Students create a graphic organizer of their findings and report their findings to the class.
> c. Require that students write a journal entry about the types and uses of television and other types of visual media found within today's society. Students then share their writing with three other members of the class to gain additional perspectives on the subject.
> d. Require that students work in cooperative groups to brainstorm a list of television programs they watch most often. Students work together in small groups to evaluate each of the programs with regard to biased, hidden, or idealized messages. Students then share their findings with the class.

A is correct. It is good pedagogical practice to require that students work in cooperative groups. This assignment also involves the students in higher order thinking as they write the survey and interpret the results.

2. Students in Mr. Holmes' 10th grade English / language arts class just completed an assignment on the Renaissance era of literature. Students worked in groups to produce PowerPoint presentations of their reports. The students were very proud of their application of technology and incorporated many of the latest PowerPoint features into their presentations. When Mr. Holmes looked closely at the projects while grading them, he noticed many incorrect facts about the content, spelling errors, and lack of citations throughout the projects. Of the following, which of the problems should most concern Mr. Holmes?

> a. Mr. Holmes should be concerned that he was not aware of the students' problems with spelling and grammar. He should have held short grammar lessons each day before students began working on the assignment.

b. Mr. Holmes should be concerned that he did not emphasize content over form in this project. Students must be made aware that a technologically enhanced presentation does not make up for poor content.

c. Mr. Holmes should be concerned that the students are not aware of the correct procedures for sighting references in their work. Mr. Holmes should have posted the correct procedures for sighting references in the room for easy student assess.

d. Mr. Holmes should feel proud of the technological advancements his students have exhibited on their projects and should grade the projects on the basis of software program application, thereby de-emphasizing the minor errors the students made on their projects.

B is correct. Classroom produced technology assignments should emphasize correct content over form.

3. The bandwagon approach used in media messages to influence people's behavior is usually characterized by:

a. Appealing to a person's need to join others and not be left behind.

b. Using music which appeals to a person's emotions.

c. Using a rock star or movie star who gives personal testimony about the use of a product.

d. Using subliminal means to manipulate the consumer into believing the message.

A is correct. The bandwagon approach used in media messages to influence people's decisions or behavior is usually characterized by appealing to a person's need to join others and not be left behind.

4. Students in Mr. Holmes' 11th grade English / language arts class are working in small groups to produce and videotape an anti-smoking advertisement. To help students prepare for this activity, Mr. Holmes shows examples of tobacco advertisements from magazines and video clips from movies that depict people smoking. After viewing the examples, Mr. Holmes asks students, "Why do you think the movie stars and models in these ads or films are all active, healthy, attractive people?" How will this question promote students' media literacy?

a. This question will help students identify effective media design elements found within the advertisements.

b. This question will help students analyze the relationship between the tobacco industry and the cost of a tobacco advertisement in an ad or a film.

c. This question will help students consider what facts about smoking were omitted in the pictures.

d. This question will help students consider how idealized and powerful visual images can be through the use of media advertisement and film.

D is the correct. This answer requires students to think critically about the influence of visual messages in film and advertising.

5. Students in Mr. Holmes 10th grade English class watch a videotaped national news story about campaign tactics used during a hotly contested political election. In the news story the reporter interviewed each contestant and asked him to give a response to the charge of mudslinging. Each contestant laid blame on his opponent's campaign. Mr. Holmes knows that it is important for his students to understand the power of visual images found within mass media. Prior to initiating a class discussion on the methods that can be used to create visual messages, which of the following teaching strategies should Mr. Holmes use first?

   a. Ask students to write a personal response in their journal about the oral responses each candidate gave during his interview.
   b. Ask students to meet in small, cooperative groups to compare and contrast the verbal responses of each contestant.
   c. Ask students to meet in small groups to discuss why this story was videotaped for national news coverage.
   d. Ask students to choose their favorite candidate in the campaign, and then write a letter from one candidate to the other describing their feelings about the mudslinging.

C is correct. This answer choice requires that students use higher order thinking as they critique the news story on its merit of creating a visual image, and is more global in scope then the other choices.

Chapter 12: Constructed Response:

Question 1: Literary Analysis and Comparison

Question 2: Three-part Writing Assessment and Pedagogy

Writing a Literary Analysis Essay

The purpose of a literary analysis essay is to carefully examine and evaluate a work of literature. As with any analysis, this involves breaking the subject down into its component parts. Examining the different elements provides a process to help readers and writers better appreciate and understand the specific aspects of a literary work. For instance, an analysis of a poem might focus on the various types of images found within the poem or with the relationship between the form and content of the poem. Analysis of a short story might include identifying a particular theme (like the difficulty of making the transition from adolescence to adulthood) and how the author reveals that theme through the point of view from which the story is told http://www.bucks.edu/. The basic elements of a literary analysis essay include the following: Thesis Statement, Introduction, Body, and Conclusion.

Thesis Statement – This statement tells the reader what to expect: it is a restricted, precisely worded declarative sentence that states the purpose of the essay.

> For example: Gwendolyn Brooks' 1960 poem, "The Ballad of Rudolph Reed," demonstrates how the poet uses the conventional poetic form of ballad to treat the unconventional poetic subject of racial intolerance.

The introduction to a literary analysis essay should try to capture a reader's interest. In order to bring immediate focus to the subject, the examinee may wish to use a quotation, a provocative question, a brief anecdote, a startling statement, or a combination of these. Moreover, the examinee may wish to include background information relevant to the thesis and necessary for the reader to understand the position taken. Additionally, it is strongly suggested that the examinee include the title of the work of literature and name of the author in the introduction.

> **Example #1 (a provocative question)** What would one expect to be the personality of a man who has his wife sent away to a convent (or perhaps has had her murdered) because she took too much pleasure in the sunset or in a compliment paid to her by another man? It is just such a man—a Renaissance duke—who Robert Browning portrays in his poem "My Last Duchess." A character analysis of the Duke reveals that through his internal dialogue, his interpretation of earlier incidents, and his actions, his traits—arrogance, jealousy, and greediness—emerge.

Example #2 (combination of a story summary / background information / statement of thesis) The first paragraph of Alberto Alvaro Rios's short story "The Secret Lion" presents a twelve-year-old boy's view of growing up as everything changes. As the narrator informs the reader, when the magician pulls a tablecloth out from under a pile of dishes, children are amazed how the dishes stay in the same spot, while adults focus only on the tablecloth itself. Adults have the benefit of experience and know the trick will work as long as the technique is correct. When people "grow up," they gain this experience and knowledge but lose their innocence and sense of wonder. In other words, the price paid for growing up is a permanent sense of loss. This tradeoff is central to "The Secret Lion." The key symbols in the story reinforce its main theme: change is inevitable and always accompanied by a sense of loss.

The Body and Important Topic Sentences of the Analysis Essay

Good literary analysis essays contain an explanation of ideas and evidence from the text (short story, poem, play) that support those ideas. Textual evidence consists of summary, paraphrase, specific details, and / or direct quotations. Each paragraph should contain a topic sentence (usually the first sentence of the paragraph) which states one of the topics associated with the thesis, combined with some assertion about how the topic will support the central idea. The purpose of the topic sentence is to relate the details of the paragraph to the thesis statement, and to tie the details of the paragraph together.

The substance of each of the developmental paragraphs (the body of the essay) will be the explanations, summaries, paraphrases, specific details, and direct quotations needed to support and develop the more general statement made in the topic sentence. For example:

> Sammy's descriptions of the A & P present a setting that is ugly, monotonous, and rigidly regulated. The chain store is a common fixture in modern society, so the reader can identify with the uniformity Sammy describes. The fluorescent light is as blandly cool as the "checkerboard green-and-cream rubber tile floor" (486). The "usual traffic in the store moves in one direction (except for the swim suited girls, who move against it), and everything is neatly organized and categorized in tidy aisles. The dehumanizing routine of this environment is suggested by Sammy's offhand references to the typical shoppers as "sheep," "house slaves," and "pigs" (486). These regular customers seem to walk through the store in a stupor; as Sammy indicates, not even dynamite could move them out of their routine (485).

This paragraph is developed through the use of quotations, summary, details, and explanation to support the topic sentence. It also relates back to the thesis statement.

The Conclusion - A concluding paragraph gives an essay a sense of completeness and lets the readers know that they have come to the end of the essay. The concluding paragraph might restate the thesis in different words, summarize the main points previously made, or make a relevant comment about the literary work from a different perspective. (Important note: do not introduce a new topic in the conclusion).

If the Duke has any redeeming qualities, they fail to appear in the poem. Browning's emphasis on the Duke's traits of arrogance, jealousy, and materialism make it apparent that anyone who might have known the Duke personally would have based his opinion of him on these three personality "flaws." Ultimately, the reader's opinion of the Duke is not a favorable one, and it is clear that Browning intended that the reader feel this way.

The Title of the Essay

It is essential to give the essay a title that is descriptive of the approach taken within the essay. Aligned with the introductory paragraph, the title of the essay should attempt to rouse the reader's attention. Be sure to move beyond simply restating the title of the work being analyzed, adding a descriptive phrase to the title which describes the theme of the essay is preferred. For example:

Robert Browning's Duke: A Portrayal of a Sinister Man
The A & P as a State of Mind
Theme in "The Secret Lion": The Struggle of Adolescence

Audience

It is important to consider the reader for whom the essay is being written. The essay should explain and interpret the work—to tell what certain elements of the work mean in relation to the central idea (thesis). When references to the text of the short story, poem, or play, are made within the essay, you are reminding the audience of something they already know, or something that had not previously considered. The principle emphasis of a strong literary analysis essay is to draw conclusions and develop arguments. Although brief summary of specific events may be included, it is important to remember that a plot summary of the entire work is not necessary or encouraged.

Using Text as Evidence

The skillful use of textual evidence -- summary, paraphrase, specific detail, and direct quotations – help illustrate and support ideas developed within the essay. However, textual evidence should be used judiciously and only when it directly relates to the topic sentence. Textual evidence is vital to a successful literary analysis essay.

Summary

If a key event or series of events in the literary work support a point made within the essay, it is important to include a brief summary, making sure that the relevance of the event or events are revealed by explicitly connecting the summary to the point being made.

Paraphrase

Make use of paraphrase when details of the original, but not necessarily the exact words of the original work are needed. For example:

Original: "I was twelve and in junior high school and something happened that we didn't have a name for, but it was nonetheless like a lion, and roaring, roaring that way the biggest things do."

Paraphrase: Early in the story, the narrator tells us that when he turned twelve and started junior high school, life changed in a significant way that he and his friends could not quite name or identify.

Specific Detail

Various types of details from the text lend concrete support to the development of the central idea of a literary analysis essay. These details add credibility to the point being developed and can be interspersed within a sentence to build a strong point.

Using Direct Quotations

Quotations illuminate and support ideas a writer is trying to develop. A judicious use of quoted material will make main points clear and convincing. As with all the textual evidence, it is important to explain how the evidence is relevant—let the reader know why the quotes cited are significant to the argument. Below are guidelines and examples for the effective use of quotations.

Brief quotations (four lines or fewer of prose and three lines or fewer of poetry) should be carefully introduced and integrated into the text of the essay. Put quotation marks around all briefly quoted material. It is also important to include page numbers or line numbers when necessary.

For example:

As the "manager" of the A & P, Lengel is both the guardian and enforcer of "policy" (487). When he gives the girls "that sad Sunday-school-superintendent stare," the reader becomes aware of Lengel's character as the A & P's version of a dreary bureaucrat who "doesn't miss much" (487).

Incorporating Quotes into a Literary Analysis Essay
Research conducted on scoring of essays reveals that longer essays tend to receive higher scores. One effective strategy to lengthen a literary analysis essay would be to include a preselected quote from a prominent figure such as: Ben Franklin, Shakespeare, Franklin Delano Roosevelt, Helen Keller, or Socrates.

When choosing quotes for a literary analysis, remember the *purpose* of using such quotes. A strong literary analysis paper develops an argument about what the author of the text is doing--how the text "works." The writer should use quotes to support this argument; that is, the writer should select, present, and discuss material from the text specifically to "prove" a point—or to make a case--in much the same way a lawyer brings evidence before a jury https://writing.wisc.edu/Handbook/QuoLiterature.html.

Popular Quotes
Ability
They can because they think they can – Vergil

Adversity
Into each life some rain must fall, some days must be dark and dreary. Henry Wadsworth Longfellow, *The Rainy Day*

Ambition
Look not too high, least a chip fall in your eye. *Proverb*

Americanism
To be prepared for war is one of the most effective means of preserving peace. George Washington, *Speech to both Houses of Congress*

Anticipation
All things that are, Are with more spirit chased than enjoyed. William Shakespeare, *Merchant of Venice*

Appearance
All that glitters is not gold,
Gilded tombs do worms enfold. William Shakespeare, *Merchant of Venice.*

Art
Art is not imitation but illusion. Charles Reade, *Christie Johnstone*

Art is the child of Nature. Henry Wadsworth Longfellow, *Keramos*

Beauty

Beauty from order springs. William King, *The Art of Cookery*

Beauty is but skin deep. *Proverb*

A thing of beauty is a joy forever; Its loveliness increases; it will never pass into nothingness. John Keats, *Endymion*

Books

Some books are to be tasted, others to be swallowed, and some few to be chewed and digested. Francis Bacon, *Essay on Studies*

Change

A rolling stone gathers no moss. Stephen Gosson, *Ephemerides of Phialo*
Life belongs to the living, and he who lives must be prepared for changes. Johann Wolfgang Von Goethe

Choice

A man is too apt to forget that in this world he cannot have everything. A choice is all that is left him. H. Mathews, *Diary of an Invalid.*

Death

All that lives must die,
Passing through nature to eternity. William Shakespeare, *Hamlet.*

He that begins to live, begins to die. Francis Qyarles, *Hieroglyph.*

Deception

Oh, what a tangled web we weave,
When first we practice to deceive. Sir Walter Scott, *Marmion*

Difficulties

All things are difficult before they are easy. Thomas Fuller, *Gnomologia.*

Disgrace

A man may survive distress, but not disgrace. *Proverb.*

Duty

I slept, and dreamed that life was Beauty;
I woke, and found that life was Duty. Ellen Hooper, *The Dial*

Education

'Tis education forms the common mind;
Just as the twig is bent the tree's inclined. Alexander Pope, *Moral Essays.*

Enthusiasm
Nothing great was ever achieved without enthusiasm. Ralph Waldo Emerson, **Circles**.

Evil
A little evil is often necessary for obtaining a great good. Voltaire, *Baron d'Otranto*.

Existence
I think, therefore I am. Rene Descartes.

Faith
Faith is a higher faculty than reasoning. Philip James Bailey, *Festus*.

Fame
Fame is a fickle food Upon a shifting plate. Emily Dickinson, *The Single Hound*.

Fate
And weather I came in love or hate,
That I came to you was written by fate. Laurence Hope, *The Complete Love Lyrics*.

Freedom
The love of liberty is the love of others; the love of power is the love of ourselves. William Hazlitt, *The Toad Eaters*.

Friendship
Friendship is Love without his wings. Lord Byron, *L'Amitie est l'Amour sans Ailes*.

Genius
Genius can only breathe freely in an atmosphere of freedom. John Stuart Mill, *Liberty*.

God
God's in His Heaven – All's right with the world. Robert Browning, *Pippa Passes*.

Greatness
Some are born great, some achieve greatness, and some have greatness thrust upon them. William Shakespeare, *Twelfth Night*.

To be great, is to be misunderstood. Ralph Waldo Emerson, *Self-Reliance*.

Happiness
One is never so happy or so unhappy as one imagines. La Rochefoucauld, *Maximes*.

Heroes
Whoe'er excels in what we prize
Appears a hero in our eyes. Jonathan Swift.

Honesty
An honest tale speeds best, being plainly told. William Shakespeare. *King Richard III.*

Honesty is the best policy. Benjamin Franklin, *Poor Richard's Almanac.*

Hope
Hope springs eternal in the human breast. Alexander Pope, *Essay on Man.*

Imitation
No man was ever great by imitation. Samuel Johnson, *Rasselas.*

Judgment
Men see a little, presume a great deal, and so jump to the conclusion. John Locke.

Knowledge
Knowledge comes, but wisdom lingers. – Alfred Lord Tennyson

Knowledge is power. Francis Bacon, *Meditationes Sacrae.*
All men naturally desire to know. Aristotle.

Love
Love's a thing that's never out of season. Barry Cornwall.

Love and a red nose can't be hid. Thomas Holcroft, *Duplicity.*

All mankind loves a lover. Ralph Waldo Emerson, *Love.*

Man
Men of few words are the best men. William Shakespeare, *King Henry V.*

Obstacles
Every path hath a puddle. George Herbert, *Jacula Prudentum.*

Order
Order is Heaven's first law. Alexander Pope, *Essay on Man.*

Peace
But the real and lasting victories are those of peace, and not war. Ralph Waldo Emerson, *Worship.*

Plenty

Plenty is the child of peace. William Prynne, Histriomastix.

Reward

The reward of a thing well done is to have done it. Ralph Waldo Emerson, *New England Reformers.*

Solitude

I was never less alone than when by myself. Lord Byron, *Childe Harold's Pilgrimage.*

Time

Sweet childish days, that were as long
As twenty days are now.   William Wordsworth, *To a Butterfly.*

Truth

Children and fools speak the truth. *Proverb*

Virtue

And virtue, though in rags, will keep me warm. Horace, *Odes*, Translated by Dryden.

War

War is just to those to whom war is necessary. Titus Livius, *History*

Water

Water water, everywhere,
Nor any drop to drink. Samuel Taylor Coleridge, *The Ancient Mariner*

Work

Labor is often the father of pleasure. Voltaire, *Discours*
Life gives nothing to mortals except with great labor. Horace

Labor has a bitter root but a sweet taste. *Proverb*

The Constructed Response Questions

The English Language Arts and Reading 7–12 test includes two constructed-response questions: a literary analysis question and a three-part writing assessment and pedagogy question. Unlike the multiple-choice questions, the constructed-response questions require the examinee to demonstrate knowledge in a subject area by providing in-depth written responses.

The two constructed-response questions account for approximately 35 percent of the total test score. For more information about scoring of the constructed response, and for additional samples and answers visit the Education Testing Service website listed below, then scroll down and click on the English Language Arts and Reading 7-12.

http://cms.texes-ets.org/texes/prepmaterials/texes-preparation-manuals/

Performance Characteristics for Constructed Response Question #1
The rubrics created to evaluate responses to the literary analysis constructed-response questions are based on the following criteria:

Purpose: The extent to which the candidate responds to the components of the question.

Demonstration of Knowledge: The extent to which the knowledge demonstrated is accurate and effectively applied.

Support: Quality and relevance of supporting details

Rationale: Soundness of reasoning and depth of understanding.

Written Expression: The extent to which the response is appropriate for the specified audience and conforms to conventions of Standard English for paragraphing, sentence structure, usage and mechanical conventions.

Sample Literary Analysis Question Prompt:

The passages below address similar related themes, either through their similarities or differences. In an essay to be read by an educator in the field of English, write an analysis of the two selections shown below. Support your analysis with textual evidence. Your evidence should:

- identify and discuss the theme/s that connect the two passages; and,
- explain how each author uses literary elements and / or literary devices to develop and support the theme/s.

Passage A: Nathaniel Hawthorne, *The Scarlet Letter*, (1849)
The excerpt below describes Hester Prenn's moral dilemma and consuming emotions as she is led before the magistrates.

The door of the jail being flung open from within, there appeared, in the first place, like a black shadow emerging into the sunshine, the grim and grisly presence of the town-beadle, with a sword by his side and his staff of office in his hand. This personage prefigured and represented in his aspect the whole dismal severity of the Puritanic code of law, which it was his business to administer in its final and closest application to the offender. Stretching forth the official staff in his left hand, he laid his right upon the shoulder of a young woman, whom he thus drew forward; until, on the threshold of the prison-door, she repelled him, by an action marked with natural dignity and force of character, and stepped into the open air, as if by her own free-will. She bore in her arms a child, a baby of some three months old, who winked and turned aside its little face from the too vivid light of day; because its existence, heretofore, had brought it acquainted only with the gray twilight of a dungeon, or other darksome apartment of the prison.
When the young woman – the mother of this child – stood fully revealed before the crowd, it seemed to be her first impulse to clasp the child closely to her bosom; not so much by an impulse of motherly affection, as that she might thereby conceal a certain token, which was wrought or fastened into her dress. In a moment, however, wisely judging that one token of shame would but poorly serve to hide another, she took the baby on her arm, and with a burning blush, and yet a haughty smile, and a glance that would not be abashed, looked around at her townspeople and neighbors. On the breast of her gown, in fine red cloth, surrounded with an elaborate embroidery and fantastic flourishes of gold thread, appeared the letter A. It was so artistically done, and with so much fertility and gorgeous luxuriance of fancy, that it had all the effect of a last and fitting de3coration to the apparel which she wore; and which was of a splendor in accordance with the taste of the age, but greatly beyond what was allowed by the sumptuary regulations of the colony.

Passage B: Frank McCourt, *Angela's Ashes*, (1996) The excerpt below is Frank McCourt's biographical account of growing up in Limmerick, Ireland in extreme poverty. In this excerpt McCourt describes his mother, Angela's, dilemma of raising four children in such raw conditions with no help from an alcoholic father.

Time and time Malachy drinks away his rent money and winds up sleeping in parks when the landlord throws him out. He's a regular disgrace, so he is, and Mr. Downes is glad McCourt is not a Limerickman bringing shame to this ancient city. The magistrates in Coventry are losing their patience and if Malachy McCourt doesn't stop the bloody nonsense he'll be kicked out of the country entirely. Mam tells Bridey she doesn't know what she's going to do with these stories from England, she never felt so desperate in her life. She can se Kathleen O'Connell doesn't want to give any more credit at the shop and her own mother barks at her if she asks for the loan of a shilling and the St. Vincent de Paul Society want to know when she'll stop asking for charity especially with a husband in England. She's ashamed of the way we look with the dirty old torn shirts, raggedy ganseys, broken shoes, holes in our stockings. She lies awake at night thinking the most merciful thing of all would be to put the four boys in an orphanage so that she could go to England herself and find some type of work where she could bring us all over in a year for the better life. There might be bombs but she'd prefer bombs anytime to the shame of begging from this one and that one.

> *No, no matter what she can't bear the thought of putting us in the orphanage. That might be all right if you had the likes of Boys' Town in America with the nice priest like Spencer Tracy but you could never trust the Christian Brothers out in Gin who get their exercise beating boys and starving the life out of them.*
> *Mam says there's nothing left but the Dispensary and the public assistance, the relief, and she's ashamed of her life to go and ask for it. It means you're at the end of your rope and maybe one level above tinkers, knackers and street beggars in general. It means you have to crawl before Mr. Coffrey and Mr. Kane and thank God the Dispensary is at the other end of Limerick so that people in our lane won't know we're getting the relief. (p.231).*

Acknowledgment

Angela's Ashes by Frank McCourt. (1996). Scribner: New York, NY, p. 231-232.
The Scarlet Letter by Nathaniel Hawthorne. Murfin R.C. (Ed). Bedford Books of St. Martin's Press: Boston, MA. 1991. p.57.

Writing Tips:
You will not be allowed to use any reference materials (dictionary, thesaurus) during the examination. It is recommended that you plan your time carefully. Read each selection more than once. It is further suggested that you break up the 90 minute block of time allotted for the literary analysis question into separate tasks:

10/15 minutes	Read and annotate the chosen poem / passage. Choose excerpts from the poem / passage for support. Create a web / graphic organizer for the response.
30/35 minutes	Draft the response – when drafting – double check to ensure that the main points address all components of the assignment.
15/20 minutes	Final edits: check spelling, grammar, and usage. (It is suggested that instead of erasing you draw a single line through any errors/words/ or phrases that you wish to omit.)

Scoring Rubric for the Literary Analysis Question
Point Score Point Description: Range from No Score to 4
The "4" response demonstrates thorough knowledge and understanding of content knowledge addressed in the question as it relates to the test framework for TExES English Language Arts and Reading 7–12.
  • The response fully addresses all components of the question.
  • The content knowledge demonstrated is accurate, appropriate and effectively applied.
  • The response provides strong support with specific, relevant details.
  • The response reflects clear, logical reasoning and a comprehensive understanding of the assignment.
  • The response is written effectively for the specified audience and is largely free of flaws in paragraphing, sentence structure, usage and mechanical conventions.

The "3" response demonstrates general knowledge and understanding of content knowledge addressed in the question as it relates to the test framework for TExES English Language Arts and Reading 7–12.
  • The response addresses most or all components of the question.
  • The content knowledge demonstrated is generally accurate, appropriate and effectively applied; minor problems in accuracy or effectiveness of application may be evident.
  • The response provides sufficient support with some relevant details.
  • The response reflects sufficient reasoning and a general understanding of the assigned topic.
  • The response is written appropriately for the specified audience, but it may have some flaws in paragraphing, sentence structure, usage and mechanical conventions.

The "2" response demonstrates limited knowledge and understanding of content knowledge addressed in the question as it relates to the test framework for TExES English Language Arts and Reading 7–12.

- The response addresses at least some of the components of the question.
- The content knowledge demonstrated is limited and/or applied with limited effectiveness; significant inaccuracies may be evident.
- The response provides limited support with few relevant details, or the support given is partially irrelevant.
- The response reflects limited reasoning and a partial understanding of the assigned topic.
- The response may not be appropriate for the specified audience and/or may contain distracting errors in paragraphing, sentence structure, usage and mechanical conventions.

The "1" response demonstrates little or no knowledge or understanding of content knowledge addressed in the question as it relates to the test framework for TExES English Language Arts and Reading 7–12.

- The response addresses few, if any, of the components of the question.
- The content knowledge demonstrated is weak, ineffectively applied and/or largely inaccurate.
- The response provides little or no support, or the support given is mostly irrelevant.
- The response reflects weak reasoning and little or no understanding of the assigned topic.
- The response is inappropriate for the specified audience and may be severely flawed by errors in paragraphing, sentence structure, usage and mechanical conventions.

NS The "NS" (no score) code will be assigned to responses that are not scorable for any of the following reasons:

- completely blank
- off topic/off task
- primarily in a language other than English
- too short or do not contain a sufficient amount of original work to score

For detailed information about scoring of the constructed response, and for additional samples and answers visit the Education Testing Service website (ets.org) listed below, then scroll down and click on the English Language Arts and Reading 7-12 exam preparation manual.

http://cms.texes-ets.org/texes/prepmaterials/texes-preparation-manuals/

Constructed-Response Question 2: Writing Assessment and Pedagogy
The second constructed-response question presents a student's draft response to an in-class writing assignment and asks you to complete three assessment tasks related to the draft.

General Directions:
Plan to use approximately 45–60 minutes to complete this question. Read the constructed-response question carefully before you begin to write your response to ensure that you address all components. Think about how you will organize what you plan to write.

The final version of your response should conform to the conventions of Standard English. Your written response should be your original work, written in your own words, and not copied or paraphrased from some other work. You may, however, use citations when appropriate.

Before attempting this practice essay, it is strongly suggested that you re-read Domain III (Chapters 8 & 9) which address basic writing skills and pedagogical practices for teaching writing.

Sample Writing Assessment and Pedagogy Question Prompt:
Read the following writing assignment and student response carefully before beginning your assessment.

In an eighth-grade English class, a teacher assigns the following 45-minute in-class writing assignment to assess students' skills in persuasive writing.

Think about a law that affects teenagers in your state that you would like to see changed or implemented. Then write a letter to a local official that explains the policy and makes a case for why you think it should be changed or implemented. Be sure to:
   • State your position clearly
   • Organize your argument appropriately
   • Support your position with specific reasons and examples
   • Choose your words carefully

The following is one student's response to the assignment.

Dear Mr. O'Dell,

The one thing teens look forward to is earning their own money, but to do so they need jobs. With Texas restrictions, requirements, and availibilty, jobs are getting harder and harder for teens to find. I am proposing that we eliminate some of these rediculus laws.

There are many requirements that teens have to meet befor they can work anywhere, one of the requirements you have to meet is your age. In Texas you have to be 15 years old to even apply for a job, let alone get jone. You also have to know what you're applying for and how to do it. I believe that the term they use for this is "work expiriance," well how are you supposed to get any work expiriance if no one will hire you till you have some.

Another thing that should change is the law that says that you can not operate any heavy machinery, which includes lawn movers, tractors, weekeaters, etc... I mean come on, lawn movers and weekeaters are not heavy macenery.

Another thing, there are very few jobs that will hirs 15 and 16 year olds, granted 16 year olds have more chances, but 15 year olds should be able to work at fast food places and stores and places like that, but they can't because the public is not comfortable bgeing served by 15 year olds, but have no problem being served by 16 year olds, which makes no sence because 1 year or less is not that much difference.

Like I've been saying, these laws are not very up to date. With our fast paced world students are needing money for more and more things like the continually raising cost of lunches and e3xtra classes. If you havn't noticed yet, money is a very important thing in our society. That is why I believe these laws should be taken out of the books and eliminated.

TASK 1
Identify one significant strength of the student's response and explain how it contributes to the response's overall effectiveness. Be sure to provide specific examples from and references to the response to support your assessment. Do not discuss the student's ability with the conventions of standard written English (e.g., grammar, usage, mechanics).

TASK 2
Identify one significant weakness of the student's response and explain how it interferes with the response's overall effectiveness. Be sure to provide specific examples from and references to the response to support your assessment. Do not discuss the student's errors in the conventions of standard written English (e.g., grammar, usage, mechanics).

TASK 3
Describe one specific, appropriate instructional activity that you, as the English teacher, would implement to address the significant weakness of the student's response that you identified in Task 2. Be sure to explain how the activity would address the particular weakness you identified and why you think the activity would be effective.

Writing Tips:

You will not be allowed to use any reference materials (dictionary, thesaurus) during the examination. It is recommended that you plan your time carefully. Read the selection more than once. It is further suggested that you break up the 60 minute block of time into separate tasks:

10/15 minutes	Read and annotate the chosen passage. Choose excerpts from passage for support. Create a web / graphic organizer for the response.
20/25 minutes	Draft the response – when drafting – double check to ensure that the main points address all components of the assignment.
15/20 minutes	Final edits: check spelling, grammar, and usage. (It is suggested that instead of erasing you draw a single line through any errors/words/ or phrases that you wish to omit.)

The scoring scale for the writing assessment and pedagogy question is 0–6.

Each rater uses the scoring criteria described in the three task-level rubrics to assess the degree to which the task responses demonstrate proficiency in fulfilling the performance requirements for each task. Each task response is given full credit (+2 points), partial credit (+1 point) or no credit (+0 points). The rater then adds together the points earned for each task and assigns a single combined score between 0 and 6. This score represents the candidate's overall proficiency in demonstrating the content knowledge and skills required by the assigned question.

For more information about scoring of the constructed response, and for additional samples and answers visit the Education Testing Service website listed below, then scroll down and click on the English Language Arts and Reading 7-12.

http://cms.texes-ets.org/texes/prepmaterials/texes-preparation-manuals/

References for Images

Achebe, Chinua www.albany.edu.writers
Ancient relief sculpture www.eawc.evansville.edu
Andersen, Hans Christian www.pacificnet.net
Angelou, Maya www.en.wikipedia
Basho, Matsuo www.poetryconnection. net
Blake, William www.onlinie-literature.com
Blake, William, The Tyger www.tangerinedream.org
Boewulf tapestry www.legends.dm.net
Bradstreet, Anne www.americanpoets.com
British Literature: The Middle Ages www.georgetown.edu
The Victorian Era www.wwnorton .com
Romanticism; Wanderer above the Sea of Fog, painting by Caspar Friedrich
www.en.wikipedia.com
Bronte sisters www.lang.nagoya-u.ac.jp
Bunyan, John www.en.wikipedia.org
Cather, Willa www.americanliterature.com
Charge of the Light Brigade, painting by Caton Woodville www.en.wikipedia.com
Chopin, Kate www.vcu.edu
Chaucer, Geoffrey www.umm.maine.edu
Chaucer's Knight's Tale www.georgetown.edu
Chaucer's Wife of Bath, Canterbury Tale www.unc.eud
Cisneros, Sandra www.lasmujeres .com
Coleridge, Samuel www.onl ine-literature.com
Cormier, Robert www.teenreads.com
Crutcher, Chris www.carmel.lib
cummings, e.e., self portrait www.english.uiuc.edu
cummings, e.e. www.americanpoems.com
Dickens, Charles www.victorianweb.org
Dickinson, Emily www.english .uiuc.edu
Defoe, Daniel www.online-literature.com
Douglas, Frederick www.fredericdouglas.org
Dunn, John www.online-literature.com
Edwards, Jonathan www.online-literture.com
Eliot, T. S. www.americanliterature.com
Emerson, Ralph Waldo www.pbs.org
Equiano, Olaudah vvww.Project_Gutenber~eeText.com
Fitzgerald, F. Scott www.onlineliterature.com
Franklin, Benjamin portrait by Jeanne Baptist Greuze, 1777 www.ushistoryorg
Frost, Robert www.ketzle.com_frost
Frost, Robert, stamp www.ssl.pro-net.co.uk

Gilgamesh, The Epic of, relief carving www.eawc.evansville.edu.grpage.htm
Hoyas, Angela de www.mandalinks.com
Hughes, Langston www.falcon.jmu.edu
Hughes, Ted www.online-literature.com
Iliad-Fallen Warrior in Homer's Iliad www.academic.reed.edu.humanities
Jarrell , Randall www.uncg.ed
Joseph, Chief www.historyplace.com
Lear, Edward www.nonsensclit.org
Lee, Robert E. www.civilwarhome.com
Lessing, Doris www.online-literature.com
Middle English Chaucer's Knight's Tale www.georgetown.edu
Milton, John www.en.wikipedia.org
Momaday, N. Scott www.english.uiuc.edu
Myers, Walter Dean www.teanreads.com
Neruda, Pablo www.Instar.com.literature
Neruda, Pablo www.nobelprize.org
Old English Woodcut www.georgetown.edu
Orwell, George www.online-literature.com
Paulsen, Gary www.teenreads.com
Petrarch, Francesco www.todayinliterature.com
Petrarchian Sonnet www.libraryupenn.eduexhibits
Pinter, Harold www.online-literature.com
Poe, Edgar Allan www.online-literature.com
Pound, Ezra www.epc.buffalo.edu
Queen Elizabeth www.accd.edu.sac_english
Shakespeare www.enwikipedia.org
16th Century Bible www.etext.viginia.edu
Solzhenitsyn, Alexander www.nobelprize.org
Steinbeck, John www.en.wikipedia.org
Tan, Amy www.luminarium.org
Swift, Jonathan www.bibliomania.com
Taylor, Edward www.spartacus.schoolnet
Tennyson, Alfred Lord www.online-literature.com
Thoreau, Henry David www.transcendentalists.com
Thomas, Dylan www. town.hall.org
Walker, Alice www.library.csicuny.edu
Wheatley, Phyllis www.earlyamerica.com
Whitman, Walt www.online-literature.com
Williams, William Carlos www.english.uiuc.edu
Wordsworth, William www.online-lierature.com
Yeats, William Butler, 1908 www.online-literaturee.com

Made in the USA
San Bernardino, CA
15 May 2017